Student, School, and Society

CROSSCURRENTS IN SECONDARY EDUCATION

Student, School, and Society

CROSSCURRENTS IN SECONDARY EDUCATION

Edited by
JOHN A. DAHL
MARVIN LASER
ROBERT S. CATHCART
FRED H. MARCUS
California State College at Los Angeles

With an Introduction by
STERLING M. McMURRIN
Professor of Philosophy, University of Utah
Formerly United States Commissioner of Education

 Chandler Publishing Company

SAN FRANCISCO

Contents

III. WHO ARE THE TEACHERS?

IV. WHO RUNS THE SCHOOLS?

Preface

The intensity of widespread interest in American public education shows no signs of abatement. Nor is it difficult to understand why this should be so. Whether for reasons of national security and international prestige (especially since the first orbit of Soviet Russia's sputnik); whether because of the increasing complexity of our industrial-technological civilization with its accompanying demands for highly skilled workers; whether because of a ballooning population which sends ever-larger numbers of pupils into already crowded schools—it is clear enough that our schools and their staffs are confronted with increasing and unprecedented responsibilities.

Moreover, while such matters as courses of study, qualifications of teachers, choices of textbooks, and details of school administration were once considered to be pretty much the domain of professional educators, today every aspect of the schools is closely scrutinized by the public at large. Thoughtful critics, extremist pressure groups, informed or uninformed laymen—all are convinced that there are urgent problems in the public schools which must be solved, and many are ready to suggest detailed reforms to bring about a school program modeled after their own heart's desire.

Particularly has the American public secondary school undergone probing investigation of all kinds. Because it is the college preparatory experience for the dramatically soaring proportion of youth who go on to higher education, or because it is the last formal schooling for those who leave for a lifetime of employment (or sporadic unemployment), the secondary school occupies a crucial position in American society. The history of the American secondary school since the start of this century, furthermore, has been a history of astonishingly rapid change from a kind of school attended by only 11 per cent of our teen-age youth to the innumerable varieties of present-day secondary schools which enroll about 95 per cent of our teen-age youth. Add to this the fact that our secondary schools today reflect significant cultural differences among communities, variations in adequacy of financial support, wide variances in the qualifications required of teachers, important differences in curricular emphases, wide ranges in grading practices, and dozens of other important differences —and it becomes immediately evident that meaningful generalizations are hard to come by, either among the critics or the defenders of the status quo. As James B. Conant has pointed out, it is a serious over-simplification to talk about *the* American public secondary school, when, in fact, there are about 22,000 public secondary schools in this country, under the jurisdiction of 16,000 different school districts.

Nevertheless, it is the belief of the editors of the present volume that there is considerable value in exploring some of the dominant themes in current discussions and controversies about the secondary school. After an examination of hundreds of books and uncounted numbers of periodicals, we reached the conclusion that most of the discussions focus on four major centers of controversy:

(1) *Who attends the secondary schools:* What are the characteristics of teen-age youth and what implications do these characteristics have for their education?

(2) *What goes on in the schools:* What are the curriculums like or, in the opinions of various critics, how should they be remodeled?

(3) *Who are our secondary school teachers:* How are they presently being prepared—or how should they be prepared—and what are the conditions under which they teach?

(4) *Who controls our schools:* What is—or what should be—the role of local districts, state or federal bodies, professional organizations, pressure groups, and community critics?

Although we recognize that a number of current and continuing issues are not represented in the foregoing framework (for example, the question of racial integration in the schools, the role of private versus public schools, the problem of the tax base for public education), we have concentrated on what we believe will continue to be widely debated issues central to the quality of public secondary education.

Several underlying principles which have governed our selection of materials should be made explicit. We have tried deliberately to bridge the gap between the generally traditional or theoretical material which comprises the content of the conventional textbook and the complex realities which are observable in the actual American public secondary schools of our era. Hence some readers may be surprised by the inclusion of attacks on the "Establishment" found in such writers as Bestor, Rickover, Koerner, or Keats, or by the inventory of shortcomings recited by a *Life* editor in an article entitled, "How We Drive Teachers to Quit." We have also ventured beyond the range of the typical textbook in sampling an unusual diversity of sources, including not only articles from various educational and professional journals, but also selections from the mass media (*McCall's, Life, Saturday Evening Post*), journals of opinion (for example, *The New Republic* and *American Mercury*), books intended for the lay audience, speeches, fictional pieces, and newspaper items. The few selections that do not focus specifically on the secondary schools are included because they are pertinent to an understanding of issues involving all of public education. The majority of our selections are reproduced intact; occasionally, however, to conserve space we have omitted some specific details, indicating all such omissions by ellipses (. . . .).

For students in college and university courses in education, but also, we hope, for teachers in service and school administrators, for members of school boards, and for citizens interested in the schools, this book will provide a convenient and compact collection of controversial statements demonstrating the liveliness of philosophical and abstract educational ideas when they are viewed through the hot light of public debate. The writers are, for the most part, among the leading contributors to the current and continuing dialogue (Woodring, Fischer, Faust, Rafferty, Hechinger, Conant, Rickover, Bruner, among others), but we have also made it a point to include articles by lesser known figures whose viewpoints, we believe, require representation.

It is scarcely necessary to state that the editors by no means subscribe to all of the opinions expressed; indeed, we hope that the reader will discover for himself that the selections range from those which are thoughtful, well-supported arguments to those which are flimsy or even specious. In any event, whether he ultimately agrees or disagrees, the reader has the first obligation, in our opinion, to attend even more closely to the views expressed by those he may initially be disinclined even to recognize as authorities.

For ourselves, we are convinced that the American public secondary school occupies a crucial position in our educational enterprise and in our society, and that neither a blind defense of the past nor an impulsive grasp at innovation will produce schools that our country and our youth deserve. As one educator puts it: "Schoolmen should learn to accept criticism and dissent, perhaps even personal attack, as evidence of a functioning democracy. . . . "

JOHN A. DAHL
MARVIN LASER
ROBERT S. CATHCART
FRED H. MARCUS

Los Angeles, California
February 15, 1964

Introduction: The Great Discussion

STERLING M. McMURRIN

Education is the basic function of any society, and the determination of its proper ends and purposes and the commitment to it of the human and material resources necessary to the achievement of those ends depend ultimately on public opinion and what might be called the public disposition. The means and methods of education, by which its ends are to be achieved, are the responsibility especially of the teaching profession, of those persons who by talent, preparation, and experience are not only best qualified to fashion the instruments for learning, but carry as well the heavy burden of responsibility for the educative process itself.

But when we raise the question of the substance of education, of what it is that is to be taught and learned if the purposes of the schools are to be realized, we seem to encounter a task that belongs properly to both the general public and the educators. It is a task that can be successfully mounted only if there is a continuing and serious discussion engaging both of these groups that comes to grips with the large problems with which education must now contend. At least four of these are outstanding at the present time: the reform of the curriculum and the improvement of the substantive content of the courses taught; improvement in the recruitment and education of teachers; the organization of the educational program to better serve the intellectual and vocational interests of individuals and the needs and purposes of society; and the resolution of fundamental issues in the administration and financing of the educational establishment.

The great value of this volume, *Student, School, and Society*, that recommends it so highly to all persons with a serious interest in the future of American education, laymen, civic leaders, students, and educators alike, is the contribution that it can make to what might be called the "great discussion." It is a discussion that now figures very importantly in our institutional, community, and national life and anyone aware of what has been going on must agree that it is one of the best things that has happened in or to our society in a long time, that its general result has been a marked advancement in the quality of our schools and, what is perhaps equally if not more important, a growing disposition within the education camp of self-criticism and determination to improve. But all too often the discussion has been uninformed, dominated by preconceived notions, by propaganda, doctrinaire slogans, and dogma, and directed more by a kind of well-disposed civic passion than by evidence and reason, descending to the questionable level of debate rather than maintaining its character as honest and open-ended discussion. It is a special merit of this volume that it not only brings into focus a variety of live and crucial issues in education, and places them in meaningful and concrete contexts, but that it provides its readers a rare opportunity to see those issues from a diversity of standpoints, to see both sides of the story, and to get the feel of the arguments pro and con that can be brought to bear upon them. It does this in a manner, moreover, that is both direct and unequivocal and with a light touch that enables the treatment of the most serious problems with a certain measure of humor and humaneness. This is no mean accomplishment. The editors have produced a volume that is pleasant to read, that clearly shows that a subject which is all too often dull and uninviting can be lively and fascinating. And they have done this not by sacrificing the quality of its content but by making sure that their book represents the diversity that actually exists in this country's educational thought. But this volume does more than represent diversity. It exhibits controversy, the real live controversy, argument, and criticism that are at once both the evidence and source of a new vitality in American education and that are in a large degree responsible for the substantial improvement that is now being made in the quality of our schools.

Few would deny that the American people have a sincere commitment to education. Perhaps nothing more fully justifies our national pride than our educational achievement, especially when this is judged by the criteria of numbers and universality. But we have all too commonly preferred to see part rather than all of the picture, to believe that we are in better shape than the facts testify, to close our eyes to failure and defeat, to solve our fundamental educational problems by pretending that they do not exist. Nothing can do more to restore our waning confidence and bring to our educational establishment the strength that it desperately needs to guarantee our future than a frank and honest recognition of our problems, failures, and successes, and a firm determination to get at the roots of our difficulties at whatever cost.

But if we have a sincere commitment to education, we nevertheless are wanting in a full understanding of its nature, its profound worth in the life of the individual, its power as the chief determinant of the character of our society, and its meaning for the strength and character of our total culture. Our native activism and practicalism have all too often restricted our conception of education simply to the cultivation of the basic intellectual skills and to vocational and professional preparation. Lacking anything like a full appreciation of education and its function, we have long taken for granted a number of things about which, fortunately, we are now asking questions. We have assumed that teaching, for instance, is a necessary, worthwhile, and pleasant task demanding at best the talents and energies of persons of second- or third-rate ability. We have assumed that the education of teachers is an important and worthy matter, but that of course it does not require or deserve the concern commonly accorded the education of doctors, lawyers, or engineers. We have taken it for granted that the compensation of teachers is a simple matter. Just pay them enough to insure a warm adult body in every overcrowded classroom and take care not to interrupt the habits of attitude and decision which guarantee that most of our teachers, including the finest among them, will have third- and fourth-rate salaries and that the total cost of education will be less than the cost of some of our ordinary national pastimes.

The financing of education is a difficult matter in the Nation as a whole largely because of our long and deeply ingrained habit of treating educational funds as items of expense, to be curtailed at every possible point, when they should be regarded rather as valuable and essential investments. And it is difficult because we have so commonly refused to tackle the money-raising problem at its root, and reform our tax system where and when reform has been indicated as necessary. But things are improving here as elsewhere. It is becoming more obvious to civic, industrial, and business leaders, that judged simply on its economic returns, to say nothing of its immense human value, quality education is of indispensable worth, and citizens' groups are widely questioning the advisability of requiring public education to depend so heavily upon the property tax. State minimum and equalization programs are widely established and are being improved, and even the uses of Federal financing for equalization among the states as well as for special purposes is now more objectively considered in some quarters than has been the case in the past. Quite certainly the condition of school finance is improving. The basic problem will not be solved, however, until we take it for granted that nothing but the highest quality of education of which we are capable will suffice for our society, and that the most affluent nation in history, enjoying a superabundance of practical ingenuity, is capable of providing whatever material resources may be necessary for its support.

In a society such as ours that has a need for and an addiction to somewhat complex organization, there is always a grave danger of over-administration. This is as true in the schools as elsewhere. Unless we are careful, our educational establishment may become top-heavy with executive and supervisory brass that will impede rather than expedite the educative process. Yet there is no good reason for supposing that the format of American educational administration needs radical revision. The state control of the public schools should be protected, for this provides our best guarantee of variety, diversity, and competition in the educational program and these are essential to the pluralistic quality of the culture that is the foundation of our democratic institutions. There is today a great hue and cry over the possibility of Federal control of the schools, and this is a matter that must always be of serious concern to the American people, for the centralized control of education could produce a monolithic structuring of the educational establishment and program that would have a deteriorating effect upon the democratic quality of American life. But history has already shown that with care and vigilance we should be able to achieve whatever Federal educational activity is essential to the strength and quality of the schools, including certain forms of financial assistance, without endangering state control. Indeed, the Federal Government appears less likely to contribute to an educational monolith in this country than do powerful nongovernmental agencies that affect education on a national scale. There is no struggle for power in education between the states and the Federal Government. That struggle is rather between the states and the local school districts, to which the states by constitutional provision or legislation have delegated authority and responsibility for the schools. In the long run it could be a major gain for American education if more of the states would strengthen their state boards and state education offices and if those less populous states that still tolerate hundreds of independent school districts would insist on reducing the number through consolidation. It would mean a gain in the efficient use of funds and talent and would result generally in a large improvement in the quality of the educational program.

The responsibility for education in its totality is shared by most of the institutions of any society. The function of a school, its reason for being, is a quite specialized one. Its broad purpose has to do with such things as the perpetuation of the culture, but its proper immediate concern is the cultivation of the intellect, induction into the right uses of reason, and the achievement, extension, and dissemination of knowledge. Whenever a school fails to fasten its primary energies upon these matters, as has been all too frequently the case, it abandons its controlling purpose and fails not only at the point of knowledge and reason but also in the accomplishment of those other ends that are appropriate goals of education: the cultivation of moral and civic character, the nourishing of artistic creativity, the refinement of aesthetic and spiritual sensibilities, and the general civilizing of the mind and passions.

A legion of forces of diverse kinds have served to distract our schools from their central task and at times have actually disqualified them for that task, forces ranging from the traditional anti-intellectualism that has been and to a considerable extent still is a habitual attitude of mind of our people, to the common presumption that the schools should perform many of the elemental social functions that belong more properly to the family or church, and to the now current imposition upon some schools of the large burden, in the instance of so-called "*de facto* segregation," of solving the problem of racial relationships that should already have been resolved through such avenues as equality of opportunity in employment and freedom and equal opportunity in housing. Often the schools, especially in our great cities, are so affected by the extraneous social responsibilities that society intentionally or adventitiously imposes upon them, that their time and vital resources are near exhaustion before they can devote their energy to the primary tasks of education.

Here is a major problem, and one of growing proportions, that confronts our schools, and only a solid interest shared by the general public can contribute effectively to its resolution. Sooner or later we must come to grips with the fact that we cannot consistently have the kind of education that is both needed and deserved by a society that has accepted such a large portion of the world's leadership and work and has developed its domestic life to such a high degree as long as we continue to attract so many of our teachers from the ranks of those with less than high intellectual stature, give them something less than the best education of which we are capable, pay them salaries that typically are too low to provide decent support for a family, and saddle them with social responsibilities both large and small that make it impossible for them to function as educators to the full extent of their abilities. Considering the degree of indifference with which in the past we have generally approached the task of education, certainly the most important function of our society, the wonder is not that our schools are not better but rather that they are as good as they are.

The public is greatly indebted to the teaching profession and especially to those teachers of first-rank ability and dedication who are chiefly responsible for the high quality that fortunately is often found in our schools.

When we consider the vast demands that the future will inevitably make upon our manpower resources, for scientific and social intelligence and technical competence of all kinds, the demands in intellectual achievement that it will make upon our leadership in government, industry, commerce, and all departments of civic life, and indeed upon all of us as citizens who must live constructively and creatively in an increasingly complex society that is rife with difficult problems both domestic and international, we may well question whether our educational establishment is adequately structured to satisfy our needs. In the presence of large-scale unemployment, we have serious shortages of technicians; with our schools and colleges overwhelmed with students, hundreds of thousands of our youth fail to complete even a minimum education and often, having no employable skills, become burdens to themselves and to society. Or consider such things as our failure in teaching economics in the presence of general economic illiteracy in a world in which the complexities of economic life daily affect every person, and where no political decision can be made in indifference to economic forces; or the sad state of the arts in countless schools even though the nurture of the artistic sensibilities is so basic to the quality of personality and, indeed, to the strength of any human society; or the inability of many schools to provide satisfactory up-to-date instruction in such basic fields as mathematics or physics because of the inadequate supply of competent teachers, or the refusal of backward administrators to take advantage of the new scientific instructional material now available, or because of the inability of schools to establish scientific laboratories due to the refusal of small backward communities to consolidate their educational resources. Clearly, there is need for a careful look at the structure of the educational establishment to make sure that in the future individual, community, and national purposes will be more adequately served than at present. There is need for a long look at the organization of the curriculum and at the substance of what is taught and learned. Fortunately this look, both careful and long, is now being taken, and with promising results. The vast gap, for instance, in what might be called our middle-level technical-manpower supply will be narrowed in the future because of recent and current examinations of the whole field of vocational and technical education. We are becoming acutely conscious of our educational failures in the social sciences. And mathematics and the natural sciences are on a considerable front achieving new levels of competency and excellence in part because of nationally and federally sponsored programs and the large interest in secondary education taken by highly competent scholars and scientists. All in all, things are moving in a good direction, but much remains to be done. The improvement of secondary scientific education, for instance, must be matched by equivalent improvements in education in the social sciences, humanities, and the arts. It is one of the great tasks of education to create the advancing technological knowledge and skill upon which so much obviously depends, and yet at the same time to build into our society those qualities of intellect, will, and spirit that will guarantee the personal quality of life against the dehumanizing forces of a mechanical, automated, technocratic age.

It is important that the concern and enthusiasm for educational improvement that are now so evident among us become and remain rational and retain their strength. We cannot afford a recession of the public interest in education and we must not permit that interest to consume itself with emotion. In a society where the people determine the course and fate of public institutions, and in a world where virtually everything will depend on the extent and character and quality of education, there is far too much at stake to warrant the risk of public apathy.

Student, School, and Society

and Society

CROSSCURRENTS IN SECONDARY EDUCATION

WHAT ARE STUDENTS REALLY LIKE? | I

The Emergence of an Adolescent Subculture in Industrial Society

JAMES S. COLEMAN

Mr. Coleman is professor of sociology at the Johns Hopkins University.

Educating its young is probably a society's second most fundamental task—second only to the problem of organizing itself to carry out actions as a society. Once organized, if a society is to maintain itself, the young must be so shaped as to fit into the roles on which the society's survival depends.

It might seem that the problem of socializing the young would be handled similarly in every society, for the young, as they enter this world, are much the same everywhere. Yet the problem is faced in very different ways. A good example of this is the recent and continuing conflict between the Amish community in Ohio and the Ohio State Board of Education. The Amish, a small Protestant sect, attempting to maintain their small society as an enclave within the larger society, have views very different from those of the Ohio laws as to what constitutes a reasonable education for their young. To quote at length a news account:

Last week, by a vote of 19–2, the Ohio Board of Education ruled that two Amish high schools—in Holmes and Tuscarawas counties—would have to measure up to state standards or close. The Amish schools, the board said, have no graded courses in geography, American and Ohio history, natural

Reprinted with permission of the publisher from *The Adolescent Society* by James S. Coleman (Glencoe, Illinois: The Free Press, 1961). Copyright 1961 by The Free Press, A Corporation. (Footnotes that appear in the original source have been omitted.)

sciences, government, and other required subjects. Some teachers, the board added, have no more than an eighth-grade education.

With few textbooks, the children spend much of their school day copying phrases from their diaries into composition books. Examples: "I plowed and cleaned raspberry patch." "Ironed all day." "In the forenoon I went to church. In the afternoon I fed the turkey broilers."

Bearded Henry Hershberger, chairman of the Amish School Committee, admitted the schools didn't meet state standards, but he hoped for a compromise. "It seems that our way is quite different from what the public demands," he said. "Worldly wisdom taught in public schools conflicts with our way of life. Our religion is built around simplicity."

One's first reaction to such an education might be one of sympathy for the children deprived of their birthright in a free society. Upon further consideration, however, the example illustrates not the depravity of the Amish parents, but the sharp difference in the educational task of a stable farming society and that of a rapidly changing, highly industrialized society. In a stable farming society—of which the Amish represent one of the few remaining examples within the United States—the problem of the society is simply to *reproduce* itself; to give its young members the values, habits, and skills of their parents. In such a stable, localized, and personalized society—which is not long past in our country as a whole—education is a simple task, and it is carried out as a part of the same "natural process" by which a parent teaches his child to walk or to talk. This is not to say that this process constitutes the "best of all educations in that best of all possible worlds." It is often far from it, for each child is at the mercy of his parents, and whether they are good citizens or ne'er-do-wells, the "natural processes" by which they socialize him make him a replica of them. Nevertheless, the problem is handled as naturally within the family as is the problem of teaching a child to walk or talk.

By contrast, in an industrial society committed to equality of opportunity, there are two facts that make the task fundamentally different and more complex. The first is the fact of change itself. Our society is changing at an ever increasing rate; adults cannot afford to shape their children in their own image. Parents are often obsolescent in their skills, trained for jobs that are passing out of existence, and thus unable to transmit directly their accumulated knowledge. They come to be "out of touch with the times," and unable to understand, much less inculcate, the standards of a social order that has changed since they were young.

Second is the fact of economic specialization. In an industrial society, each father's skills are highly specialized, while his son, if he is to start on an equal footing with his fellows, must be trained through public schooling as a *generalist*, able to choose the role in society that he wants to fill. Furthermore, the father's activities are carried out far from home, often in a place where his son never sets foot. Neither the son of a steelworker nor the son of a business executive may become an apprentice at age thirteen or fourteen. While their fathers vanish into their respective worlds of work, the sons must prepare themselves for an uncertain future—neither for steelworker nor for business executive, but for a range of possibilities.

The child can no longer help the family economically; in turn, the family has little to offer the child in the way of training for his place in the community. The family becomes less and less an economic unit in society, and the husband-wife pair sheds its appendages: the grandparents maintain a home of their own, often far away, and the children are ensconced more and more in institutions, from nursery school through college.

This age-segregation is only one consequence of specialization: another is that the child's training period is *longer*. With every decade, more of the jobs available in our society require a high level of training. As our industrial economy comes of age, it has less and less room for laborers and skilled workers, more and more room for engineers and managers. Thus not only do we relegate education to an institution outside the family, we must keep a child there longer before he is "processed" and fit to take his place as an adult in society.

This setting-apart of our children in schools—which take on ever more functions, ever more "extracurricular activities"—for an ever longer period of training has a singular impact on the child of high-school age. He is "cut off" from the rest of society, forced inward toward his own age group, made to carry out his whole social life with others his own age. With his fellows, he comes to constitute a small society, one that has most of its important interactions *within* itself, and maintains only a few threads of connection with the outside adult society. In our modern world of mass communication and rapid diffusion of ideas and knowledge, it is hard to realize that separate subcultures can exist right under the very noses of adults—subcultures with languages all their own, with special symbols, and, most importantly, with value systems that may differ from adults. Any parent who has tried to talk to his adolescent son or daughter recently knows this, as does anyone who has recently visited a high school for the first time since his own adolescence. To put it simply, these young people speak a different language. What is more relevant to the present point, the language they speak is becoming more and more different.

As if it were not enough that such an institution as today's high school exists segregated from the rest of society, there are other things that reinforce this separateness. For example, adolescents have become an important market, and special kinds of entertainment cater almost exclusively to them. Popular music is the most important, and movies, since television took away their adult audience, have moved more and more toward becoming a special medium for adolescents.

To summarize: in a rapidly changing, highly rationalized society, the "natural processes" of education in the family are no longer adequate. They have been replaced by a more formalized institution that is set apart from the rest of society and that covers an ever longer span of time. As an unintended consequence, society is confronted no longer with a set of *individuals* to be trained toward adulthood, but with distinct *social systems*, which offer a united front to the overtures made by adult society.

Thus, the very changes that society is undergoing have spawned something more than was bargained for. They have taken not only job-training out of the parents' hands, but have quite effectively taken away the whole adolescent himself. The adolescent is dumped into a society of his peers, a society whose habitats are the halls and classrooms of the school, the teen-age canteens, the corner drugstore, the automobile, and numerous other gathering places. Consequently, the non-occupational training that parents once gave to their children via "natural processes" has been taken out of their hands as well, not by the school teachers—many of whom are dismayed at the thought of having to take over parental functions—but by those very social changes that segregated adolescents into a society of their own.

A good index of those changes is given by the number of teen-age youths in high school. We think of high school in our society as having been in existence for a long time. But in 1900, only 11 per cent of this country's high-school-age youth were *in* high school; as late as 1930, the proportion was only 51 per cent. Sometimes this is viewed as "progress" toward making our society more democratic, but there is considerable evidence to suggest that these changes are simply necessary consequences of industrialization. For example, a parallel trend, thirty years delayed in time, has occurred in the Soviet Union. Fifty years ago, in an earlier stage of industrialization, comparatively few persons needed the lengthened training that high school represents. The rest were learning their work on the farms or in the stores or in the trades of their parents and neighbors.

Perhaps it is self-evident that the institutional changes that have set apart the youth of our society in high schools should produce an "adolescent culture," with values of its own. These changes have been discussed speculatively by numerous authors. Whether or not there is a separate adolescent subculture is partly a matter of definition as to what constitutes a separate subculture. However, there are several items from the present study that give a sense of the degree to which these adolescents are oriented to parents and peers. In one set of questions, they were asked whether they would join a club in school (1) if their parents disapproved, (2) if their favorite teacher disapproved, and (3) if it would mean breaking with their closest friend ... Then they were asked whose disapproval would be most difficult to accept—parents', teacher's, or friend's (see Table 1).

The responses indicate a rather even split between friend and parent, while the teacher's disapproval counts most for only a tiny minority. The balance between parents and friends indicates the extent of the state of transition that adolescents experience—leaving one family, but not yet in another, they consequently look both forward to their peers and backward to their parents.

Thus, teen-agers are not oriented solely to one another; yet the pulls are extremely strong, as the responses in Table 1 show. It seems reasonable, however, that those adolescents who are more oriented to their parents might "set the standard" in school, while those more oriented to their peers would tend toward delinquency or at least enjoy less esteem than those who are parent-oriented. If this were so, then the adolescent cultures existing in the school would be oriented

Table 1—*Which one of these things would be hardest for you to take—your parents' disapproval, your teacher's disapproval, or breaking with your friend?*

	Boys	Girls
Parents' disapproval	53.8%	52.9%
Teacher's disapproval	3.5	2.7
Breaking with friend	42.7	43.4
Number of cases (*excluding non-responses*)	(3,621)	(3,894)

toward parents to a greater degree than the individual responses indicate, because the central persons in the schools were more oriented to parents. But this is not at all so; a slight reverse tendency exists.

This can be seen by looking at those students who are named most often (ten times or more) by their fellows in response to the following question: . . . "If a fellow came here to school and wanted to get in with the leading crowd, what fellows should he get to be friends with?" Quite reasonably, we can infer that the students named in response to this question include most of the "leaders" or the "elite" of the adolescent culture in the schools. For this group and for the students as a whole, the proportion who say parents' disapproval would be hardest for them to take is shown in Table 2.

The elites in the school are not closer to their parents than are the students as a whole, but are pulled slightly farther from parents, closer to fellow-adolescents as a source of approval and disapproval. Thus, those who "set the standard" are more oriented than their followers to the adolescent culture itself. The consequences of this fact are important, for it means that those students who are highly regarded by others are themselves committed to the adolescent group, thus intensifying whatever inward forces the group already has. . . .

In sum, then, the general point is this: our adolescents today are cut off, probably more than ever before, from the adult society. They are still oriented toward fulfilling their parents' desires, but they look very much to their peers for approval as well. Consequently, our

Table 2—*Proportion who say that "parents' disapproval would be hardest to take"*

	BOYS		GIRLS	
All boys	Leading crowd	All girls	Leading crowd
53.8%	50.2%	52.9%	48.9%
(3,621)	(167)	(3,894)	(264)

society has within its midst a set of small teen-age societies, which focus teen-age interests and attitudes on things far removed from adult responsibilities, and which may develop standards that lead away from those goals established by the larger society.

Given this general condition, there are several directions in which educational efforts could turn. One is toward a channeling of the adolescent societies so that the influence they exert on a child is in the directions adults desire. Rather than attempting to motivate children one by one, each parent (with teachers' assistance) exhorting his own child in one direction while the adolescent culture as a whole pulls in other directions, efforts can be made to redirect the whole society of adolescents itself, so that *it* comes to motivate the child in directions sought by the adult society. This is not a new device; "playing by ear," perceptive principals and teachers have long attempted to do this. Yet it has never been the focus of any general philosophy of education, nor have any general means for redirecting the adolescent society been set forth in schools of education, perhaps because we know too little about the ways in which subsocieties, such as those of our teen-agers, can be guided and directed.

Before any such attempts are made in this direction, it is important to examine carefully the ways in which these subsocieties operate, the kinds of effects they have on the teen-agers within them, and the elements that shape them in one direction or another. This will be the intent of the succeeding chapters of this book [*The Adolescent Society*].

The values, activities, and interests characterizing the "teen-age culture" as a whole will be examined first. But of primary importance will be the ways in which these adolescent societies differ from school to school, from community to community, so that some insight can be gained into the factors shaping them in one or another direction. Looking both at the separate schools and at the various "crowds" or groups within the schools, it will be possible to achieve some understanding of how the climate of education within a school may better implement the hopes and ideals of our society.

2

The Impact of the School:
The Clarification of Experience

EDGAR Z. FRIEDENBERG

*Mr. Friedenberg is professor of social science and education
at Brooklyn College, New York.*

In what ways does the school influence the growth of adolescents?
It is society's formal provision for them. It is charged with their intellectual and moral development. In a culture like ours, in which
tragedy is regarded as a problem and problems are assumed to have
solutions, the school is held responsible for observable deficiencies in
the adolescent much as a department store is held responsible for defects in the quality of its merchandise.

For the most part the school accepts this responsibility. It tries to
meet it professionally; that is, by means of a program planned to meet
stated objectives through techniques derived from empirical research.
The statements of objectives are often so naïve philosophically, and
derived from so vulgar a conception of what life will demand of its
students, as to be indefensible; the research is often so stupidly planned
and executed as to be irrelevant to the conclusions drawn from it.
But the school is seldom frivolous or irresponsible in its attitude
toward youngsters; it tries to understand its job and do it as conscientiously as the quality of its staff permits.

Indeed, in discussing the role of the school in the social order, professional educationists are frequently unrealistic through being *overly*

From *The Vanishing Adolescent* by Edgar Z. Friedenberg (Boston: Beacon Press,
1959). Reprinted by permission of the Beacon Press, © 1959 by Edgar Z.
Friedenberg. (Footnotes that appear in the original source have been omitted.)

responsible and conscientious in their point of view. They see the school as a much more active influence on society than it is. They may regard the school as primarily the agent of society, but they still perceive it as an *agent*. They assume that it can and does *act* rather independently, on behalf either of society or of its own educational ends, and that its policies, if properly executed, ought decisively to influence the outcome of events.

In this conception of the function of the school there is some truth; but the school overstates its agency. It takes too much on itself, and speaks as if it were responsible for the outcomes of social processes that it has scarcely influenced. For in much that transpires within the school—and that is undoubtedly highly educational—the school is not an agent. It is the arena in which social forces interact, employing students, teachers, and administrative officials in roles with which they have become familiar but into which they have not developed much insight. The committee reports and public statements by which the school attests its professional orientation and benevolent concern are as sincerely meant as Polonius' advice to Laertes. But the school's intentions are seldom independent influences on educational events. The drama of Prince Hamlet did not work out quite as Polonius intended; and Polonius was not its hero. Too many other people were trying to do too many other things; and even the adolescent Hamlet, who came closest, did not quite grasp all that was going on.

What *is* going on? If we were to attempt to analyze the complex web of activity of a typical American high school with the affectionate but detached interest of an observer from another planet, what social functions would be discernible? They will obviously vary from one school to another and, more significantly perhaps, according to the categories of thought of the observer. But I think we might expect to find something like the following social processes occurring simultaneously and in interaction. I indicate them here in order of the importance I would attribute to their actual impact on the adolescent and on his subsequent life as an adult in society.

First: The school is where you learn to be an American. Americanization is a process, not a result; it is carried on chiefly by the youngsters themselves. The teachers play a fairly important role as manipulators of the *mise en scène;* but they do not much influence the process by direct instruction. There is plenty of nationalist propaganda in our textbooks and courses, but there is not much evidence that it influences the students. The informal processes of Americanization produce, in fact, so stubborn a resistance to direct indoctrination with any ideology that we have had to evolve other means of propagating our own. They are effective, and the school is one of the principal loci of their application; but they are informal and fit cleverly into our image of ourselves as an independent people given to irreverence.

Second: The school serves as a hydraulic mechanism designed to provide a measure of fluidity and stability of equilibrium for a society which is far more stratified than its members care to admit. How a youngster reacts to the school largely determines his chance to get on in the world; whether he wants to get on in the world largely determines what his attitude toward the school will be. What the school contributes in the process is complex, and formal instruction is probably not a very important part of it. Those who set themselves professional goals receive some elementary instruction in the relevant sciences and techniques; it is not usually very good. For the rest, the vast majority, the school serves as what C. Wright Mills has called "a seed-bed of . . . white collar skills." For all, it is the source of the certification prerequisite to getting a decent job in a society grown much too impersonal to depend on face-to-face assessment of competence.

Third: The school transmits some of the knowledge and some of the intellectual skills and attitudes on which the tradition of Western civility depends—depends more precariously than ever. The quality of general education in the American high school is not high, particularly in comparison with a European secondary school of university preparatory grade. But it is probably underestimated by most observers. It has contributed substantially to the development of a middle class which is interested in the arts, capable of quite fine discrimination in consumption, intellectually alert and anxious to maintain a broad and just interest in its involvement in world affairs. This class continues, however, to lack sufficient depth of education and confidence in the authority of the mind to use its intellectual capacities fully.

Fourth: The school functions as an administrative and records center for various activities with reference to the young. The high school adds substantially to the dossier which has now become standard equipment for Americans. It records a youth's intelligence, interests, medical history, and emotional stability. It notes, should it occur, the rare complication produced by the development of political interests. It observes—and often sets down on microfilm, for permanence and economy—its appraisal of his personality and of his over-all promise for the future, and its transmits this appraisal, and sometimes the raw data on which the appraisal is based, in response to what it regards as legitimate inquiry, forever afterward.

It is probably idle to question at this point whether these processes are conducive to the good of society; they are in any event part of its workings. Processes having a similar function have always occurred in schools. One can hardly imagine a school system which did not somehow provide an ambience congenial to the values and attitudes of the culture which supported it. In every society complex enough to provide formal schooling for postpubescent youngsters, the schools strongly influence the social mobility of individuals. In every culture education aims to develop individuals whose sensitivities and whose anxieties will be useful and reassuring to the kind of people who already wield power. (Indeed, the distinction between liberal and professional education seems to be peculiar to an age of self-made men. Harvard College was founded as a vocational school for clergymen; it was hardly necessary to stipulate that it should also turn out Harvard men.) And schools have doubtless always managed to provide interested authorities with estimates of their students' character and potential for various kinds of action; in this, as today, their judgments were colored by the ideologies then prevailing.

These functions are traditional, but their impact upon the adolescent is new. They become something different in a society in which school attendance is universal and compulsory, the educational establishment

correspondingly enormous, the teaching staff correspondingly specialized, bureaucratic, and lacking in prestige and self-esteem.

Regardless of the uses to which any society may put its schools,
education has an obligation that transcends its own social function and
society's purposes. That obligation is to clarify for its students the
meaning of their experience of life in their society. The school exists
fundamentally to provide the young people of a community—a nation
may be a community; it had better be—with a fairly tough and firmly
fixed philosophical apparatus for making a certain kind of sense out
of their lives, and communicating with other people who may be
assumed to have a basically similar apparatus.

This does *not* mean propagating similar views, or social attitudes
and beliefs as such. A great deal of this sort of propagandizing does
go on concomitantly and perhaps inevitably, but it is not helpful in
accomplishing the purpose of clarification. Neither does it mean
teaching the truth—though it certainly does mean not teaching the
false—for the truth usually cannot be taught; it is too subtle and
iridescent, and can only be recognized by persons who expect that it
will look entirely different when viewed from different angles. The
first and fundamental step is certainly to get the relevant facts right,
if facts are involved, and deal with them honestly and consistently;
facts can be taught. But they are not the truth.

What it does mean is teaching people to mean the same thing by
the truth; to establish in their minds similar categories of thought; to
approach understanding with roughly the same unconscious predispositions; to admit the same considerations as relevant; to share
a common intellectual—though it sometimes is scarcely that—
methodology. In any generation, a few souls will use this apparatus
to formulate the truth about themselves and the world they live in;
and they do not necessarily go mad or get themselves hanged. We
simply remember more vividly those who do. But the social purpose
of education is not to create a nation of actively insatiable truth-
seekers; truth-seeking is a highly specialized function. It is to create
a nation which can see clearly, and agree on what it sees, when it
looks in certain directions.

The American school seems to do this. We do indeed share a common culture. There is as yet no other nation in which individual regional differences have been so swamped. Whether the man from the car rental agency meets you at New York, Miami, New Orleans, or San Francisco International Airport hardly matters. And the commonness goes further: American mass gratifications, from soft drinks to comic books and movies, have turned out to be the common coin of mass culture the world over; so that it hardly matters either whether he meets you in Ankara, Tokyo, or Rome. This is not conquest, but genuine cultural diffusion. All over the world, man in the mass has turned out to be exactly our type of fellow.

It is nearly as deep as it is wide, too. As we view ourselves being ourselves, the differences between the patterns of lives of city folk and country folk, rich people and poor ones, those with a Ph.D. and those who never finished grade school, are minimal. There are, of course, superficial differences in *how* and *where* people of different social groups spend their leisure, but not fundamental differences in what they *do* with it and what it does to them.

Our schools are a precise expression of our culture; they do prevent it flying apart; they do polarize our vision in certain directions; they do certainly establish in young Americans common categories of thought and unconscious predispositions. But they do not clarify the meaning of experience.

Our schools act as if America were still a melting pot. This is a strong tradition that developed through the decades when the nation was being built up through immigration. Free public secondary education was created in the United States in order to supply its expanding economy with a labor force and a technical staff equal to its growing demands. In order to do so, it had to take youngsters from the most diverse ethnic backgrounds and turn them into an article sufficiently standardized to fit efficiently into a productive system that had very little interest in their personal characteristics and no wish to be troubled by them. In return, the youngsters could count on a rising standard of living. The high school was intended to produce not an industrial proletariat, but a group of individuals who could be trusted with complex technical and administrative machinery and trusted not to raise awkward questions about the place of that machinery in the universe of values. The youngsters by and large agreed with the high school that they were being given an unprecedented opportunity.

Still, adolescents need clarity. If adolescence is the process of defining oneself through conflict with society, it is helpful if the educational institutions with which the adolescent must deal remain loyal throughout the struggle to the task of clarifying the meaning of experience. For him this amounts, after all, to the same thing: one defines oneself by clarifying the meaning of one's experience. As an individual, he is responsible for achieving more clarity than the school can give him; for the school's cultural biases will in any case camouflage many vitally important phenomena and relationships. Each youngster must correct as best he can for the astigmatism induced by social institutions. But if the school is consistent, honest, and sufficiently sophisticated to be aware of important things and coherent about the relations between them, it will be of great assistance in giving the adolescent something on which to build himself.

Adolescents are ill-served by schools which act as melting pots. When they get into a stew, it is best if the stew is like a properly prepared Japanese soup: crystal clear, with the individual qualities of all the odd ingredients preserved; the soft things soft, the tough things tough, the green things green, and the yellow things yellow. From this kind of heterogeneity it is possible to learn something.

In this respect, the high school has been getting worse for years, for society has. It has always devoted itself to the interests of uniformity more than to individuality; but the uniformities used to be more *external* than they are now. I shall not labor this point, which has already been dealt with so thoroughly by Riesman, W. L. Whyte, and many others; but will simply point out that the school today is less a stew pot than a blender. What comes out, when it is functioning effectively, is not merely uniform but bland and creamy; by its very nature inimical to clarity, yet retaining in a form difficult to detect all the hostile or toxic ingredients present in the original mixture.

This is really serious. It is one thing for the schools of a culture to impart to adolescents a distorted picture of reality, seen from a limited point of view, but *clearly*. So long as the school is not simply an agent of propaganda, or psychotic—so long, that is, as what it talks about is really there, even if what it says is much different from the whole truth—it may still contribute effectively to adolescent growth. Adolescents are alive, and the school is not the whole of life; given a consistent, honest, and coherent picture of the world, they can correct for themselves its biases and omissions. But it is quite another thing for the school to limit perception and responsiveness in every direction to what the society can tolerate without discord. Society thereby establishes within its members a cut-off point; no matter what happens, they do not see too much, get too involved, or try to overthrow the system.

This is happening increasingly in our schools; though nobody intends that it should—in principle, that is; the school staff do intend that it should in particular instances. When a specific conflict arises, the school almost automatically seeks to *mediate* rather than to clarify. It assesses the power of the conflicting interests, works out a compromise among them, and keeps its name out of the papers. The loyalty oath is accepted with gentle chidings about singling out teachers for undue suspicion; *The Merchant of Venice* is omitted from the reading list in favor of something just as good in which all the Jewish characters are pleasant; the aggressive candidate for student council member is quietly barred from office on grounds of emotional immaturity.

We do not know that universal education can retain a commitment to clarity; being in the business, I am sometimes skeptical of it myself. The problem is one of dignity. We have had in all history no experience of any society in which a large proportion of the members could take a good hard look at life without breaking and running. The examined life has always been pretty well confined to a privileged class. Liberal thought has held that this confinement was deliberate: the members of the privileged class knew that knowledge was power, and excluded those subordinate to them so as to maintain the existing inequities. Liberal thought was here based on sound observation. But it was inclined to overlook certain converse processes.

The most important privilege of a privileged class is freedom from some of the vicissitudes of fortune. Its members are running the show and can divert much that is disagreeable elsewhere. It is often easier, therefore, for them to be honest with themselves about what they see and about what it portends. They can afford to be; they have to be if they are not to lose control, and control is important to them. Ruling classes differ, of course, in the degree to which they understand this and can bear to go on understanding it. De Tocqueville, standing at the point of no return in history, noticed that the *ancien régime français* had forgotten it, and that we had not learned it. Most elites do forget it, and become convinced that destiny, rather than equestrian skill, is keeping them in the saddle. Their members can be distinguished in historical engravings by the hoofprints in the small of their backs.

With respect to this issue, our expectations of education are mixed and conflicting. Our public-school system was not designed to nurture an elite—just the contrary; it was designed to train the boys who would work uncomplainingly in its mills and vote unquestioningly for its measures. The school, by and large, is still devoted to the twin ideals of success and contentment, though it pursues them with greater technical sophistication. But our cultural tradition is a lot broader than our school system, and is less purely pragmatic. It is slightly Hellenistic, a good deal more British, and in any case humanistic and Western. Whether we want to or not, when we think of education—rather than of what school was really like—we think of a process which is expected to prepare the young to accede as well as to succeed. Educators like Robert Hutchins have maintained that democracy demands just this view of public education because in it every man must behave as a ruler of men.

This seems to me rather fanciful, because what actually happens in a modern democratic state seems to be abdication of popular sovereignty in favor of an equally undistinguished and ephemeral ruling clique. But this does not erase the connection, established in our minds by a hardy tradition of our culture, between education and a large measure of responsibility, detachment, and discipline.

In this tradition the common man, exposed as he is to economic, social, and personal pressures, has never fully shared. That, given the opportunity, he would consent to do so is merely an educated guess. He has not yet received the protections of status and property on which the tradition was based; these, or their equivalent, are only now being devised in the form of a less completely material conception of the welfare state in which new social forms guarantee leisure and continued high-level economic security rather than bare survival.

New and more widely applicable sources of security and status also lead to a clearer sense of self. *Lucky Jim* is just as trustworthy and really just as brave as Archdeacon Grantly, as well as a great deal more human. But he is far less sure of himself; he cannot count on his nerves and judgment as well in a threatening situation, and situations have much more power to threaten him. He is more vulnerable; he has a much shorter lease on life.

The modern school, then, serves people who lack the protections enjoyed by those who taught us what to expect of an educated class. It is also staffed by people who are, in fact, vulnerable to public opinion and dependent on the approval and support of their colleagues, even in matters of detail, in order to be effective. We cannot be sure that they will ever feel free themselves, or accept any large measure of responsibility to teach youngsters to examine what they are learning against the criteria of their own values, traditions, and experience of life. It may be that we cannot expect them to analyze experience sharply, and tell the truth about what the analysis reveals.

It is difficult to put what we feel to be wrong into words, and we very often use the wrong ones. We complain that standards are too low; yet research report after research report confirms that students, by and large, are learning more rather than less of the kind of fact and simple skill on which schools conventionally base their claim. We feel that the students are getting lazier; but they seem to work hard, and the worst of all often work the hardest of all; they voluntarily assail the teacher with volumes of mediocrity because, they say, they want to raise their grade. Students who do badly in a course frequently argue that they should have a higher mark because what they did took them so long. We feel the students are duller, and it is true that the public school reaches students of lower ability than it was formerly able to enroll. But it is not they who are the focus of public concern; in fact it is precisely with them that the school often does its most clearly professional and original work. We feel that the students are less disciplined, and are here a little closer to the mark. But it is an inner discipline that is lacking; the school fails to provide a basis for it. The undisciplined behavior which sometimes results is often a sign of the anguish which results from having no core of one's own.

Standards are unsatisfactory, not because they are low, but because they are fragmentary and incoherent. They exist, and to the extent that they exist, they add to the general confusion. The academic curriculum consists of shards of a pre-democratic academic culture; relics of a way of life in which many of the people who had gone through school read poetry for fun, spelled properly and wrote cogently because they sometimes worked on public documents, spoke French correctly and fluently because they occasionally had to communicate as equals with civilized Frenchmen. Their schools were technically far worse than ours; the teachers untrained in the special concerns of education, usually unimaginative and occasionally brutal. But in that culture, as in ours, the students were quick to learn what made sense in relation to their view of themselves and their social role, either with the school's help or despite it.

The problem today is to determine what does make sense in terms of one's view of oneself and one's social role. Our schools are socially heterogeneous, and deeply riven by discontinuities of experience between the staff, the students, and those earlier individuals who wrote the major works and participated in the events with which the curriculum must deal. Between the high-school staff and the street corner boy there is no common ground. Between the high-school staff and Shakespeare there is not likely to be much common ground either. If

Sir John Falstaff can only reach the corner boy—who would find him very meaningful—by passing through the high school, he is pretty sure to get lost on the way.

This social heterogeneity is not simply a matter of incongruous courses of study and students with very diverse cultural backgrounds. These would be, as they are commonly thought to be, unique strengths of our system, if only the school had a philosophical structure by which to order them—not into a hierarchy, but according to the existing and potential relationships among them and a coherent set of values. A school having white and Negro students ought to be able, for example—if it is sustained by a conception of democracy that is both profound and sophisticated—to make use of the problems attending desegregation as a living exercise in American social democracy as it actually is. This would require intense historical scholarship and keen and detached sociological analysis. But neither the teachers nor the students are usually capable of either; faced with so controversial an issue they would more likely panic when they found that they lacked the necessary scholarly skills and discipline, and each would run to his particular pressure group to try to get his story in first. . . .

3

One in Three

FRANK RIESSMAN

*Mr. Riessman is chairman of the department of psychology, Bard College,
Annandale-on-Hudson, New York.*

In 1950, approximately one child out of every ten in the fourteen largest cities of the United States was "culturally deprived."[1] *By 1960, this
figure had risen to one in three.* This ever increasing trend is due to their
rapid migration to urban centers. By 1970, it is estimated there may be
one deprived child for every two enrolled in schools in these large
cities.

When one considers that almost one-sixth of the population of the entire
nation resides in these cities; that between 1940 and 1950 eighty per cent of
the national growth in population occurred in metropolitan areas; and that
between 1950 and 1957 ninety-seven per cent of the national growth occurred
in these same areas, the dimensions and urgency of the problem are readily
apparent.[2]

Clearly one of the most pressing problems facing the urban school
today is the "culturally deprived child." . . .

Why is education of this disadvantaged group so important? It
would be easy to answer that we must educate the deprived because
they are a source of needed manpower, or because everyone deserves

---

"One in Three" is from *The Culturally Deprived Child* by Frank Riessman (New
York: Harper & Row, 1962). Copyright © 1962 by Frank Riessman. Reprinted
with permission of Harper & Row, Publishers, Incorporated. (A number of
footnotes that appear in the original source have been omitted.)

[1] The terms "culturally deprived," "educationally deprived," "deprived,"
"underprivileged," "disadvantaged," "lower class," "lower socio-economic
group," are used interchangeably throughout . . .

[2] "The Great Cities School Improvement Studies," Ford Foundation Project,
mimeographed, 1960.

an education. But perhaps there is a deeper reason. It is essential to democracy to combat the anti-intellectualism, prejudice, and intolerance that are bound to be characteristic of any educationally deprived group, and are, in fact, dominant motifs of the disadvantaged in America. Fundamentally, education combats narrow thinking. The groups who lack education have contributed disproportionately to discrimination, bigotry, and attacks on freedom of thought. Education is not merely something that we would like all groups to receive for their own good; it is as vitally necessary to us, the educators, as it is to the uneducated.

There is another reason why a meaningful approach to the deprived is important to the educator. Most teachers who work with underprivileged children today find this a most unattractive, unrewarding task. It can be both a challenging and an interesting assignment if a different approach is used.

What is needed is a sympathetic, noncondescending, understanding of the culture of the underprivileged. We need to comprehend the deprived person's attitudes toward education, the school, and the teacher. Many of his attitudes toward education are more positive than we might think, although his attitudes toward the school and the teacher may be negative. This contradiction between education and the school must be resolved.

We will endeavor to show why the deprived individual, although desiring education, is antagonistic toward the school. Although we recognize that both the school and the parents are at fault in producing the existing educational problems, we wish to emphasize the need for corrective action in the school—for it is there that we are more likely to produce large-scale changes than in the home, which we can influence but little.

While there may be aspects of the culture of the deprived individual that would be better changed, it is necessary for the educator to work within the framework of the culture as it exists. In other words, the culture should be accepted as given. There is one fundamental exception to this principle—one area in which the educator avowedly attempts to oppose the culture of the underprivileged, and that is with regard to anti-intellectualism and narrow pragmatism. While we may understand the reasons for the anti-intellectualism, we are not required to be uncritical of it.

CULTURALLY DEPRIVED OR EDUCATIONALLY DEPRIVED?

A word is necessary about the term "culturally deprived." While lower socio-economic groups lack many of the advantages (and disadvantages) of middle-class culture, we do not think it is appropriate to describe them as "culturally deprived." As we shall see, they possess a culture of their own, with many positive characteristics that have developed out of coping with a difficult environment. The term "culturally deprived" refers to those aspects of middle-class culture—such as education, books, formal language—from which these groups have not benefited. However, because it is the term in current usage, we will use "culturally deprived" interchangeably with "educationally deprived" to refer to the members of lower socio-economic groups who have had limited access to education.

WHO ARE THE DEPRIVED?

Paul Goodman points out that "In our economy of abundance it is still subject to discussion whether or not there is as much poverty as there was in the Thirties when 'one third of a nation was ill-housed, ill-clothed, ill-fed.' Some say 20 per cent are poverty-stricken, some as many as 40 per cent. Census, 1958: 31 per cent."

A large portion of the current disadvantaged population is composed of cultural and racial minorities.

When we think of the deprived sub-culture, we do not take as our model that segment which is most disorganized by the environment. This group, despite the disproportionate public attention it receives, is surprisingly small. We do not think that much can be learned about how to educate the mass of the underprivileged from examining this small element. On the contrary, from investigating the main disadvantaged groups and their cultures, we may gain insights that are valuable in dealing with the disorganized minority.

A quotation from Robert Weaver, the new Housing Administrator, is useful in characterizing the mainstream of the deprived:

> Slums in American cities today house families which hold a wide range of values and evidence a variety of behavior patterns. Some are households with female heads and are stable none-the-less; others may be ungrammatical but adhere to high moral standards; still others evidence all the attributes of middle-class behavior and are dedicated to its values, if not recipients of its rewards. All three groups have ambition and talent, but fight an uphill battle in maintaining respectability and achievement for themselves and their children. . . .

Weaver also characterizes the disorganized minority element in the following way:

> Certain elements now concentrated in the slums, however, present clear well-defined problems; they include the confirmed middle-aged winos, the established prostitutes, the overt homosexuals, the hardened criminals, and the like, who either resist rehabilitation, or require long-term assistance of a most intensive type. They are multi-ethnic and constitute the real "hard core."

The main groups in the underprivileged communities strongly dislike this anarchic, criminal element, and thus represent important allies for the social practitioners.

WHY JOHNNY CAN'T LEARN

Countless reasons are offered to explain why underprivileged children do poorly in school. Here is a partial list of the conventional reasons:

1. The lack of an "educational tradition" in the home, few books, etc.

2. Insufficient language and reading skills.

3. Inadequate motivation to pursue a long-range educational career, and poor estimate of self.

4. Antagonism toward the school, the teacher.

5. Poor health, improper diet, frequent moving, and noisy, TV-ridden homes.

Undoubtedly there is much truth in this listing and we will attempt to illuminate some of these factors and what may be done about them. But implicit in this list is the emphasis on the non-school environment, the parents, and the child himself, as the central determinants of the failure to learn. What has happened to the old idea that held if the children aren't learning, look to the teacher? Scant attention is given to the faults of the school in the present-day analysis of the problem. It is almost as though the school were saying: "We want to teach these kids—we try very hard—but they don't want to learn because their parents and friends don't want them to."

By refocusing on the school's contribution, we think we may be able to make suggestions on which the school can take direct action, rather than blaming a home environment over which the school has little power. Furthermore, some of the conventional causes given for Johnny's failure to learn may now be recast in a new light. For example, instead of talking about poor motivation and antagonism toward the school, reference will be made to the rejecting attitudes of the teacher toward Johnny, and the resulting anger and loss of interest on the part of the child.

Let us then try to reformulate some basic factors deterring Johnny from learning, with which we shall be concerned . . .

1. The discrimination, frequently unintentional, seen in the class-room, Parent-Teacher Association, guidance office, psychological testing program, etc., which alienates Johnny and his family.

2. Johnny's *ambivalence* toward education—not simply rejection of it—his lack of school know-how, test-taking skills, information concerning college, and his anti-intellectualism.

3. The culture of the school which overlooks and underestimates his particular skills and mode of intellectual functioning that arise out of his culture and way of life.

4. The deficits in Johnny's background which necessitate special *transitional* techniques to bring him into the academic mainstream.

These do not require a "soft" approach, a lowering of standards, a capitulation to his deficiencies.

A CULTURAL APPROACH: CULTURE VS. ENVIRONMENT

It is easy to say that we must understand the culture of the under-privileged. Most people would agree. The question is, what do we mean by a cultural approach? Some people seem to think that the culture of a group is equivalent to its environment. Therefore, the culture of lower socio-economic groups is seen to include inadequate housing, limited access to leisure facilities, and the like. We prefer to distinguish between the environment, or conditions of life, of a group, and the culture of that group. We conceive the latter to be the methods that have evolved for coping with the conditions of life. Thus, "culture" would include the traditions, values, and mores of a specific group, many of which have a long history. Values and attitudes of the underprivileged that are relevant for the educator would include beliefs about punishment, authority, games, cooperation, competition, introspection, intellectuals, etc.

Along with customs and traditions, culture consists of the institutions, the structures, and the methods of organization of the people involved. The storefront church and the protest movement, the trade union and the fraternal lodge, the large extended family, the neighborhood club or gang, are illustrative here.

Thus, we view culture as an effort to cope with the surrounding environment. Many of the coping techniques are ineffective or devious, of course, but we believe that only if they are seen in terms of an effort to grapple with the milieu will they be properly understood. If we fail to see the struggle, the attempts to combat the difficult environment, and instead seize upon the failures, the ineffectiveness, we will not understand the behavior of the educationally deprived, or, at best, will see it only one-sidedly.

IMITATION AND REBELLION: TWO SIDES
OF THE SAME COIN

An important question that arises here concerns the formation of this culture. It is easy to believe that the underprivileged, surrounded as they are by television, movies, and the other mass media, simply mimic the dominant mores of the society. Carrying the process one step further, it is often contended that minority members incorporate the dominant group's views of them; therefore, they have low self-esteem and sometimes self-hatred. Undoubtedly there is some truth to these assertions; the underprivileged are unquestionably affected by the mass communications system and the images of the deprived presented therein. But culture is not primarily determined by words and symbols, but by people. Perhaps the culture of the deprived is not decisively produced by the mass media, but rather by the interactions of disadvantaged groups and individuals with each other, over a long period of time.

Alongside the view that the deprived person's culture is largely reflective of the mainstream culture, an apparently opposite thesis has emerged. Here the culture of the deprived is seen as a contra-culture, in which the characteristic feature is rebellion and opposition to the dominant way of life. This culture is supposed to be typical of many delinquent gangs. Again, there is a measure of truth in this view—the culture of the disadvantaged does have certain rebellious, angry features, and certainly some of the sub-cultures within the deprived society could be most aptly characterized in this fashion. But again, the implicit, somewhat ethnocentric, belief seems to hold that under-privileged culture is fundamentally determined by the dominant society—this time not as a simple mirroring, but in direct opposition. It is as though we were saying "These people have no way of shaping their own lives other than by trying to do what we do or by doing just the opposite—they can't think for themselves and find their own paths."

THE VALUE OF THE CULTURAL APPROACH
FOR THE TEACHER

There are two ways in which a cultural approach can aid the educator. One has to do with the social-emotional relationship between the teacher and the educationally deprived child; the other is more directly concerned with the way subject matter can best be taught.

A sound cultural understanding should enable the teacher to establish a much better relationship with the deprived child who is typically antagonistic toward the school and, on the surface at least, unmotivated to learn. Through an empathic understanding of his culture, the teacher will begin to see why the deprived child is hostile, what he expects of her, why he wants her to prove herself. The teacher will come to learn why he needs a structured classroom, how she can utilize his in-group loyalty, informality, equalitarianism, humor, and the like. She will come to understand why he does not need "love" but respect. And finally, she will be able to interpret in a new light much of the behavior which appears negative. What previously appeared to be emotional imbalance and supersensitivity to minor frustrations can now be seen anew.

An interesting illustration of how knowledge of the culture of the underprivileged can be useful, not only to the teacher, but to other social practitioners as well, can be seen in regard to low-income public housing. Often politically minded people are astonished at the lack of interest which disadvantaged groups manifest toward the public housing movement. Believing that these projects are essentially valuable for lower socio-economic groups, they cannot comprehend the resistance frequently encountered.

Only when it is realized that the rules governing admission into public housing violate the traditions and mores of the deprived culture does this resistance become comprehensible. In order to obtain an apartment in a public housing project, it is necessary to have a standard family unit of father, mother, and children. Grandparents, aunts, uncles, and other relatives, with whom the deprived family may have been sharing an apartment, are not accepted as part of the basic family unit. The extended family pattern, which is an important part of the culture of the deprived and plays a major communal role in their lives, is thus ignored. It is no wonder then that they have misgivings about public housing. Also, the housing administrations will not accept families in which the parents are unmarried. Furthermore, projects are constructed in so-called "slum neighborhoods," and the large numbers of people in these areas who do not qualify for public housing are swept back ("relocated") into other areas, which are further over-crowded. The communal ties which existed in the original neighbor-hood are thereby destroyed.

To sum up: effective education of the "one in three" who is de-prived requires a basic, positive understanding of his traditions and attitudes. . . .

4

Are Schools Doing Their Part?

ROUL TUNLEY

Mr. Tunley is a reporter who was commissioned by the Greater Philadelphia Movement to complete a worldwide study of juvenile delinquency.

Dr. Negley Teeters, the fire-eating criminologist of Temple University, was in an incendiary mood when I went to see him.

"I didn't want this interview, you know," he said, when I entered his office. "I've nothing against you, mind, but people write so much and so little is done. I don't think we're getting anywhere with Senate investigations and conferences and headlines. I'm so sick of hearing that the broken home is the cause of delinquency, or the motion picture, or our speeded-up life. The fact is we've *got* to live with our culture. And if you ask me, the crux of our delinquency is not the parents; it's the schools. Our schools are filled with misfits, kids who don't belong. Our education is geared for *all* our kids and that's the heart of the problem. We need some kind of program for the kids who *don't* fit into our school picture, who are *not* interested in middle-class norms or in becoming a lawyer someday."

Dr. Teeters was expressing a point of view which more and more people have come to hold, namely, that our schools are not doing their job. As Dr. William Kvaraceus, of Boston University, has put it: "Our schools face the imminent danger of becoming the most expensive irrelevancy of the twentieth century."

Consider a typical delinquent youngster we'll call John Morris. . . . John is fifteen. He has a slightly lower-than-average I.Q., and his

---

"Are Schools Doing Their Part?" is from *Kids, Crime and Chaos* by Roul Tunley (New York: Harper & Row, 1962). Copyright © 1962 by Roul Tunley. Reprinted with permission of Harper & Row, Publishers, Incorporated.

school grade is a year lower than his age would indicate. His report cards have shown a long list of failures, and he's never really learned to read properly. All his teachers have been women, and he has somehow got the impression that reading, writing and spelling are feminine accomplishments. His family, which is in middle-class circumstances, has moved frequently because his father, working for a large company, has been shifted around. Since John has never been able to understand properly what he's been called upon to study, school to him is pure drudgery, boredom and, worse, humiliation. In the past year or two, finding the situation intolerable, he has played truant more and more. Once he got into trouble for breaking into a store, and he was put on probation. Although he likes to work with his hands and would have made a good gardener, or perhaps a bricklayer, his parents feel this is not in keeping with their status aspirations. Besides, he can't leave school until he's sixteen anyway. Consequently, John sits out the extra year, unhappy, sullen and building up habits of idleness and mischief. He's a headache to the school, and the school is a headache to him.

Now let's look at what might have happened to John if he'd been an Austrian or a Dane or a German.

First of all, he would not have attained his present grade without a good working knowledge of reading and writing, even if he had had to go to school six days a week to do it. Furthermore, the chances are that along the way he would have been exposed to many male teachers and would definitely not have gotten the notion that literacy is largely a female accomplishment. At the age of fourteen, since he did not plan to follow an academic career, he would have been allowed to leave school with the proviso that he enter into an apprenticeship as a stonemason or a gardener or a forester or some other trade. Under this arrangement, he would have had from four to seven years of on-the-job training with a first-rate master. During this time, he would also have had to go to a trade school one day a week.

The U. S. answer to the European approach is the vocational high school. This exists in many large cities, but on the whole it is for boys and girls with fairly good academic qualifications. There are some exceptions. A few—very few—of our big cities have trade programs which take youngsters of lower-than-average ability and attempt to instruct them in paperhanging or upholstering or needlework. But such programs touch the merest fraction of our high school enrollment. Speaking for the country at large, there is little place in our system for the boy or girl with few or no academic qualifications, for the child, as some people put it bluntly, who would make a good second-class citizen.

In accordance with the American dream, everybody must want to be, and be able to be, a first-class citizen. Anything less is un-American. Consequently, a largely uniform school system has been geared to this ideal. It is book-centered and college-oriented, which is fine for those going on to higher education. But it leaves no alternatives for a fellow like John.

The results of this rigid approach are crushing. Almost one million youngsters a year drop out of high school. Many just sweat it out, doing little or nothing, until the legal age of leaving (sixteen in some states, seventeen in others). Some are embittered, frustrated and, worse, functionally illiterate. In the name of democracy and with high humanitarian purpose, we have short-changed a large segment of our juvenile population and not given them the kind of education *which would have been right for them*.

Realizing that something was wrong and unable to lower the legal age at which kids might leave school, the education authorities have tried to fill the gap with substitutes—counselors, psychologists, playgrounds, "practical" courses and extracurricular activities. Some of these have been helpful, but they have not got to the heart of the problem. Counselors are worthwhile, for example, but there are only eleven thousand counselors for nine million high school students. One can see how little individual help can be given, especially when there are no adequate educational alternatives for the counselors to recommend anyway.

Dr. Kvaraceus estimates that only about 35 per cent of our youth have the ability to profit from a traditional college-preparatory curriculum, and that the academically untalented youngster, the "reluctant learner" as some educators like to call him, is unprovided for. This point of view was confirmed by a recent National Education Association study of the teachers themselves. After listing "overlarge classes" as their number one problem, the teachers designated "the reluctant learner" as problem number two. Forty-five per cent of the teachers urged that some provision be made outside the regular classroom for nonlearners, and almost half the principals endorsed this suggestion. Moreover, the Conant report subtly urged that these youngsters might be eased out of school at fourteen, if they couldn't, or wouldn't, learn.

It might be interesting at this point to take a look at the I.Q. distribution of the nation's children as a whole.

They run roughly as follows:

2.5% I.Q. lower than 70	25% I.Q. 70–90	45% I.Q. 90–110	25% I.Q. 110–130	2.5% I.Q. higher than 130

The first two sectors, comprising 27.5 per cent of our juvenile population, is the segment of our youth that is most handicapped under our educational system. These youngsters are being pushed through the same system as everybody else, in the illusion that such things are more democratic.

Far from being democratic, this situation is highly undemocratic in that it denies to a large group of youngsters a training which is geared *for them*. This might be faced with some complacency were is not for the fact that from this "nonlearning" group we draw a good deal of our juvenile delinquency, especially the kind which becomes statistical.

According to judges who handle delinquency cases, a large percentage of the youngsters involved are unable to read. One of New York's children's courts reported that 75 per cent of its delinquents had difficulty reading, and that "there is a definite link between reading retardation and delinquency." Street workers have found many gang members unable to read at all, and some have been reported who couldn't ride the subways because they couldn't understand the signs.

In the Gluecks' study of five hundred delinquents matched with five hundred nondelinquents of the same basic intelligence, age, size and background, it was found that while the former were filled with the "spirit of adventure," they were not at all filled with an equal interest in school. In fact, they were a full year behind the nondelinquents in their grades. Moreover, a recent Ford Foundation report found that the incidence of delinquency is much higher among the nation's drop-outs than among those who continue on through high school. It would seem fairly obvious, therefore, that a very large segment of our youth are not in tune with our educational setup, and because of this, are getting into trouble.

Consequently, it seems to me there are two possible solutions:

1. Such youngsters can leave school earlier.

2. If they are required to stay until present age limits, schools can provide educational alternatives to them, things which will interest the so-called "nonlearner" who can make a good gardener, cook, nursemaid or maintenance man, but is not a potential lawyer, school-teacher or business executive.

"What perversion of democracy makes us feel that everybody must *want* to be a general, never a sergeant?" a school principal once asked me.

In other parts of the world this problem is often approached more realistically. In Thailand, for example, which devotes a far larger share of its national budget to education than we do (30 per cent), education is compulsory only to the age of fourteen. However, schools, colleges and universities are free to all, and those interested in an academic career can go on to higher learning if they want to and if they are capable of it.

As we have seen in Germany and Austria, a boy or girl not inter-ested in books can leave school at fourteen, but he is not just thrown on the street corner. Alternatives have been set up, generally of an ap-prenticeship nature. In France, where one can leave school at fifteen, there is a similar setup. Denmark also has a fourteen-year-old limit for school, *but those who leave must definitely be embarked on other careers.*

England had a school limit of fourteen years until recently, when it raised the age to fifteen. It is interesting that when this happened, the peak of juvenile delinquency suddenly rose from fourteen to fifteen. It is equally interesting to note that in Sweden, which has a very high delinquency quotient, the legal age at which one can leave school is sixteen—*the same as ours!*

These experiences would seem to indicate that leaving school earlier—at least leaving the *conventional* type of school—tends to curb delinquency. But on the other hand, such implications do not mean that formal education must be stopped. They simply mean that *different kinds* of learning must be arranged, within the school system if we wish.

During the past decade a concerted campaign has been waged to curb dropouts and try to get everyone through our high schools. It has largely failed. Some improvement was noted in the first few years of the campaign, but now the number has leveled off, suggesting that under our present curriculum probably very few more youngsters can be induced to stay.

Says Dr. Kvaraceus: "Indications are that the holding power of the public schools, presently graduating sixty out of a hundred persons, seventeen years of age, has probably reached its peak. Unless the curriculum is broadened . . . universal secondary education will remain an American myth."

Although very few alternatives to the present curriculum have been created, and although we have more or less insisted that everybody conform to a uniform approach, here and there a breakthrough has occurred—a glimpse of what could be done. This has not been accomplished, though, without strong opposition. . . .

A study of unwed mothers ten years ago revealed that less than 10 per cent of the girls returned to school. Furthermore, many of them, because of a lack of supervision or of any compelling interests, had a second child born out of wedlock. Most of the girls were embarrassed to return to school, and those who did created a problem by talking too freely about their escapades. Consequently, the school officials, with the help of private funds, started a project to provide vocational training for the unwed mother—in dressmaking, beauty culture, baby care and office work. The project has a nursery attached where mothers leave their babies while attending classes but where they can go when their infants require feeding. While they learn to take responsibility for their children, they also learn a salable skill. The whole project is under the supervision of a director who helps the girls plan their futures.

Programs like these in delinquency prevention are far too few in the United States. A few school systems have been imaginative enough to set up projects to deal with kids who don't conform to the usual standards, but there are not many. Since schools are one agency of society that touches the life of every child in his most formative years, and through him his family, most schools could do much more in spotting delinquency and setting the wheels in motion to curb it. Very few delinquents who turn up in court at fifteen, sixteen or seventeen arrive there as a result of a single act. Offenders are rarely created overnight. Mostly, they have a long history of misbehavior which was first noticed at nine or ten years of age in the schoolroom, but nothing was done about it. With the proper facilities, most of our delinquents could be pinpointed and set straight before they got too deeply involved.

This will not be accomplished, however, merely with counselors and case workers. These are important, of course, especially for the maladjusted youngsters with home problems, medical problems or personality problems. But what is even more important is to have basic educational, or training, alternatives for that percentage of our children who do not fit into the conventional picture—the non-learners who find it hard to work with books.

"So long as the school lacks a varied curriculum to meet the needs of *all* youngsters," says Dr. Kvaraceus, "the effectiveness of the counseling, the social work, the psychological and attendance services will be severely circumscribed."

In sum, our schools are potentially one of our best weapons in the fight against delinquency. But they often lack the funds, the imagination, the public backing, or all three, to do the job. In effect, as far as the country as a whole is concerned, they have been warring with popguns rather than with heavy artillery.

5

Cult of the Slob

MAX RAFFERTY

Mr. Rafferty is California's State Superintendent of Public Instruction.

Is this the Thing the Lord God made and gave
To have dominion over sea and land ... ?
—Markham

We speak today of changes—desirable or necessary—in the high schools of the land. Gentlemen, I invite you to consider with me the case of the triumphant Slob . . .

He stands before us at this moment, unwashed and unregenerate. His hair is agleam and adrip with oil, kneaded behind into strange whorls and sinuosities. Below the ears and following the slack jaw-line, it descends in bristling tufts, and with an exuberance unknown since the more militant days of the late General Burnside. Hairiness, in fact, is the very badge and symbol of the Slob. He spends a considerable portion of his day coiling and matting, as the Mock Turtle did reeling and writhing.

Our Slob is apt to wear his clothing much as the ladies of Regency days flaunted their bodices—for purposes of revealing rather than concealing. His shirt is open to the fourth button, coyly baring naked flesh down even to the navel. Trousers are slick denim, buckled low upon the hips and hinting at an eager willingness to go even lower. Boots are standard Slob attire, as is the cheap leather jacket with "GENTS" or "ROADRUNNERS" blazoned luridly upon its back.

His stance approximates the so-called "debutante slouch" of a generation ago. His walk is an exaggerated, hip-swinging roll which

From *Phi Delta Kappan*, November 1958. Reprinted by permission.

harks back to the gait of the old salt-water sailor temporarily marooned on land. His talk is a modern thieves' jargon, relying strongly
upon scarcely-disguised obscenity and intelligible mainly to other
members of the cult. His music is the monotonous and nerve-racking
drumbeat of the primeval jungle.

If we were to overcome our instinctive revulsion long enough to
institute a more intimate search of the Slob's person, we should find
exotic treasure indeed. Aside from the miscellaneous and unprintable
items of pornography which we may expect as a matter of course, we
are bound to come upon several pieces of equipment which will cause
even our experienced eyebrows to do a demivolt. I do not refer here to
the ubiquitous switch-blade knife, normally used to enforce terrorized
quiescence upon the victim of a mass rape. Nor do I allude to the
bicycle chain, commonly swung menacingly about the heads of
smaller boys in order to collect protection money, nor even to the zip
gun which lends a deadly note to the gang rumbles.

No, I have reference rather to the inked or tattooed device worn
upon the hand or arm, strikingly suggestive of an unholy brotherhood
of crime and startlingly reminiscent of the Mafia. I allude in passing
also to such esoteric appurtenances as the razor-studded cap brim for
slashing faces, and the shortened tire-iron for breaking legs. Surely,
such a walking chamber of horrors should at least cause us to pause for
consideration.

I am reminded in this connection of the Duke of Wellington's comment when confronted with a somewhat similar situation. During the
Peninsular Campaign, the Duke kept the sea-lanes to London sizzling
with his insistent demands for reinforcements. After an interminable
delay, the laggard troops arrived in Spain, but to everyone's horror,
they turned out to be jailbirds and sturdy rogues, the scourings of the
London streets. As the Iron Duke sat glumly on his horse before the
heights of Torres Vedras watching the clumsy recruits attempting to
drill, an eager aide approached him.

"Tell me, m'Lord, d'ye think these blighters will frighten old
Boney?"

The Duke regarded him grimly.

"I can't say about Boney, but by God they frighten *me!*"

I must confess that I am with the Duke in this matter. They frighten *me*.

STUDY SLOBBISM—IN SELF-DEFENSE

It is these added refinements, these supererogatory icings on the cake of delinquency, which in my opinion constitute ample cause for our serious study of the Slob in any symposium on high-school problems. In sober truth, and especially since educators have of late become prime targets of the Slob's more lethal aggressions, we are left with little choice other than to initiate an examination of Slobbism, if only out of self-defense.

After all, so long as the characters who lurched menacingly about our high-school corridors and snarled defiantly at their teachers confined their activities to mere lurching and snarling, it was expedient for us to chalk up such behavior to "release of tensions" and "animal spirits," and to let it go at that. A good many of our abler instructors, it is true, dropped out of the business, unable or unwilling to assume the role of Frank Buck constantly challenging the carnivores, and some of the hardier souls who stuck it out were carried out feet first as the result of brushes with certain of their pupils whose tensions they had unwittingly helped to release. But minor blood-letting such as this was dismissed by school administrators as statistically inconsequential, and life in the Great American High School rocked and rolled along its accustomed path.

Until recently . . .

When, a few months ago, a junior-grade disciple of Slobbism toted his rifle to school for kicks, and spent the better part of a half hour chivvying his startled principal from office to lavatory as the hot lead flew.

And a short time later, another junior high principal was so bedeviled and intimidated and just plain scared that he chose to solve his problems by jumping off a roof and spattering himself all over a playground, while the Slobs stood by and sniggered.

Then, just recently, the crash of shotgun fire added a touch of piquancy to the run-of-the-mill noises of a California campus as a sulky Slob blew the leg off an athletic director who had been unwise enough to intervene between the grinning gunman and a potential victim.

It may seem at first glance that these examples of Slobbism are excessively sanguinary, but simple assault and battery in the schools is, quite frankly, too common to talk about. Almost every edition of your favorite newspaper contains a matter-of-fact story about some school man who has been slugged or roughed up by a pack of punks. Such treatment is coming to be regarded as just another occupational hazard, ranking somewhere on the scale between simple writer's cramp and accumulation of chalk dust in the lungs. So long as this one-sided tong war took place outside the inner sanctum of the principal or the superintendent, we administrators were inclined to shrug it off.

Isolated instances, you know . . .

Or, "Mr. Jones brought it on himself, in a way. Had trouble establishing rapport."

But recent happenings have placed things in a somewhat different light. The zip gun sights have been raised, and Mr. Administrator is finding himself uncomfortably in dead center. His concern has ceased to be academic, and is rapidly becoming personal. I can only assume that a good many of my colleagues, in the face of imminent stabbing or shooting, are going to revise their priority listings of significant high-school problems to place Slobbism somewhere up near the top.

At least, they will if they are as downright cowardly as I am.

SCHOOL NOT BATTLEGROUND, HUNTING PRESERVE

Even if school men turn out to be heroes, however, it is still high time to concern ourselves seriously with the peculiar problem posed by this twentieth century version of *homo neanderthalensis*. A school is neither

a battle ground nor a hunting preserve, and unless we address ourselves energetically to the solving of this puzzle, we are going to find
ourselves increasingly beset within our ivory towers by baying bands
of Slobs. So perhaps the mills of the gods, by grinding perilously near
our persons, may compel us at last to take the action which the scandalous and pitiful plight of our normal, decent pupils, terrorized by these
creeps, has so long demanded of us.

The old head-in-the-sand technique of minimizing or ignoring the
size of the Slob in the hope that he will somehow get lost won't work
anymore. It has been fashionable to say smugly that these are maladjusted boys, thrown up through no fault of their own from the modern
maelstrom of wars, depressions, and broken homes. To this pious
platitude is usually appended the magnificent *non sequitur* that, after
all, these social deviates compose but a very small fraction of the total
adolescent population. A similar observation, of course, might be
made with equal truth about the cholera bacillus.

LET'S UNDERSTAND THE ENEMY

It is important that we understand our enemy. And it is an enemy we
are talking about, not just a misunderstood by-product of the machine
age. The Slob, or more importantly the whole insitution of Slobbism,
is the mortal adversary of Education.

Slobbism negates all the values which we teach.

It convulses hysterically against all disciplines.

It derides morality in any form.

It persistently seeks out ugliness and filth in preference to beauty
and decency, like the unlovely but irreproachably Biblical dog which
insisted on returning to its vomit.

Above all, it takes pleasure in inflicting pain.

The Slob is thus the exact opposite of the gentleman, who is defined
by Newman as one who never willingly inflicts pain. Our Slobbish
citizen not only inflicts pain; he revels in it. The threatening note, the
obscene phone call, the ravaging of women and children—these are the

Slob's stock in trade. Indeed, it has been truly said that his sole interests are sadism, sex, and speed, in that order.

The Slob's mental processes are so rudimentary as to be almost nonexistent, although a certain amount of animal cunning is sometimes to be found in his agile twisting and turning to avoid work and to remain out of jail. The brain, however, is not so much deficient as unused. It has been short-circuited by a constant succession of appeals to the emotions. The Slob is ruled by his passions. He warms easily to rage. He burns with lust upon the slightest pretext. He shivers, occasionally, with clammy fear. He is adrenal rather than cerebral, physical rather than mental.

He is, in short, the perfect antithesis of everything Education stands for. The paradox lies in the fact that he is also the product of Education. A dozen years ago, he was in our kindergartens. He went on our field trips to the bakery, and danced around ribboned poles at our May Festivals. Only yesterday, he was studying "social living" in our junior highs. He has been tested and guided and motivated. It has cost the taxpayers, over a decade or so, several thousand dollars to produce a Slob. It hardly seems worth it, does it?

To wax classical for a moment, we may compare Education to old Cronus, who produced a numerous family, only to find himself in his old age hunted down mercilessly and mutilated by his own children. This is a melancholy prospect indeed. Let us see if, from our knowledge of Slobbism, we can avert from our profession the fate of Cronus.

First, let us clear the ground by conceding in advance some of the more obvious truisms. Let us concede that the great majority of our high-school pupils is as yet free from the grosser manifestations of Slobbism. We can agree, too, as to the essentially non-school origins of the phenomenon. No one doubts the intricately complex causes which rub against each other long enough and intimately enough to produce the smolder or the flash of blind violence. But, when all this has been said, it does not follow that Education is absolved of all responsibility for the golems who stalk its halls.

Whose fault is it that no more exciting and rewarding goal than sheer sensuality has succeeded in capturing the imagination of these people? Hedonism, after all, is as old as the hills. Its lure was exploded before Christ. Surely Education can, if it tries, break in upon the sterile, revolving-door cycle of liquor and licentiousness.

Who is to blame for the pathological inability of these persons to concentrate for more than a few fleeting moments on anything less basic than feeding, fighting, and fornicating? Could it possibly stem from the kaleidoscopic and chaotic mishmash of canal-building, Hopi Indians, tomato growing, air transport, and steel puddling through which we have merry-go-rounded our pupils in recent years? Is it possible that we have produced a group unamenable to discipline simply because we have never insisted upon their mastering anything which required discipline to overcome?

TO THE SLOB, LIFE IS A DIRTY JOKE

It is barely conceivable that, by destroying the hierarchy of values which placed mastery of specific subject matter in a position of paramount importance, we have persuaded these already confused minds that nothing in life, including life itself, is of any particular importance. We have required them to go to school, but we have not required them to do any work. Instead, we have created special "courses" wherein they might sprawl and leer in company with one another, and where constructive learning is laughed out of court. To the Slob, life is a dirty joke, with school the cream of the jest and educators the buffoons.

We talk of change in the nation's high schools.

Here is a change which must be made, and soon, if we are to avoid destruction.

SOCIALLY UNEDUCABLE MUST BE EXCLUDED

One way or another, the Slob must go. Those of his ilk who have passed the point of no return must be excluded from our schools as socially uneducable, even as we exclude the unfortunate imbecile as mentally uneducable. And let no one challenge our right to take this step. The Slob is more dangerous to his classmates than a walking case of typhoid or tuberculosis. We have not only the right, but the clear and positive duty to quarantine him. It is our shame that we have not done so sooner. What will become of him? When he has reached this stage, he has passed beyond our power to correct. He is no longer susceptible to Education. He has become a subject for criminology.

As Dr. Johnson said of the Scotchman, much may be done with the Slob if he be caught young enough. With a program of specific goals, scientific testing, understanding guidance, and consistent discipline, a school should be able to nip a great deal of Slobbism in the bud. If the school is fortunate enough to be located in a community where the police are alert, the courts tough, and the citizenry concerned, the cult of the Slob can be broken by the united action of all. Where such a happy combination of attitudes is not present, it becomes the positive duty of the school administration to work diligently within the community to produce it.

We have gone overboard on universal education. It has become a fetish, instead of a logically considered objective. By our stubborn refusal to exclude clearly pathological cases from school, we are presently permitting this fetishism to work irremediable wrong upon the great majority of normal children whom we are exposing to this moral plague. It is my conviction that Slobbism is a highly contagious disease. It must be treated as such. Isolation and prophylaxis are strongly indicated.

Law cannot help the deliberate homicide. He defies it.

Medicine cannot help the would-be suicide. He rejects it.

Religion cannot help the hardened atheist. He disbelieves it.

Even so, Education cannot help the full-blown Slob. He loathes it.

It is a sorry tribute to our perspicacity as schoolmen that we have let this thing drift to the point where many of us have become quivering quarry in our own classrooms. I submit that it will be pointless and tragic folly for us and for our country if we stand dithering by while the throat of Education is slowly cut with a switch-blade knife.

6

We Don't Like Youth Very Well

EARL C. KELLEY

Mr. Kelley is professor of secondary education at Wayne State University, Detroit, Michigan.

I have come to this conclusion [we don't like youth very well] reluctantly. . . . our literature during the last 2400 years at least reveals this fact. Today's magazines and newspapers probably devote as much space to this topic as to the bomb and our threatening doom. Our youth, when they are talking about their elders among themselves, reveal it. The wrangling that goes on in many homes attests to this fact. The conflict between age and youth is one of the saddest aspects of our culture. And the saddest fact of all is that age always strikes the first blow.

I am aware that many adults do love youth. Earlier I referred to the oratory at the service clubs. The speakers and the listeners are both sincere, at least at the moment. Some forget their noble sentiments when they go back to getting and spending; others do not. I have known men and women who cared so much about the welfare of youth that they gave all of their time and spent much of their money for youth's betterment.

It is the manner in which our society as a whole—our parents, our teachers, our government, our citizens—behaves regarding youth that we have to examine here. The good people cited above are not enough. No one person, no hundred persons, can do enough on this huge problem to accomplish more than to set an example. We who want our democracy to survive have to see where our values lie and have to learn to give not only our money, but our attitudes and our love. Hostile attitudes on the part of the elders are quickly sensed by youth whose response in many instances is hostility and aggression.

WE PROVIDE POORLY FOR THEM

A good measure, however, of our attitudes toward youth may be gained by the money we are willing to spend for them. The young have many needs, but a good place to start would be to provide them with good schools taught by well-educated, competent, well-paid teachers. This would not answer all of youth's needs, but it would be a good beginning. On the whole, however, we seem to be unwilling to do even this much. I do not know, except by inference, how the schools are faring in other parts of the country, but in Michigan we are in a continuous uproar about getting the voters to approve taxes for our schools. Many of the proposals turned down by the voters are most niggardly to begin with. In many cities of this state schools are being operated on half-time schedules. Parts of the curriculum enjoyed by youth are being cut out, leaving only the parts young people dislike. The building of new schools is being discontinued. Old buildings are being left to deteriorate. One community has two new buildings already finished which are standing idle because there is no staff for them. All this goes on at the very time when the burgeoning crop of postwar babies is coming to school, and the trend is toward larger and larger families.

This is also the time when we have never before been so wealthy. It will not serve any good purpose here for me to quote statistics on annual income and related evidences of wealth. I think no one will question the fact that the United States today has more wealth and a higher standard of living than any large country has ever had at any time in the history of mankind. Yet it is not uncommon to read in the public press that we simply cannot carry the tax load needed to support good schools.

Sidney Harris, whose daily column is filled with intelligent comment on the current scene and whose writings I recommend most highly to any who may read these words, treats of our penury in regard to the support of education (April 1, 1959; Detroit *Free Press*). He says in brief that we are schizophrenic in this matter. We all believe in good schools but seem also to believe in magic and think that if we go to enough PTA meetings, or find enough fault, or pick on our youth enough, our schools will become magnificent institutions by magic and without cost.

He goes on to say that we do not apply magic to our businesses or any of our many other enterprises; that we know these take money, effort, planning, and a goal. He calls attention to the fact that when many children die in a school fire, as happened in Chicago recently, we pass resolutions forbidding the use of fire traps but provide nothing to eliminate them. This, Mr. Harris says, is schizophrenia. Such a society, I say, does not let the right hand know that the left hand is not doing anything. Anybody who wants to verify the above should read the minutes of the Detroit Common Council shortly after the Chicago school fire.

When the great depression of 1929 struck us, the first thing we did was to cut many facilities for youth. Schools needed then to be greatly expanded with much broadening of their offerings. This is obvious because there were so many youth who had no place else to go. But we cut school budgets severely, reduced the salaries of our teachers below what anybody could survive on, and took out all parts of the curriculum which might appeal to idle and disinherited youth. All other agencies for youth suffered similarly. Organized recreation, for example, was eliminated or greatly reduced. Idleness became the unwilling lot of our young. Despair followed closely. Some of our youth sat at home, some went out into our streets and found release from boredom in anti-social behavior, some took to the road. There was a time, so it is said, when there were a million and a half boy and girl tramps on the highways of the richest country on earth. These young people became known as the lost generation. Why were they lost, and what was the cost?

They were lost because we cared more about our money than we did about our young. Of course, these were hard times for all of us. They were much harder than they needed to be, as we can see now. We thought we were financially ruined. It was said that our national debt was twenty billions and could not stand to be raised. If it was raised, the national credit would be gone. The last I heard, our federal debt now is 289 billions, and Uncle Sam's credit is still good. Most of this increase came during World War II. We found that to save our own hides we could get money. In 1933, perhaps our blackest year, we still had our beautiful land, our farms, our factories, and our houses. We simply did not know how to use them. So we saved on the most helpless in our society.

There is a large segment of the lost generation which we usually forget to count. It is the large number who never got started because our economic system prevented their being born. The number of unborn during the thirties must be in the millions. How many scientists, how many teachers, artists, musicians did we lose? We note that tax experts are aghast at the present birth rate. Do they want to wish away human beings with all of their unique potentialities? The only real value in this world is human beings, not forests, oil wells or mines. It is humans which give all of those things value. Each human being that might have been born and was not represents an irreplaceable loss.

The lost generation were not, of course, all lost. Many were damaged needlessly, and some were indeed lost, in that they became criminals as a product of the lives we required them to live. Some became insane. Some were rescued by the creation of two federal agencies, the Civilian Conservation Corps (C.C.C.) and the National Youth Administration (N.Y.A.). Some were just too resilient to be ruined. It takes a lot of doing to spoil a boy or girl. This is a good thing for us older ones. For this lost generation was the one which heroically threw itself in front of the oncoming war machine of the Nazi.

Those who survived this ordeal—and hundreds of thousands of them did not—are now in the early stages of middle age, heads of families, holding responsible positions in our society, reproducing like mad, and causing all kinds of future trouble for the taxpayers who think we are too poor to care for our own.

I have dwelt on the plight of the schools partly, I suppose, because I am a teacher, and educational problems are closer to me than are some others. It also seems to me that for the citizen who is not schizophrenic, paying taxes for schools would be the easiest thing he could do for youth. This is the way he would get most for his money and effort. It would be much cheaper and easier than opening and supporting a teen canteen, for example, and would do more for youth if we really care about them.

Our record in providing other institutions is even more deplorable. Unfortunately, some of our youth, for the safety of the community and for themselves, have to be isolated and secured. Until quite recently we thought nothing of throwing them in jail or penitentiary with older, hardened criminals to absorb all of the fine points of crime and to learn all kinds of depravity. Some time in the early part of this century we saw that this was a harmful way to treat children. We built detention homes, and our state penitentiaries for youth were called schools. In most states youth under a certain age could not be charged with a crime but could only be judged to be delinquent.

This was a big step in the direction of more humane treatment of a segment of our youth. Of course, now when a boy is especially sick and commits a particularly violent act, there is a great cry that he must be "bound over" from the juvenile court to the criminal court where we can do a better job of "getting even" with him for what he has done. In other words we say "This boy is too sick for the best treatment we know about. Because he is so sick, we must give him our worst medicine."

Having established special institutions for youth, we have then failed to support them. Because of our parsimony these detention homes and state "schools," overcrowded and inadequately staffed, have had to become more and more like jails. We still dump dependent children, who are guilty of nothing but having no one to take care of them, into these "homes."

For the past five or ten years a great hullabaloo has been heard in the state of Michigan over the location of a new state school for boys. For many years the so-called "Vocational School" for boys, in Lansing, was outdated, overcrowded and inadequate. What is perhaps even worse, it occupied considerable space right in the city—space that would be very valuable if it were sub-divided. The legislature had finally appropriated funds—no small achievement if you know our legislature—to build a new school out somewhere where there will be more space and property will be cheaper. But whenever a site was chosen, lawsuits and injunctions were brought by citizens who lived near the site and who thought some other part of the state would be better. It appeared that we would never get the new school because nobody wanted it in the same county with him. We had a few bleak and desolate spots in the northern part of our otherwise beautiful state, far from friends and relatives, and it appeared that one of those places, where there were only pine stumps to protest, would have to be used for our new boys' school. We did, however, finally get a good location for the new school.

It will not profit us, I think, to pursue further this story of adult neglect of the needs of youth. The failure to provide adequately for the brain-injured, the spastics, the mentally ill would only labor the point. "Oh masters, if I were disposed to stir your hearts and minds with mutiny and rage . . ."

We use our youth as scapegoats. Often when we ourselves fail, we blame it on our young. This is not new, but recent events point to this fact dramatically.

When Russia launched her first satellite in October, 1957, it not only scared the living daylights out of us, but hurt our pride almost beyond repair. Up to that time we had assumed that we could do everything better than anybody else anywhere. And when our armed forces began to shoot those Roman candles which fell at their feet on Cape Canaveral in an absurd effort to show that we are as smart as anybody else, we almost died of humiliation.

When we looked around for someone to blame, we did not see the Pentagon, large as it is. We did not see the Congress, which appropriates funds for such matters. We did not see the Commander-in-Chief who, within the limits of what Congress provides, controls such matters. Whom did we see? We saw our youth! Here was the perfect scapegoat—perfect because youth has little power to strike back. The logic is clear. (Logic is often a way to get the wrong answer in an orderly fashion.) We did not beat Russia because we have inferior scientists. This is true because our youth are lazy, indolent, fun-loving, and will not study "hard" subjects. This in spite of the fact that the scientists who were working on our missiles were educated in "the good old days," which are never further back than the childhood of the complainers.

I am still enough of a hundred per cent red-blooded American to think that we could have launched the first satellite if we had been willing to make the sacrifice and had not starved or hounded some of our best scientists out of government service.

Then began the most vicious vilification of our youth that has ever occurred in our history. This never could have happened before, because we did not have the mass media previously. Nearly every newspaper, magazine, radio and television station took up the hue and cry. Facts and truth were quite forgotten and ignored. In attacking youth it was logical to include their teachers, who also were relatively helpless and who were, of course, partly to blame for youth's shiftlessness which bordered on treason. A sad aspect of it was that many teachers were stupid enough and masochistic enough to join the pack. It was scapegoating at its worst.

As a result of this reaction to fear and hurt pride, we now find our youth under pressure as never before. And this at a time in their growth when they ought to be expanding into life. This pressure is particularly severe if a youth is so unfortunate as to be considered "gifted." He has had his homework doubled, and some otherwise sane people recommend as much as six hours a night. He has had his grades reduced, despite the fact that he is doing more work than ever. This is the way teachers show that they do too have high standards. I believe that at this particular time our so-called gifted youth are more discriminated against than any other group.

How much leisure does the adult who thinks six hours of homework is about right demand for himself? Even though he may not know any better than to overwork, he hardly would commit himself to that much work after hours. But it's good for growing youth!

To be sure our youth are a good deal more intelligent than we give them credit for, and many have found that the best thing to do is to fail tests so they will not be chosen for special punishment. It is the medium smart who are really catching it.

We use our youth as means to our own ends. This is what is going on with the present demand that every child shall be a scientist and a mathematician. There has been no outcry from youth for this. It is entirely because adults are frightened and think that if the whole population were making missiles, they would somehow be safe. As is always the case, when anyone sticks his nose into business he does not understand, he runs the chance of looking silly.

When we got into World War II we dearly loved the youth we had neglected. Nothing was too good for our boys as long as they went out and fought our battles. Even the colleges, which found themselves nearly devoid of students, found that they could take some who would previously have been rejected. Welcome signs hung from every elm on the campus, and almost any 4F whose body was warm could get in. That was because adults work in colleges, and while students are an awful nuisance to some of them, they still must have a student body.

Terrible things portend for the next war, if it comes, but next time youth will not be in any more jeopardy than anyone else. Indeed, the armed services may be the safest place to be.

Thus I am forced to the sad conclusion that we do not like youth very well. If we did, we would not quarrel with them so much. We would not use them as scapegoats. We would not use them as means to our own ends. We would be more willing to spend our riches on them. We would learn better how to live with them.

7

Facts and Fancies About Talent

JOHN W. GARDNER

Mr. Gardner is President of the Carnegie Corporation and of the Carnegie Foundation for the Advancement of Teaching.

The strategy a society adopts in dealing with differences in ability may depend in part on its views concerning the hereditary nature of such differences. As we shall see, the genetic facts cannot be wholly decisive for social policy. But in the past, certain widely held views concerning heredity have played a powerful role in buttressing social policy with respect to differences in ability.

In societies of hereditary privilege it is usually widely believed that the social strata correspond to hereditary differences in human quality. The society is stratified, the argument runs, because people do differ in quality; and since these differences are hereditary, the stratification is hereditary. This view is most strongly held by the upper classes of a stratified society, of course, but it is apt to be partially accepted throughout the society. It is always startling to the American traveling in a stratified society to discover that though the lower classes may resent certain social inequalities, they more than half accept the ideology that supports those inequalities. I recall the astonishment of a young American soldier in Italy in 1944 when an elderly Italian servant patiently explained to him that the social hierarchy was based on the unshakable facts of human heredity.

"Facts and Fancies About Talent" is from *Excellence* by John W. Gardner (New York: Harper & Row, 1961). Copyright © 1961 by John W. Gardner. Reprinted with permission of Harper & Row, Publishers, Incorporated. (Footnotes that appear in the original source have been omitted.)

The democracies, of course, officially rejected the idea that differences in social status were due to differences in hereditary quality. But even in the democracies the notion refused to die. Herbert Spencer, for example, believed that the poor were "unfit" and should be eliminated. Criticizing this view, Henry George once wrote:

> Mr. Spencer is like one who might insist that each should swim for himself in crossing a river, ignoring the fact that some had been artificially provided with corks and others artificially loaded with lead.

But Mr. Spencer's view of the unfitness of the poor did not die. It was too tempting for the rich and wellborn to suppose that the stratification existing at any given moment was rooted in enduring human qualities. It was too easy to imagine that the latest crop of immigrants was humanly incapable of rising from ignorance and poverty. Thus H. G. Wells wrote in 1906:

> I doubt very much if America is going to assimilate all that she is taking in now; much more do I doubt that she will assimilate the still greater inflow of the coming years. . . . I believe that if things go on as they are going, the great mass of them will remain a very low lower class—will remain largely illiterate industrialized peasants.

The view that the social strata coincided with a natural hierarchy of ability received a shattering blow with the development of relatively objective measures of mental performance. The earliest wide-scale use of objective tests, in World War I, made it clear that intelligence was broadly distributed in the population and that there were rich resources of ability at every social level.

Though the tests made it clear that mental performance did not follow the lines of social stratification, they did not settle the question of whether ability was hereditary. For years this was one of the liveliest topics of debate among research people in psychology.

It is sufficiently controversial as a purely intellectual question; it becomes more so because of its implications for social theory. The argument quickly takes on political overtones. Individuals whose weighing of the evidence leads them to believe that heredity is the dominant factor in intelligence find that this conclusion endears them to some conservative elements in the society, and gains the hostility of certain left-wing thinkers. Lewis Terman was bitterly criticized by the Communists for placing what they considered to be too much emphasis on heredity and too little on environment in the determination of the IQ. On the other hand, the individual whose weighing of the evidence persuades him that environment is more important than heredity finds himself applauded by some liberals who want very much to believe that the intellectual inequalities between men are due to social inequalities.

It is not easy to settle an intellectual question when people have a powerful emotional stake in one or another outcome. As a matter of fact, the experts have long since concluded that for most purposes the question is neither profitable nor meaningful. They point out that it is simply unreal to ask how much of behavior is determined by heredity and how much by environment as though one were asking how many eggs and how much milk went into a pudding. The question oversimplifies an enormously complex matter and treats as separate and self-contained ingredients two factors which are essentially inseparable.

But the layman is not concerned to achieve clarity in matters of theory. He wants to know what it all means for him and for his child. And the truth is that most experts are in reasonable agreement (though they would never admit it) as to what it means for him.

It is clear, for example, that the striking differences in environment that exist do have some effect upon intellectual performance. One youngster may find himself in a stimulating and instructive environment from the first days of infancy. Intelligent adults may give him immeasurable help in learning the names of objects, understanding the consequences of acts and seeing the connections between things. An environment rich in toys, pictures, books and responsive people may give him abundant opportunities for learning and for broadening his horizon. The next child may have a barren and impoverished environment, little or no attention from parents or other children and no tutoring at all in the simple lessons of childhood.

There is evidence that such differences do affect intelligence as measured by tests. But there is also ample evidence that the effect of environmental circumstances on test performance is rather limited.

This has been demonstrated in studies of identical twins reared apart. It is also suggested by the relative stability of the IQ. If environmental circumstances powerfully affect the IQ, one would not expect the IQ to be a very stable measure. The IQ is far from constant—it can be affected in a variety of ways by environmental factors, and in any substantial batch of cases it is possible to point to some fairly marked changes in individual IQs over a period of years. But considering the wide range of environments through which human beings pass, the remarkable thing about the IQ is its relative stability.

The precise degree of stability of intelligence, as measured by tests, is the subject of considerable debate among some of the experts. But the majority of modern workers in the field have a balanced view of the question. They recognize the relative stability of intelligence, but they are willing to accord ample weight to environmental influences.

When we examine the appropriate social policy to be adopted in the light of these findings, we are faced with a simpler task than the behavior theorists are faced with. For purposes of social policy, precise answers on this question are not necessary. Even if environment were a modest factor in determining intelligence, social policy would necessarily emphasize the importance of taking this factor into account. Even if only one child in ten could gain in intellectual effectiveness through a more favorable environment, we would still be bound to make the effort.

The other major factor in social policy must be a straightforward admission of the fact that individuals do differ greatly in their capacities, and each must be enabled to develop the talent that is in him. *Whether individual differences in ability are innate or are due to environmental differences, we must deal with them imaginatively and constructively.*

If we are going to develop a sensible approach to the encouragement of talent, we shall have to dispose of a good many myths surrounding the talented individual.

One such myth is summed up in the phrase "early bloom, early fade." There is an old wives' tale to the effect that most highly gifted children "burn themselves out" and never amount to anything as adults. The companion belief is that great men were almost invariably either dull or fractious children. Neither is true.

There is something immensely satisfying about both beliefs and it is a pity to explode them. What could be more comforting to ordinary mortals than the thought that Winston Churchill was an unpromising youngster? Or that Charles Darwin had trouble in school? Or that William Faulkner was a poor student? But it has been demonstrated over and over that youngsters who show early promise tend to perform better in later life than youngsters who do not show early promise. . . .

. . . The classic research in this field is of course the work of Lewis Terman, who selected a group of 1,000 gifted children for long-term study. The study has been going on for approximately 40 years now, and the evidence of continued high performance is impressive.

Another popular misconception is the notion that great talent is usually highly specific. We tend to assume that the man of extremely high talent is narrowly gifted. But the research evidence indicates that gifted individuals generally have many talents rather than a single talent. If the individual is promising in one line, the best guess is that he will be promising in a number of lines.

He probably will not develop his gifts along all the lines open to him, so in later life he may seem less broadly talented than he actually is. Some narrowing is inevitable. There are limitations of time and energy. And there is a "tyranny of talent" which tends to force the narrowing of anyone with extraordinarily high ability in a specific line. Once the talent is discovered it is often so highly rewarded that the individual is apt to neglect (or not to discover) his other talents; and society abets him in this neglect. With all those clavichord recitals at age seven, Mozart could not have had much time for exploration of his other gifts. Such one-sided development may be essential to the highest reaches of performance, and it might be foolish to try to prevent it in people of great talent. But anyone responsible for very gifted young people would do well to assist them in exploring the full range of their talents where possible, and to postpone at least for a time the tyrannical narrowing down.

Still another misconception concerning talented individuals is that they are indecisive, impractical, unreliable in positions of responsibility, and unfit for active life. This is certainly not true of talented people generally. As a matter of fact, large numbers of highly talented individuals choose managerial or other "practical" activities as the chief outlet for their talents. And even those who choose more cloistered paths are not necessarily forced to do so by their own limitations. During World War II many gifted scholars proved themselves extremely able administrators in emergency assignments. And it is a fallacy, in any case, to suppose that responsibility, decisiveness and judgment are qualities which can be tested only in the market place. It is true that the decisions involved in a normal business day might be torture to the average professor, but it is equally true that the decisions involved in composing a lecture would be torture to the average business executive. And the practical realities of faculty politics would test the shrewdness of a congressional party whip.

This is not to say that there is nothing to the legendary impracticality of the talented individual. There are certain fields—art and music, for example—in which society encourages the individual of great gifts to be impractical, and many individuals accept that invitation. But this may be a culturally determined trait. If they lived in a society which defined great artists as highly practical, they might well be so.

Still another myth is that the extremely gifted individual is unstable. In this case the myth is particularly hard to disprove because of the vivid examples which seem to support it. One thinks of Van Gogh cutting off his ear, of Poe's alcoholism, of Nietzsche's incoherent end. But again, the weight of solid evidence is in the other direction. Whenever systematic data have been gathered on a wide range of gifted individuals it has been found that they are apt to be more stable than the less gifted.

8

The Conant Report

PAUL B. DIEDERICH

Mr. Diederich is a Senior Research Associate with Educational Testing Service, Princeton, New Jersey.

As we consider the recommendations of the Conant Report that are likely to have most influence on school policies, "There is need," as the man who rises to speak so neatly puts it, "for a return to basic fundamentals." By this redundant expression I mean the fundamentals we sit on.

Those in the top sixth in scholastic ability, according to this report, ought to sit on hard chairs seven or eight class periods a day listening to other people talk. Five of these periods are for English, a foreign language, mathematics, science, and social studies; two or three more for everything else the school teaches. After school, students have a little time for work, practicing an instrument, games, hobbies, talking with friends, and blowing off steam, but right after supper they must settle down to what Dr. Conant optimistically estimates as three hours of homework. Perhaps he is counting on what we shall get, flesh and blood being what it is, not what teachers will assign, since five subject-matter specialists per day—each smitten with zeal to get as much of his subject as possible into students' heads—will not assign a total of just three hours a night. My own children spent about four during their last two years in high school and a large portion of their weekends, and their interests were not very scholarly, nor were their

---

"The Conant Report" is an unpublished letter written by Paul B. Diederich, Educational Testing Service (Princeton, N. J.), July 6, 1959. Reprinted by permission of Paul B. Diederich. (Mr. Conant's views are expressed on pp. 117–127 of the present volume.)

records unusually good. They were always behind in their work and always feeling guilty about it.

As we advocate a "get tough" policy with these superior students, we should realize that we are advocating a daily schedule for growing boys and girls, at the most social and fun-loving period of their lives, that is a lot tougher than any adult puts in—except a few harassed executives with ulcers. Whenever we teachers go to educational conventions, do we regularly go to seven or eight meetings per day, sitting on hard chairs in cramped quarters the whole time, and then return to our hotel rooms to put in three or four more hours boning up on what the speakers wanted us to know, so that we could prove that we understood it and remembered it when they quizzed us about it next day? This is really too easy a comparison, since the speakers have a long time to prepare what they have to say and try hard to make it interesting, while teachers have to make it up as they go along. If we ever tried this routine for three consecutive days, would we then prescribe that our dearly beloved sons and daughters should undergo an even tougher routine, not for just three days but every day of their lives while they are fizzing with all the juices of adolescence? Would we further prescribe that even this inhuman schedule would never be enough to satisfy the demands of their teachers, so that they would regularly go back to their chairs the following day with feelings of inadequacy and guilt, and be publicly put to shame if their sins of omission were found out?

You may say, "This is sheer exaggeration. Surely going to high school is much nicer than this." No, it is not, and I know whereof I speak. I have just been sitting in classes day after day all over the sixteen excellent school systems participating in the "lay reader study," trying to find out what their above-average teachers are teaching about English. I solemnly declare that at the end of each day visiting classes—even though I am treated as a VIP, not as a guilty student— my fundament is sore, my legs are cramped, my eyes are tired, my brain is reeling, and I would rather do anything else on earth than study for three or four more hours what these students are supposed to study. It is not that the teaching is bad; there is simply too much sitting down, listening to talk, talk, talk. We say that these students ought to learn to "work hard," and they would not mind that in the least; it is the sitting and listening all day in a space half the size of a grave that gets them down. If they seem lazy to us when movement is called for, remember that we have conditioned them only to sitting in chairs and listening. Naturally they droop like a lily when they are up-rooted from this unnatural habitat.

It is equally deadening to teachers who have to impose discipline on five successive large groups of lively, wiggling adolescents whose whole instinctive drive is to stand up, move around, do things, and talk to people, while we have to make them sit still and listen. The teachers come out of it as scarred and tired as the students. The art of teaching is so delicate and difficult that I would be willing to bet that we shall wind up the next century of experimentation with the fully documented conclusion that no one can do it effectively for more than two hours a day—each class hour accompanied by at least two hours of preparation, checking students' work, and conferring with those who need special help. We could put in more time than this by including meetings with students, teachers, and parents, supervising extra-curricular activities, and professional reading and research, but not more time in teaching that would do anyone any good.

All of this dreary, ineffectual round is based on the assumption that learning proceeds best when administered in doses of five periods a week plus homework for all academic subjects. This assumption is unsupported by a shred of evidence in all experimental literature, contrary to common sense, and contrary to the practice of almost all colleges in every country for hundreds of years. Dr. Conant does not say one word to justify it. There is not a word to say that has any rational or experimental foundation.

I append a neat schedule that will teach everything that Dr. Conant wants us to teach in just *two* periods per subject per week. It averages out to just two subjects a day with homework, which will mean an average of two hours of homework per school night if each academic class requires an hour of homework. There is plenty of time left in the daily schedule for art, music, shop, labs, library reading, and all those activities of a modern school that involve standing up, moving around, doing things, and talking to people. It is unfair to condemn such activities with the label "progressive education." They go on in the most conservative schools, and students obviously learn a great deal from them. They also reduce the tail-sitting and listening to the span of time

Illustrative Weekly Schedule

Class Day	All Mon.	Grade 7 Tu-W	Th-F	Grade 8 Tu-W	Th-F	Grade 9 Tu-W	Th-F	Grade 10 Tu-W	Th-F
9–10	CORE	Sci.	Soc.	Soc.	Sci.	Math	Lang.	Lang.	Math
10–11		Math	Lang.	Lang.	Math	Sci.	Soc.	Soc.	Sci.
11–1	LUNCH, independent study, conferences Assembly, music, theater, school government								
1–2	TRIP	Labs	Eng.	Eng.	Labs	Arts	Lib.	Lib.	Arts
2–3		Arts	Lib.	Lib.	Arts	Labs	Eng.	Eng.	Labs
3–5	SPORTS Arts and Labs have a double period once a week. Thus, grade 7 would have a lab on Tuesday and an art on Wednesday.								

that youngsters can endure. If you think that two periods per subject per week would teach only two-fifths as much of the academic fare as Dr. Conant wants, my best guess—after a quarter-century in educational research—is that they would learn as much as they do now, or more. This guess is supported by the fact that nearly all students report that they learn more per year in college, where each class meets only two or three times a week. Why we think youngsters thirteen to seventeen years old can stand more of a classroom grind than college students is something for the historians of our culture to figure out.

The only course in my proposed schedule that might properly be labeled "progressive" is what I have called the "core," for want of a better short name. It is all that remains of the core courses that were so popular and, on the whole, so invigorating during the Eight Year Study. The chief subject I would recommend for this "core" is a careful, systematic study of how the people of the community organize and carry on their work. The rest of the schedule is good, solid, academic fare with English, a foreign language, mathematics, science, and social studies for everyone every year, interspersed with enough ambulatory activities to relieve the tail-sitting. We think of superior students as cherubs in Italian renaissance paintings—all heads and wings, no bottoms. Let us return to fundamentals. They have a bottom and it is sore.

9

Live Students and Dead Education:
Why the High School Must Be Revived

OSCAR HANDLIN

Mr. Handlin is a professor of history at Harvard University.

More money will help. But it will not itself solve the problem. American schools, particularly the high schools, are entering a prolonged crisis, obscured by the debate over the ways and means of financing them. However the funds will be raised, we shall have to reconsider the function of secondary education if we wish to spare our children the chaos that now threatens them in the most vulnerable years of their lives.

The evidence is clear. The number of high school students is larger than ever before, and it will continue to increase for years to come. In this group are boys and girls of types that did not formerly ascend to this level of instruction; it will be dangerous to neglect their needs and interests. Above all, the high schools operate in a new social context, of which they must take account. These developments pose a challenge so serious that we can disregard it only at our peril.

The federal census conveniently tabulates the population by age groups and projects its size into the future. The number of Americans aged fifteen to nineteen grew from slightly more than eleven million in 1955 to well over twelve million in 1958. At that point we began to feel the effects of the post-war baby boom. The size of the group grew more rapidly. In 1965 it will amount to more than seventeen million; in 1970, to well over nineteen million. There is no guesswork to these

From *Atlantic Monthly*, September 1961. Copyright © 1961 by Oscar Handlin. Reprinted by permission of Willis Kingsley Wing.

estimates; these children are already born and on their way toward adolescence. They will enormously expand the pool from which the high school population of the future will be drawn.

An ever-larger percentage of the eligible age group will demand and receive a secondary education. Almost twice as large a proportion of entering students will receive high school diplomas in 1961 as were able to do so twenty years ago. More than 90 per cent of the boys and girls over five and under eighteen are now enrolled in some school; before long *almost all of them will be.* The high school population has already soared under these pressures. From six and a half million in 1950, it has risen to over ten million in 1961.

One can anticipate an even larger increase in the decade ahead, for the high birth rate and the rising level of expectations throughout American society show no signs of subsiding. In addition, the dominant economic trends of our period literally drive young people into the schools.

There is nothing else for them to do. The range of unskilled jobs open to youths of under eighteen years of age is steadily shrinking. The decline of the family farm and mechanization and automation of industry continually reduce the number of places for which they can qualify. The talk of a thirty-hour week to spread employment reflects the desire to limit the size of the labor force, a situation not likely to make attractive openings for the very young. The number of white-collar jobs has grown, but these jobs generally require a high school diploma. As the long process of formal education becomes the universal norm, the thing to do, those who lack education suffer increasingly and are compelled to adhere to the general pattern. All the ways up now lead through the high school, and only the misfits or the children of the very poor and underprivileged are pushed into the narrowing range of employments from which there is no exit. It is not in the least likely that these trends will be reversed in the future.

The high school cannot meet the challenge of the oncoming tide of new students simply by increasing its existing facilities. The high school was an institution developed for a rather select student body, and this much larger aggregate will not fit into its established forms.

THE TOTAL STUDENT BODY

Our students vary greatly in intelligence; as many are below as are above average. The problems of the high school change radically as it begins to serve a clientele unselected as to ability.

The situation of the talented boys and girls is clear-cut. The old curriculum was made for them; the road ahead to college and the professional schools is open; and a good deal of attention is already being devoted to them. They will have to learn to avoid being dragged down by the average of the mass about them. But success in doing so is one of the tests of their ability.

The high school has had less experience in dealing with those who, lacking competence or motivation, are euphemistically called the "academically untalented." The traditional course of study is above their grasp, and the careers open to them are by no means clear. Yet the untalented will comprise a rising percentage of the total student body. They cannot be thrown into a labor market which has no room for them, but the imperatives of a democratic society demand that they have their chance. Formerly, it was possible to shunt them off into various vocational educational programs. Rarely did these programs reflect a positive comprehension of the students they served; all too often they aimed simply to get the less able out of the way of the more able. Characteristically, they absorbed the underprivileged, who lacked the opportunity to develop their ability. It was no coincidence, for instance, that Georgia in 1958 had three times as many students enrolled in such programs as did Massachusetts.

In any case, the old forms of vocational education will be even less useful in the future than in the past; the very same economic changes that drive more students into the schools also undervalue the handicraft skills that can be taught there. These vocational programs are therefore growing at a far lower rate than are other sectors of secondary education.

A large part of the high school population consequently finds itself enmeshed in an institution that has little relevance to present or future needs. These boys and girls have drifted on into the ninth grade because it follows after the eighth. They are told to study subjects they cannot grasp and to acquire skills they may never use. Only athletics, marching bands, and their own social life rescue them from total boredom.

And they are adolescents! Growing into maturity, they feel the need to test their powers and assert their individuality. Lacking recognized means for doing so, confined to a round of purposeless tasks, some become utterly apathetic. Others divert their vitality into the rebellion of juvenile delinquency.

The secondary school must adjust to meet the needs of all these young people. In the 1960s, either it will prepare or it will fail to prepare them for citizenship and for careers. . . .

. . . A large percentage of our boys and girls will resist the efforts of the school to stuff such culture into them. It does not matter. They will make good citizens, businessmen, and parents despite the lack of Latin or of history, if they can grow through the difficult years of adolescence, learning by experience to relate themselves to the world about them.

What is important is that the high school do well what it can do. It serves a democratic society at a point in the lives of its young people when their future is still vague and undefined. It can do no more, but it must do no less, than to endow them, to the limits of their abilities, with the common attributes of our culture.

WHAT DO THE SCHOOLS TEACH? II

1

From Alice's Adventures in Wonderland

LEWIS CARROLL

Lewis Carroll was the pen name of Charles Lutwidge Dodgson (1832–1898), a story writer and an Oxford professor of mathematics.

. . . The Mock Turtle went on.

"We had the best of educations—in fact, we went to school every day——"

"*I've* been to a day-school, too," said Alice. "You needn't be so proud as all that."

"With extras?" asked the Mock Turtle, a little anxiously.

"Yes," said Alice; "we learned French and music."

"And washing?" said the Mock Turtle.

"Certainly not!" said Alice indignantly.

"Ah! Then yours wasn't a really good school," said the Mock Turtle in a tone of great relief. "Now, at *ours*, they had, at the end of the bill, 'French, music, *and washing*—extra.' "

"You couldn't have wanted it much," said Alice; "living at the bottom of the sea."

"I couldn't afford to learn it," said the Mock Turtle with a sigh. "I only took the regular course."

"What was that?" inquired Alice.

"Reeling and Writhing, of course, to begin with," the Mock Turtle replied; "and then the different branches of Arithmetic—Ambition, Distraction, Uglification, and Derision."

"I never heard of 'Uglification,' " Alice ventured to say. "What is it?"

The Gryphon lifted up both its paws in surprise. "Never heard of

From *Alice's Adventures in Wonderland* (1864) by Lewis Carroll.

uglifying!" it exclaimed. "You know what to beautify is, I suppose?"

"Yes," said Alice doubtfully; "it means—to—make—anything—prettier."

"Well, then," the Gryphon went on, "if you don't know what to uglify is, you *are* a simpleton."

Alice did not feel encouraged to ask any more questions about it; so she turned to the Mock Turtle, and said "What else had you to learn?"

"Well, there was Mystery," the Mock Turtle replied, counting off the subjects on his flappers, "Mystery, ancient and modern, with Seaography; then Drawling, the Drawling-master was an old conger-eel, that used to come once a week: *he* taught us Drawling, Stretching, and Fainting in Coils."

"What was *that* like?" said Alice.

"Well, I can't show it you, myself," the Mock Turtle said; "I'm too stiff. And the Gryphon never learnt it."

"Hadn't time," said the Gryphon; "I went to the Classical master, though. He was an old crab, *he* was."

"I never went to him," the Mock Turtle said with a sigh. "He taught Laughing and Grief, they used to say."

"So he did, so he did," said the Gryphon, sighing in his turn; and both creatures hid their faces in their paws.

"And how many hours a day did you do lessons?" said Alice, in a hurry to change the subject.

"Ten hours the first day," said the Mock Turtle; "nine the next, and so on."

"What a curious plan!" exclaimed Alice.

"That's the reason they're called lessons," the Gryphon remarked: "because they lessen from day to day."

This was quite a new idea to Alice, and she thought it over a little before she made her next remark.

"Then the eleventh day must have been a holiday?"

"Of course it was," said the Mock Turtle.

"And how did you manage on the twelfth?" Alice went on eagerly.

"That's enough about lessons," the Gryphon interrupted in a very decided tone. "Tell her something about the games now." . . .

2

Traditional Versus Progressive Education

JOHN DEWEY

Mr. Dewey (1859–1952), a widely known American philosopher and educator, was the father of the "progressive education" movement in the United States. Mr. Dewey served as a professor of philosophy at the Universities of Minnesota, Michigan, and Chicago, and at Columbia University. School and Society *is one of his still-influential books.*

Mankind likes to think in terms of extreme opposites. It is given to formulating its beliefs in terms of *Either-Ors*, between which it recognizes no intermediate possibilities. When forced to recognize that the extremes cannot be acted upon, it is still inclined to hold that they are all right in theory but that when it comes to practical matters circumstances compel us to compromise. Educational philosophy is no exception. The history of educational theory is marked by opposition between the idea that education is development from within and that it is formation from without; that it is based upon natural endowments and that education is a process of overcoming natural inclination and substituting in its place habits acquired under external pressure.

At present, the opposition, so far as practical affairs of the school are concerned, tends to take the form of contrast between traditional and progressive education. If the underlying ideas of the former are formulated broadly, without the qualifications required for accurate statement, they are found to be about as follows: The subject-matter of education consists of bodies of information and of skills that have been worked out in the past; therefore, the chief business of the school is to transmit them to the new generation. In the past, there have also

From *Experience and Education* by John Dewey (New York: The Macmillan Company, 1938). This excerpt if used by permission of Kappa Delta Pi, owners of the copyright.

been developed standards and rules of conduct; moral training consists in forming habits of action in conformity with these rules and standards. Finally, the general pattern of school organization (by which I mean the relations of pupils to one another and to the teachers) constitutes the school a kind of institution sharply marked off from other social institutions. Call up in imagination the ordinary schoolroom, its time-schedules, schemes of classification, of examination and promotion, of rules of order, and I think you will grasp what is meant by "pattern of organization." If then you contrast this scene with what goes on in the family, for example, you will appreciate what is meant by the school being a kind of institution sharply marked off from any other form of social organization.

The three characteristics just mentioned fix the aims and methods of instruction and discipline. The main purpose or objective is to prepare the young for future responsibilities and for success in life, by means of acquisition of the organized bodies of information and prepared forms of skill which comprehend the material of instruction. Since the subject-matter as well as standards of proper conduct are handed down from the past, the attitude of the pupils must, upon the whole, be one of docility, receptivity, and obedience. Books, especially textbooks, are the chief representatives of the lore and wisdom of the past, while teachers are the organs through which pupils are brought into effective connection with the material. Teachers are the agents through which knowledge and skills are communicated and rules of conduct enforced.

I have not made this brief summary for the purpose of criticizing the underlying philosophy. The rise of what is called new education and progressive schools is of itself a product of discontent with traditional education. In effect it is a criticism of the latter. When the implied criticism is made explicit it reads somewhat as follows: The traditional scheme is, in essence, one of imposition from above and from outside. It imposes adult standards, subject-matter, and methods upon those who are only growing slowly toward maturity. The gap is so great that the required subject-matter, the methods of learning and of behaving, are foreign to the existing capacities of the young. They are beyond the reach of the experience the young learners already possess. Consequently, they must be imposed; even though good teachers will use devices of art to cover up the imposition so as to relieve it of obviously brutal features.

But the gulf between the mature or adult products and the experience and abilities of the young is so wide that the very situation forbids much active participation by pupils in the development of what is taught. Theirs is to do—and learn, as it was the part of the six hundred to do and die. Learning here means acquisition of what already is incorporated in books and in the heads of the elders. Moreover, that which is taught is thought of as essentially static. It is taught as a finished product, with little regard either to the ways in which it was originally built up or to changes that will surely occur in the future. It is to a large extent the cultural product of societies that assumed the future would be much like the past, and yet it is used as educational food in a society where change is the rule, not the exception.

If one attempts to formulate the philosophy of education implicit in the practices of the newer education, we may, I think, discover certain common principles amid the variety of progressive schools now existing. To imposition from above is opposed expression and cultivation of individuality; to external discipline is opposed free activity; to learning from texts and teachers, learning through experience; to acquisition of isolated skills and techniques by drill, is opposed acquisition of them as means of attaining ends which make direct vital appeal; to preparation for a more or less remote future is opposed making the most of the opportunities of present life; to static aims and materials is opposed acquaintances with a changing world.

Now, all principles by themselves are abstract. They become concrete only in the consequences which result from their application. Just because the principles set forth are so fundamental and far-reaching, everything depends upon the interpretation given them as they are put into practice in the school and the home. It is at this point that the reference made earlier to *Either-Or* philosophies becomes peculiarly pertinent. The general philosophy of the new education may be sound, and yet the difference in abstract principles will not decide the way in which the moral and intellectual preference involved shall be worked out in practice. There is always the danger in a new movement that, in rejecting the aims and methods of that which it would supplant, it may develop its principles negatively rather than positively and constructively. Then it takes its clue in practice from that which is rejected instead of from the constructive development of its own philosophy.

I take it that the fundamental unity of the newer philosophy is found in the idea that there is an intimate and necessary relation between the processes of actual experience and education. If this be true, then a positive and constructive development of its own basic idea depends upon having a correct idea or experience. Take, for example, the question of organized subject-matter . . . The problem for progressive education is: What is the place and meaning of subject-matter and of organization *within* experience? How does subject-matter function? Is there anything inherent in experience which tends towards progressive organization of its contents? What results follow when the materials of experience are not progressively organized? A philosophy which proceeds on the basis of rejection, of sheer opposition, will neglect these questions. It will tend to suppose that because the old education was based on ready-made organization, therefore it suffices to reject the principle of organization *in toto*, instead of striving to discover what it means and how it is to be attained on the basis of experience. We might go through all the points of difference between the new and the old education and reach similar conclusions. When external control is rejected, the problem becomes that of finding the factors of control that are inherent within experience. When external authority is rejected, it does not follow that all authority should be rejected, but rather that there is need to search for a more effective source of authority. Because the older education imposed the knowledge, methods, and the rules of conduct of the mature person upon the young, it does not follow, except upon the basis of the extreme *Either-Or* philosophy, that the knowledge and skill of the mature person has no directive value for the experience of the immature. On the contrary, basing education upon personal experience may mean more multiplied and more intimate contacts between the mature and the immature than ever existed in the traditional school, and consequently more, rather than less, guidance by others. The problem, then, is: how these contacts can be established without violating the principle of learning through personal experience. The solution of this problem requires a well thought-out philosophy of the social factors that operate in the constitution of individual experience.

What is indicated in the foregoing remarks is that the general principles of the new education do not of themselves solve any of the problems of the actual or practical conduct and management of progressive schools. Rather, they set new problems which have to be worked out on the basis of a new philosophy of experience. The problems are not even recognized, to say nothing of being solved, when it is assumed that it suffices to reject the ideas and practices of the old education and then go to the opposite extreme. Yet I am sure that you will appreciate what is meant when I say that many of the newer schools tend to make little or nothing of organized subject-matter of study; to proceed as if any form of direction and guidance by adults were an invasion of individual freedom, and as if the idea that education should be concerned with the present and future meant that acquaintance with the past has little or no role to play in education. Without pressing these defects to the point of exaggeration, they at least illustrate what is meant by a theory and practice of education which proceeds negatively or by reaction against what has been current in education rather than by a positive and constructive development of purposes, methods, and subject-matter on the foundation of a theory of experience and its educational potentialities.

It is not too much to say that an educational philosophy which professes to be based on the idea of freedom may become as dogmatic as ever was the traditional education which is reacted against. For any theory and set of practices is dogmatic which is not based upon critical examination of its own underlying principles. Let us say that the new education emphasizes the freedom of the learner. Very well. A problem is now set. What does freedom mean and what are the conditions under which it is capable of realization? Let us say that the kind of external imposition which was so common in the traditional school limited rather than promoted the intellectual and moral development of the young. Again, very well. Recognition of this serious defect sets a problem. Just what is the role of the teacher and of books in promoting the educational development of the immature? Admit that traditional education employed as the subject-matter for study facts and ideas so bound up with the past as to give little help in dealing with the issues of the present and future. Very well. Now we have the problem of discovering the connection which actually exists *within* experience between the achievements of the past and the issues of the present. We have the problem of ascertaining how acquaintance with the past may be translated into a potent instrumentality for dealing effectively with the future. We may reject knowledge of the past as the *end* of education and thereby only emphasize its importance as a *means*. When we do that we have a problem that is new in the story of education: How shall the young become acquainted with the past in such a way that the acquaintance is a potent agent in appreciation of the living present?

3

How Can the Junior High School Curriculum Be Improved?

A. H. LAUCHNER

Mr. Lauchner was principal of the Thornburn Junior High School in Urbana, Illinois, when this article was written.

How can the junior high school curriculum be improved? The powers that be have given me the sixty-four dollar question. Just take a semester's leave of absence and travel over the United States, visiting junior high schools, talking with administrators, teachers, students, and patrons. Then, read newspaper editorials and comments from readers. Finally, in light of all this, cast your eyes on articles in leading periodicals of our profession . . . and try to come up with a story on improving the junior high curriculum.

Know what I mean? Sit with a principal and most likely the conversation will run to a discussion of problems, needs, and interests of boys and girls. The school administrator may speak of club work, assemblies, student council, intramurals, plays, committees, field trips, exhibits, and programs of one sort or another as being proper activities for the curriculum designed to meet such needs.

Visit with the classroom teacher and chances are that she too will mention problems and needs of youth . . . but start talking about those school activities mentioned by the administrator and like as not she will make the comment that "They take too much time from regular classes."

Corner some of those students about whose future we are so vitally

Reprinted by permission from the *Bulletin of the National Association of Secondary-School Principals*, March 1951. Copyright: Washington, D. C.

concerned . . . and hear them question the value of "what they are giving us."

Now watch editorials in the daily press. Hear the cry about schools "losing their standards." Read the reports of "softening up" . . . of "getting away from the real purpose of the school." Note the reports on what today's graduates "are like."

Read the article in a national periodical—a story prepared by a teacher in an institution of higher learning—and return in your thinking to needs, problems, interests.

With all this on your mind, become a little bird and listen to a group of mothers discussing Junior across the fence. "I tell you," says one, "the children cannot spell as well as they could when I went to school." A neighbor agrees, and quickly protests the school's "doing so many things it isn't supposed to do." The group decides that their junior high school must return to the three R's.

And someone asks yours truly to attempt an essay on improving the junior high curriculum! Well, I shall do it, win or lose.

What is the school for, anyway? Try to secure agreement on that one. I shall not try; it is my intention to state what I think . . . and let it go at that.

I believe the purpose of the school—in a democracy—should be to turn out young men and women *who can and will live useful, thoughtful, happy lives.*

If that be true, then something of the true nature of improving the junior high curriculum should at once come to light. *The curriculum should seek to bring about the desired goal.*

Now let us give consideration to the arguments presented by those folks who wish to contend that schools should return to the job for which they were founded, that task being to teach the three R's. Thousands, perhaps millions, of today's older folks are seeking to lay the blame on the school's failure to do the old-fashioned teaching as they wish it done for all the sins and woes that this day beset us.

What are some of these troubles of 1951?

I should say that difficulties within individual families is one. The divorce rate is appalling . . . but that tells only part of the story. Millions of homes from which no divorce story is forthcoming nevertheless live in constant strife. Dare anyone say that a stricter adherence to a program of the subjects of reading, writing, and arithmetic would have improved the pattern of family living? I hope no one cares to argue the point, for many of these men and women who fail to get along in family responsibilities these days were in school back when "standards were high."

A second ill of this day lies in the trend of getting more and more on the outs with those who have been more successful than we. In nearly all walks of life is this true. Millions of us look upon anyone who does well as being dishonest; since we fail to get along ourselves, we just can't see how anyone can manage. And so there is in this country today an eternal strife between those who succeed and get ahead and those who sit around and blame others. What has brought this about? Is it a lack of training in math or any other of the good, old subjects? I doubt if there's much argument on the question.

As I am writing this, a call comes over the radio. "If you drink, don't drive" says the voice. Yes, brother, that's a problem in this enlightened country of ours. And if you think all of those drivers who kill innocent people because they mix drinking and driving are folks who weren't taught the "things for which school's for" you've another guess coming; not a few of them are college graduates. It seems we've done a better job teaching math than we have abstinence.

Shall we speak of tossing money away? I am nearing the end of a tour of the country which has taken me through the Middle West, East, West, and South. It is no untruth when I make the statement that I've seen thousands of folks competing with one another to get rid of their money. And for nothing of value. Take the funds spent in the United States for drinking, gambling, and betting on the horses and the schools could get along with it quite well, thank you. *But that's not all of it;* add the dollars that are lost in so-called petty gambling, throw in the thousands that carnivals remove from communities, plus half a dozen other "expenditures" most of us know about, and you will be thinking about another source of unhappiness that cannot be laid to failure of traditional subjects.

As I have traveled from one community to another, I have noted that Community Chest organizations are having their usual tough time in raising funds for what any right-thinking man knows is a good cause. Boy Scouts, Y.M.C.A.'s, Salvation Army, the church . . . nearly always it's a task to secure what they need. Why? Well, I know one argument folks can't raise; they cannot lay this to poor spelling or reading. It may be poor figuring, but not the kind they're yelling about.

And here's another illness of today's generation; most of us do not know what to do with our leisure time. And that's fatal, for we are having more and more idle-hours laid at our doors. Time was when a man worked sixty hours a week and thought nothing of it. I'm not the one to argue that was good, but I'll suggest that working forty hours a week and squandering the rest is not good either. Does anyone think the millions of our citizens are going to use this newly-discovered time to continue further learning in the three R's? Let's be honest.

These are just some of the more pressing problems that are apparent to the casual observer who may be wondering what the junior high should do about improving the curriculum.

What can be done?

———

1. A lot of us are going to have to do the best job of our lives in the matter of public relations. We shall need to make a sale to our classroom teachers and to John Q. Public. It will not be easy. Through the years we've built a sort of halo around reading, writing, and arithmetic. We've said they were for everybody . . . rich and poor, brilliant and not-so-mentally-endowed, ones who liked them and those who failed to go for them. Teacher has said that these were something "everyone should learn." The principal has remarked, "All educated people know how to write, spell, and read." When some child declared a dislike for a sacred subject, he was warned that, if he failed to master it, he would grow up to be a so-and-so.

The Three R's for All Children, and All Children for the Three R's! That was it.

We've made some progress in getting rid of that slogan. But every now and then some mother with a Phi Beta Kappa award or some employer who has hired a girl who can't spell stirs up a fuss about the schools . . . and ground is lost.

Math has not been the all-important subject they told me it would be. The facts I learned in history have for the most part passed by the boards. The algebra I didn't learn hasn't been needed.

Not everyone needs all this. Especially is it true since we are being called upon to keep all the children of all the people in school until they are sixteen years of age.

Furthermore, not all children can get these subjects.

When we come to the realization that not every child has to read, figure, write and spell . . . that many of them either cannot or will not master these chores . . . then we shall be on the road to improving the junior high curriculum.

Between this day and that a lot of selling must take place. But it's coming. We shall some day accept the thought that it is just as illogical to assume that every boy must be able to read as it is that each one must be able to perform on a violin, that it is no more reasonable to require that each girl shall spell well than it is that each one shall bake a good cherry pie.

We cannot all do the same things. We do not like to do the same things. And we won't. When adults finally realize that fact, everyone will be happier . . . and schools will be nicer places in which to live. (Some of my colleagues will want to root me out of the profession for these statements.)

2. If and when we are able to convince a few folks that mastery of reading, writing, and arithmetic is not the one road leading to happy, successful living, the next step is to cut down the amount of time and attention devoted to these areas in general junior high school courses.

Let those boys and girls who have the ability and inclination in these areas go along.

But for those thousands who have neither capacity nor desire to work in those areas, the school must provide other types of activities they can and will do. It's high time for us to stop cramming these subject materials down all mouths. Too many of the mouths have to be pried open . . . and too many of the stomachs cannot or will not digest the materials forced into them. When there is no assimilation, food cannot be said to have value.

When I think of the many, many hours we struggle with young men and women in junior high, laboring to teach them the multiplication tables (in remedial classes), I wonder! When I step into a school that is working day and night to get everyone to spell, I do a bit of debating in my mind. When I visit a school that worries and frets constantly because "so many of the children cannot read," I find myself asking the question if these teachers know that thousands of youngsters never will be able to read. One junior high in the East has, after long and careful study, accepted the fact that some twenty per cent of their students will not be up to standard in reading . . . and they are doing other things for these boys and girls. That's straight thinking. Contrast that with the junior high which says, "Every student must know the multiplication tables before graduation."

Such a requirement attaches more importance to those tables than I'm willing to accord them.

3. Having reached the point at which we are willing to admit that these subjects . . . and I shall now include history, geography, Latin, algebra . . . are not worth the stress we've been giving them, we may then turn to two topics for consideration.

First, there is the possibility of combining. Here in Long Beach where I am writing this article a Social Living course includes grammar, literature, reading, writing, spelling, library work, citizenship, and history. Students meet with a teacher two periods per day.

In Minneapolis, they call it *common learnings*. In the Folwell Junior High of that city pupils of grades seven, eight, and nine have social studies and language arts under the direction of one teacher who builds around student needs and interests.

In Battle Creek, the *core* has been in use for some time. This is a program which brings together much of the materials we used to think should be departmentalized. Here, as at Minneapolis, students remain longer than a single period with a core teacher.

In Baltimore, at Garrison Junior High School, they are working with a *home-room-centered curriculum*. Several seventh grade groups remain with the home-room teacher for half of each day, while teachers in charge work around problems of interest and value.

In Denver, it's called *general education*. They are not seeking to do away with the three R's, but rather to make them "function for pupils in everyday living." At Byers Junior High School they are striving to develop three more R's . . . successful human Relationships, Responsibility, and Rectitude.

In Elizabeth, New Jersey, this plan has been given the name, *Unified Studies*. In junior highs of that city the attempt is to integrate, to correlate, to unify, to weave together in related pattern . . . rather than to pour knowledge in from so many different sources which may not know too much about each other.

Other cities are carrying on similar programs in junior high, and hundreds of junior high schools which make no claims regarding unifying or fusing of subject matter have nevertheless placed the teaching of two subjects (usually language arts and social studies) under the direction of one teacher in what is known as block of time instruction. A few are adding mathematics or science to the block and making it a triple period. The Jennings Junior High of Akron has a math-science block, giving them a double block of time.

There is a lot of howling about the block of time . . . and more about common learnings programs. It must be admitted that: (a) Few teachers are trained for it. (b) Not many principals and administrators have made a careful study of it. (c) Not much training is going on . . . though a good many clinics and workshops are springing up. (Strong in-service programs are the answer.) (d) The public does not seem ready. (e) Not too much evidence of success has been presented.

On the other hand, some of the schools which have carried on such programs for five or more years claim: (a) With such a program, attendance at school is much more satisfactory. (b) There is less skipping. (c) More books are read. (d) Students show more interest in school. (e) Both teachers and students are more at ease. (f) The program calls for and results in much wider use of materials.

---

4. Having done some combining, the next step is that of adding, changing, enriching.

This is the thing nearly every principal wants to do . . . but "just can't work it into the program." The combining makes such a course possible.

In Jefferson Junior High School of Dubuque, Iowa, time has been found for an auditorium class. Students meet in groups, weigh matters of interest to school and community, determine courses of action, appoint committees, and work at problems. They learn business procedures, abiding by decisions of majorities, and a lot more that I have not time to relate in this story. (Many schools reserve this experience for a mere handful of students.) Roosevelt Junior High of Rockford, Illinois, is another school where I found auditorium classes in session; Principal Welsh is sold on the value of such a class. So am I.

In Bret Harte Junior High, Los Angeles, and Wilson Junior of Appleton, Wisconsin, interesting co-educational physical education classes are being conducted. They, and a few other schools I've visited, have caught the idea of wholesome development of boy-girl relationships. (It's surprising the number of schools which seem afraid or unwilling to have girls and boys play together.) At Bret Harte Junior High School boys and girls are organized into forty groups to engage in volleyball, table tennis, paddle tennis, handball, shuffleboard, folk dancing, square dancing, and social dancing. (Note that these are activities which have carryover value; students may use them for leisure-time pursuits later on in life.)

One school in San Francisco, the James Denman Junior High, has set up a course, designed "to introduce students to a variety of fundamental experiences in the fields of Home Mechanics, Home Economics, and Home Arts." Units include Electricity in the Home, General Household Maintenance, The Family Car, Decoration and Redecoration, Family Foods, and Crafts for Leisure Time. This is co-educational.

Southwest Junior High of Battle Creek and South Park Junior of Oshkosh are among other schools which have broken away from traditional and are providing co-educational classes in arts and crafts.

In the new junior high at Elmhurst, Illinois, may be found a shop for girls and a home mechanics area for boys.

The junior high in New Castle, Indiana, has organized a fine program for boys in the field of home mechanics.

Many junior high schools have complete home units in which girls are trained to keep a home neat and attractive. Test Junior High of Richmond, Indiana, has a cottage for this purpose.

A large number of junior high schools have little theater programs, and some, including the Wilson Junior High of Muncie, Indiana, have their own radio stations in the operation of which students receive real training.

Scores of junior high schools include detailed study of campaigns and elections in their program and provide real activity to permit students to engage in all phases of this practice in citizenship. At Bloomfield, New Jersey, I observed all this in practice.

I've visited schools where much is made of banking and saving, but in general, it must be admitted that most of our junior high schools do little to encourage thrift. By a bit of effort on the part of a staff the curriculum can be made rich in matters of taking care of money.

In more than a dozen junior high schools, I have noted campaigns for Community Chest in progress; but again, it must be said we've merely scratched the surface in such phases of community endeavor. Teaching anyone to share is much to be desired.

Since wholesome family relationships mean so much in lives of people, there should be courses in this area of living in junior high schools where children are so impressionable. I grant you that finding the proper folks to teach these classes is no easy job . . . but securing excellent teachers for any field is not always a simple matter.

———

What to do with high-ability students is always a question; many is the teacher who finds herself unable to keep up with them or cope with them when they find things boring. Some schools are pioneering in doing things for such children. In one school they are permitted to miss classes now and then and given something to do that will make use of their talents. A lad is allowed to spend several days at the art museum, a young lady is given the chore of arranging materials in display cases in corridors, another student spends a week at work in the library, and yet another takes the school's projector apart, oils proper parts, and puts it back together again. Certain gifted students are put to work aiding others who cannot do the work without a great deal of help. Some of the gifted children serve in the office, others in corridors. A young man does all the cartoons for the annual. Now and then one finds a school in which superior students are permitted to browse in the library when they've completed work in a given lesson. (We used to assign them extra problems in math or give them added words to spell; for their ability to learn quickly they were rewarded by having more of what they could already do so well heaped on their shoulders.)

The important thing to remember in setting up a program for top-ability children is to help them escape boredom, to challenge their abilities and talents to productive endeavor, to use them to stimulate others wherever and whenever possible, and to lead them to broadness of mind.

The idea that such children should be in their "regular" classes all of the time must be abandoned if the curriculum is to be enriched as far as they are concerned.

———

Now, what to do with the slow ones? (Not all of us serve in schools where the average I.Q. is 125, with practically no one under 100. I visited one.)

There was a time, years ago, when most junior high schools practiced "grouping." Then, for a while, a majority dropped the idea as being undemocratic.

We are grouping again. This is particularly true of the slow learners. I have observed one school after another in which small classes of boys, girls, or both are working under the direction of teachers who have them in all academic areas.

In one junior high many of these youngsters have reading ability at only second or third grade level, but they are reading the same stories . . . brought down to their level . . . as are their fellow students in regular classes. Their language lessons are at their level, as is spelling, science, and other academic work. In music, shop, home making, crafts, and physical education some of these children do as well as any.

In Grant Junior High of Syracuse some of these low-ability boys may be seen together in a Junior Trades Class while certain girls who would find the regular curriculum impossible attend Girls Trade Class. I observed them and was quite impressed by their happy attitudes.

Some people object to separating such boys and girls from other children with more ability, but to me it makes sense. It does less harm to the self-respect of a young man than leaving him to flounder among others with whom he cannot keep the pace. With normal children he can have no feeling of success; he is a failure . . . but with other boys of somewhat equal ability he can be and is successful. That develops security . . . and belongingness. All children deserve to have these feelings.

To improve the curriculum within its walls each junior high school must plan to make adequate provision for the education of its "highs" and "lows." That offers a challenge.

————

This brings me back to the point at which this story began. Is the junior high a building in which young men and women are brought to be crammed with facts, tables, dates, rules, and other such elements of the curriculum which have been handed down from one generation to another? Is it a day-home in which citizens of today and tomorrow learn to serve, share, save, select, sing? Or is it a place where young people are taught to cook and sew, put in a fuse or repair a screen, make articles from metal, clay, or plastic material, or do a sketch?

Put all of that together and it will approach what the junior high should be like.

Establish such flexibility in the curriculum as will permit realization of the dream . . . and the improvement will have come about.

4

A Crisis of Purpose

ARTHUR E. BESTOR

Mr. Bestor, a professor of history at the University of Washington, formerly taught at the University of Illinois. He has been president of the Council for Basic Education and his two books, Educational Wastelands *(1953) and* The Restoration of Learning *(1955), are frequently referred to in debates on education.*

The present crisis in the American public-school system is, at bottom, a crisis of purpose. Low achievement is the consequence of low aims. Confusion about the purposes of the high school has produced the shortcomings so appallingly evident today. In an article published in 1952 I spoke of the problem as "Aimlessness in Education." May I repeat what I said then, five years before Sputnik: "If we really believe that education is vital to our safety, then we need to know exactly what kind of schooling constitutes genuine education, and what kind is merely a gaudy show."[1]

For twenty-five years, at least, the purposes of our high schools have been determined by a narrow group of educational theorists who like to describe themselves as "professional" educators—thereby implying that a college professor in the liberal arts or sciences (who may devote a lifetime to teaching) is somehow an amateur in education. Contemptuously rejecting the views of the scholarly and scientific world, these professional educationalists have redefined the purposes of both elementary and secondary schools in terms that are almost completely non-intellectual, and that are often belligerently anti-intellectual. Year by year, the high-school curriculum has come to have less

From *Vital Speeches of the Day*, September 15, 1958. Reprinted by permission of the publisher and the author.

[1] *Scientific Monthly*, vol. 75, pp. 109–116 (August 1952).

and less connection with the real world of mature intellectual activity. As a consequence, the American high school now prepares its students for a grotesque dream world, where science and mathematics do not count (though in the real world they underlie our whole technology), where foreign languages are unnecessary (though in the real world our responsibilities as a world power make them indispensable), where history can be overlooked (though the real world is a changing world, which history alone can interpret).

The educational theory that dominates our public-school system today is an attempt to escape from reality, not an effort to grapple with the actual intellectual problems of the contemporary world. To conceal this fact, professional educationists insist that the school should not be judged in terms of the intellectual achievement of its students. The school is to be looked upon as a welfare agency performing a variety of social services, of which intellectual training is merely one and a relatively minor one. Let us examine this argument in its own terms.

The public schools enroll virtually all the young people of the nation. These young people are facing all sorts of personal problems. They must all eventually make a living, hence the question of a well-paid future job is much on their minds. They are all growing up—a disconcerting, even painful, experience—and they can well be "mixed up" without being "crazy." A substantial number of these young people have a most unsatisfactory home life. Poverty, the divorce of their parents, discriminations practised against them as members of a minority group create in them deep-seated emotional and psychological disturbances. Problems like these are much more real to vast numbers of the young people than are the problems presented by *Macbeth*, by algebra, by grammar, by the American Constitution, or by the reaction of hydrochloric acid with zinc.

Taking these facts as their starting point, professional educationists insist that the public school must try to solve all the resulting problems. "It is the job of the school," according to a pronouncement of one of the most influential bodies of American professional educators, "to meet the common and the specific individual needs of youth."[2] Because a young man's need for a job is so evident, the school should make every effort to help him "develop salable skills." For a young woman, cooking and sewing and homemaking should be a central feature of the program. If a child comes from a broken home, then the school must devote its main effort to giving him a sense of security. When young people reach adolescence, and begin to feel excited and disturbed about the opposite sex, the school must move in on the problem with courses in sex education. If accidents are increasing, the school must teach youngsters to drive. Since personal appearance counts for so much, the school ought to show girls how to dress attractively and how to use make-up, and boys how to be well-groomed.

Educationists who look upon the school's responsibility in this way believe that every school activity must be placed on a par with every other. If a pupil is getting some kind of practical training that he needs, then he is being "educated," regardless of any intellectual content in what he is doing. To say that one activity is any more "educational" than another—to treat one kind of study as intrinsically more worthwhile and important than another—would be undemocratic. The Educational Policies Commission (set up by the National Education Association and one of its departments) undertook a few years ago to describe an ideal school program in an imaginary community, which it called Farmville. The Commission stated the principle thus: "There is no aristocracy of 'subjects' in the Farmville curriculum. Mathematics and mechanics, art and agriculture, history and homemaking are all peers."[3]

Intellectual training gets short shrift in such a conception of education. Educationists who view the school program in this way are apt to think of intellectual training as simply a special form of vocational training, rather than as an exciting venture in ideas, important in its own right and vital to intelligent citizenship. Science and mathematics,

---

[2] National Association of Secondary-School Principals, *Planning for American Youth* (Washington, 1944), p. 10.

[3] Educational Policies Commission, *Education for All American Youth* (Washington, 1944), p. 142.

these educationists assume, are appropriate only for the few who are going to be scientists or engineers or doctors. History and English, they believe, are for the minority who plan to be writers or historians or lawyers. Pupils destined for other jobs, the educationists insist, can get along without these forms of knowledge, or with minimum dosages.

Another aspect of this philosophy must be noted. Many of the social and psychological problems of young people can be handled more effectively through extra-curricular activities—editing the school paper, planning class parties, running student government, managing athletic teams, and the like—than in a formal classroom. Because the handling of these personal problems is so important, educationists wish to erase the traditional line between the curriculum (the course of study) and the other activities connected with the school, thus permitting youngsters to devote all or most of their time to activities rather than studies.

This shift of emphasis from intellectual to non-intellectual activities in the school leads to some extremely odd statements about the things with which the school should concern itself. One such document from Illinois is worth citing. Under the auspices of the state, a certain professor of education undertook to list the "real-life problems" of young people, which the school should attempt to deal with by a "reorientation" of its curriculum. Among the fifty-five items on the list there was no mention whatever of any branch of science or mathematics, though "camping" and "doing parlor stunts" rated specific attention. Here are some of the problems, put forward in all seriousness as proper concerns of the school: "The problem of developing one or more 'making things,' 'making it go,' or 'tinkering' hobbies," "The problem of improving one's personal appearance," "The problem of developing and maintaining wholesome boy-girl relationships," and "The problem of selecting a 'family dentist' and acquiring the habit of visiting him systematically.[4]

I have no doubt that some thoughtless adolescents consider these

---

[4] Harold C. Hand, "Problems of High School Youth," in Illinois Secondary School Curriculum Program, Bulletin No. 11, pp. 30–32 (August 1950).

"problems" significant enough for them to spend precious school time—*their* time, paid for by their parents and by the rest of us—in learning the answers. Did the American people, however, create a nationwide public-school system to deal with problems like these? They did not. Neither parents nor citizens at large originated these proposals. They were devised by doctrinaire educational theorists. Whatever public acceptance they have won is the result of irresponsible, high-pressure salesmanship on the part of professional educationists.

The argument, briefly put, is that because a social need exists the school must therefore attempt to satisfy it. This is a complete *non sequitur*. The school is only one of the agencies that exist to satisfy the needs of society. Each agency has its own area of responsibility, because each possesses a particular sort of competence. The particular competence of a school is in providing intellectual training. It was created for this purpose and its facilities and techniques—classrooms, laboratories, libraries; assignments, recitations, lectures, examinations—are adapted to this particular end. To subordinate this end to something else (no matter how worthy) is to deprive society of a vital service that no other agency can provide.

When a school takes over a function that it is less competent to perform than some existing social agency, the net effect is to impair the welfare of society, not to improve it. Family life is said to have deteriorated in the United States. The public schools have made a great fuss over courses in "home and family living." Nothing in the present situation suggests that such courses have succeeded in reducing the divorce rate or accomplishing any of the other results so glowingly promised. On the other hand, there is good reason to believe that the influence of the home upon young people has been seriously undermined by the very effort of the school to take over functions properly belonging to the family. The promise that the school will effectively perform these functions is a promise that cannot possibly be kept. Nevertheless the irresponsible utterances of educationists about taking over responsibilities that the home has neglected contribute to the very breakdown they are talking about. Their words are an encouragement to weak-minded parents to dump their problems on the school instead of dealing with them as they should.

There is, of course, one kind of school that can and does assume responsibility for the entire life of the young person in its charge. This is the full-time residential or boarding school. Such a school stands *in loco parentis*, exercising the authority and assuming the responsibility of the home. It provides medical services. It enforces discipline twenty-four hours a day. It furnishes recreation. It usually sponsors religious services, making itself the channel through which the church performs its functions. Under these circumstances the influence of every social agency except the school is suspended, and the school not only can but must take over their duties.

A strong argument can be made (as, indeed, Admiral Rickover has done) for creating in the United States a large number of full-time residential schools, in which public funds would provide both subsistence and tuition for the students enrolled. Such schools would be capable of assuming the responsibilities that American educationists are talking about. But educationists are not urging the creation of such schools. They are asking that the public schools, as they now exist, assume these wide-ranging responsibilities. They close their eyes to the basic fact that the American public school is a *day school*, which has charge of the student for no more than half (and usually much less than half) of each waking day, for only five days out of each week's seven. During the greater part of his conscious life, a student is under the influence of—within the sphere of control of—other institutions of society, upon which responsibility also rests. There must be a distribution of function among the various agencies of society, the school included, because there is a distribution of time among them. The school has responsibility for part, but only part, of his time. *Which* part of the child's upbringing, given this distribution of function, is the peculiar and inescapable responsibility of the school?

The experience, practice, and policy of a residential school is peculiarly relevant in this connection. Though such a school must assume responsibility for the entire life of its students, it never permits a blurring of the line that separates the curriculum from the rest of its activities. Formal classroom periods are devoted to basic intellectual disciplines and uninterrupted study periods are set aside. All other functions are performed outside the curriculum. Now, the time available to the day school is roughly the equivalent of the time devoted in a residential school to the curriculum proper. A student can expect to receive an education of equal depth and value in a public day school, only if the same number of classroom periods are devoted to serious intellectual training as would be the case in a residential school, and only if the public school insists upon homework equal in amount to the work done in the study periods that a residential school sets aside in the evenings and on weekends and holidays. If a public day school purports to offer a genuine education—rather than a watered-down imitation—then it must prevent any and every encroachment upon the time that students devote to study of the fundamental intellectual disciplines. School administrators must draw a sharp line between the curriculum and extra-curricular activities. In the time available to the school for the latter—for activities over and above the basic curriculum—it can accomplish many desirable vocational and social ends. Athletics, shop-work, cooking, and driver-training are perfectly legitimate *extra-curricular* activities, recognized as valuable in the most traditional schools. "The battle of Waterloo," Wellington is supposed to have said, "was won on the playing fields of Eton."[5] Every good school accomplishes much besides intellectual training. Only by distinguishing clearly between the classroom and the playing field, however, can serious and honest results be achieved by either.

The school must plan its program in terms of the time that has been made available to it. Most of the time made available in America to the public school is *curricular* time, within which the school is under solemn obligation to plan a continuous, cumulative, uninterrupted program of intellectual training. A small balance of time is also available for extra-curricular activities under supervision of the school. The school, if honest and responsible, must promise, in the way of vocational training and social conditioning, no more than it can perform within the

---

[5] *Oxford Dictionary of Quotations* (2nd ed., London, 1953), p. 564.

limits of this *extra-curricular* segment of time. Before embarking on vast programs purporting to advance social, psychological, and vocational purposes, the school must demand and receive from society whatever additional allotments of student time (as well as whatever additional allotments of money) may be necessary to carry out such programs. If, for example, the school is really to take over the responsibilities of the home, it must take time away from the home life of the student and must be vested with the disciplinary authority of the home. Barring such a grant of time, authority, and money (a grant most unlikely to be forthcoming), the school has no business promising—or even consenting—to assume responsibility for tasks that are outside its province. Indeed, until the school has proved itself willing to carry out honestly, thoroughly, and unremittingly its assigned task of intellectual training, there is no reason in the world for society to say to it, "Well done, thou good and faithful servant: thou hast been faithful over a few things, I will make thee ruler over many things."

The contention that American public schools can carry on the miscellany of activities that professional educationists advocate, can introduce these activities into the curriculum itself, and can at the same time provide basic intellectual training of undiminished quality is a preposterous contention on its very face. The hard, unyielding statistics, moreover, show that American public schools, taken as a whole, have failed—calamitously failed—to provide the mass of our young people with intellectual training of the quality and thoroughness required in the modern world.

5

From The Saber-Tooth Curriculum

HAROLD BENJAMIN

Mr. Benjamin has taught at the Universities of Minnesota and Colorado, Stanford University, the George Peabody College for Teachers in Tennessee, and Glassboro State College in New Jersey. He is the author of Building a National System of Education *(1950).*

The first great educational theorist and practitioner of whom my imagination has any record (began Dr. Peddiwell in his best professorial tone) was a man of Chellean times whose full name was *New-Fist-Hammer-Maker* but whom, for convenience, I shall hereafter call *New-Fist.*

New-Fist was a doer, in spite of the fact that there was little in his environment with which to do anything very complex. You have undoubtedly heard of the pear-shaped, chipped-stone tool which archeologists call the *coup-de-poing* or fist hammer. New-Fist gained his name and a considerable local prestige by producing one of these artifacts in a less rough and more useful form than any previously known to his tribe. His hunting clubs were generally superior weapons, moreover, and his fire-using techniques were patterns of simplicity and precision. He knew how to do things his community needed to have done, and he had the energy and will to go ahead and do them. By virtue of these characteristics he was an educated man.

New-Fist was also a thinker. Then, as now, there were few lengths to which men would not go to avoid the labor and pain of thought. More readily than his fellows, New-Fist pushed himself beyond those lengths to the point where cerebration was inevitable. The same quality of intelligence which led him into the socially approved activity of producing a superior artifact also led him to engage in the socially disapproved practice of thinking. When other men gorged themselves on the proceeds of a successful hunt and vegetated in dull stupor for many hours thereafter, New-Fist ate a little less heartily, slept a little less stupidly, and arose a little earlier than his comrades to sit by the fire and think. He would stare moodily at the flickering flames and wonder about various parts of his environment until he finally got to the point where he became strongly dissatisfied with the accustomed ways of his tribe. He began to catch glimpses of ways in which life might be made better for himself, his family, and his group. By virtue of this development, he became a dangerous man.

This was the background that made this doer and thinker hit upon the concept of a conscious, systematic education. The immediate stimulus which put him directly into the practice of education came from watching his children at play. He saw these children at the cave entrance before the fire engaged in activity with bones and sticks and brightly colored pebbles. He noted that they seemed to have no purpose in their play beyond immediate pleasure in the activity itself. He compared their activity with that of the grown-up members of the tribe. The children played for fun; the adults worked for security and enrichment of their lives. The children dealt with bones, sticks, and pebbles; the adults dealt with food, shelter, and clothing. The children protected themselves from boredom; the adults protected themselves from danger.

"If I could only get these children to do the things that will give more and better food, shelter, clothing, and security," thought New-Fist, "I would be helping this tribe to have a better life. When the children became grown, they would have more meat to eat, more skins to keep them warm, better caves in which to sleep, and less danger from the striped death with the curving teeth that walks these trails by night."

Having set up an educational goal, New-Fist proceeded to construct a curriculum for reaching that goal. "What things must we tribesmen know how to do in order to live with full bellies, warm backs, and minds free from fear?" he asked himself.

To answer this question, he ran various activities over in his mind. "We have to catch fish with our bare hands in the pool far up the creek beyond that big bend," he said to himself. "We have to catch fish with our bare hands in the pool right at the bend. We have to catch them in the same way in the pool just this side of the bend. And so we catch them in the next pool and the next and the next. Always we catch them with our bare hands."

Thus New-Fist discovered the first subject of the first curriculum— fish-grabbing-with-the-bare-hands.

"Also we club the little woolly horses," he continued with his analysis. "We club them along the bank of the creek where they come down to drink. We club them in the thickets where they lie down to sleep. We club them in the upland meadow where they graze. Where-ever we find them we club them."

So woolly-horse-clubbing was seen to be the second main subject in the curriculum.

"And finally, we drive away the saber-tooth tigers with fire," New-Fist went on in his thinking. "We drive them from the mouth of our caves with fire. We drive them from our trail with burning branches. We wave firebrands to drive them from our drinking hole. Always we have to drive them away, and always we drive them with fire."

Thus was discovered the third subject—saber-tooth-tiger-scaring-with-fire.

Having developed a curriculum, New-Fist took his children with him as he went about his activities. He gave them an opportunity to practice these three subjects. The children liked to learn. It was more fun for them to engage in these purposeful activities than to play with colored stones just for the fun of it. They learned the new activities well, and so the educational system was a success.

As New-Fist's children grew older, it was plain to see that they had an advantage in good and safe living over other children who had never been educated systematically. Some of the more intelligent members of the tribe began to do as New-Fist had done, and the teaching of fish-grabbing, horse-clubbing, and tiger-scaring came more and more to be accepted as the heart of real education.

For a long time, however, there were certain more conservative members of the tribe who resisted the new, formal educational system on religious grounds. "The Great Mystery who speaks in thunder and moves in lightning," they announced impressively, "the Great Mystery who gives men life and takes it from them as he wills—if that Great Mystery had wanted children to practice fish-grabbing, horse-clubbing, and tiger-scaring before they were grown up, he would have taught them these activities himself by implanting in their natures instincts for fish-grabbing, horse-clubbing, and tiger-scaring. New-Fist is not only impious to attempt something the Great Mystery never intended to have done; he is also a damned fool for trying to change human nature."

Whereupon approximately half of these critics took up the solemn chant, "If you oppose the will of the Great Mystery, you must die," and the remainder sang derisively in unison, "You can't change human nature."

Being an educational statesman as well as an educational administrator and theorist, New-Fist replied politely to both arguments. To the more theologically minded, he said that, as a matter of fact, the Great Mystery had ordered this new work done, that he even did the work himself by causing children to want to learn, that children could not learn by themselves without divine aid, that they could not learn at all except through the power of the Great Mystery, and that nobody could really understand the will of the Great Mystery concerning fish, horses, and saber-tooth tigers unless he had been well grounded in the three fundamental subjects of the New-Fist school. To the human-nature-cannot-be-changed shouters, New-Fist pointed out the fact that paleolithic culture had attained its high level by changes in human nature and that it seemed almost unpatriotic to deny the very process which had made the community great.

"I know you, my fellow tribesmen," the pioneer educator ended his argument gravely, "I know you as humble and devoted servants of the Great Mystery. I know that you would not for one moment consciously oppose yourselves to his will. I know you as intelligent and loyal citizens of this great cave-realm, and I know that your pure and noble patriotism will not permit you to do anything which will block the development of that most cave-realmish of all our institutions—the paleolithic educational system. Now that you understand the true nature and purpose of this institution, I am serenely confident that there are no reasonable lengths to which you will not go in its defense and its support."

By this appeal the forces of conservatism were won over to the side of the new school, and in due time everybody who was anybody in the community knew that the heart of good education lay in the three subjects of fish-grabbing, horse-clubbing, and tiger-scaring. New-Fist and his contemporaries grew old and were gathered by the Great Mystery to the Land of the Sunset far down the creek. Other men followed their educational ways more and more, until at last all the children of the tribe were practiced systematically in the three fundamentals. Thus the tribe prospered and was happy in the possession of adequate meat, skins, and security.

It is to be supposed that all would have gone well forever with this good educational system if conditions of life in that community had remained forever the same. But conditions changed, and life which had once been so safe and happy in the cave-realm valley became insecure and disturbing.

A new ice age was approaching in that part of the world. A great glacier came down from the neighboring mountain range to the north. Year after year it crept closer and closer to the head waters of the creek which ran through the tribe's valley, until at length it reached the stream and began to melt into the water. Dirt and gravel which the glacier had collected on its long journey were dropped into the creek. The water grew muddy. What had once been a crystal-clear stream in which one could see easily to the bottom was now a milky stream into which one could not seen at all.

At once the life of the community was changed in one very important respect. It was no longer possible to catch fish with the bare hands. The fish could not be seen in the muddy water. For some years.

moreover, the fish in this creek had been getting more timid, agile, and intelligent. The stupid, clumsy, brave fish, of which originally there had been a great many, had been caught with the bare hands for fish generation after fish generation, until only fish of superior intelligence and agility were left. These smart fish, hiding in the muddy water under the newly deposited glacial boulders, eluded the hands of the most expertly trained fish-grabbers. Those tribesmen who had studied advanced fish-grabbing in the secondary school could do no better than their less well-educated fellows who had taken only an elementary course in the subject, and even the university graduates with majors in ichthyology were baffled by the problem. No matter how good a man's fish-grabbing education had been, he could not grab fish when he could not find fish to grab.

The melting waters of the approaching ice sheet also made the country wetter. The ground became marshy far back from the banks of the creek. The stupid woolly horses, standing only five or six hands high and running on four-toed front feet and three-toed hind feet, although admirable objects for clubbing, had one dangerous characteristic. They were ambitious. They all wanted to learn to run on their middle toes. They all had visions of becoming powerful and aggressive animals instead of little and timid ones. They dreamed of a far-distant day when some of their descendants would be sixteen hands high, weigh more than half a ton, and be able to pitch their would-be riders into the dirt. They knew they could never attain these goals in a wet, marshy country, so they all went east to the dry, open plains, far from the paleolithic hunting grounds. Their places were taken by little antelopes who came down with the ice sheet and were so shy and speedy and had so keen a scent for danger that no one could approach them closely enough to club them.

The best trained horse-clubbers of the tribe went out day after day and employed the most efficient techniques taught in the schools, but day after day they returned empty-handed. A horse-clubbing education of the highest type could get no results when there were no horses to club.

Finally, to complete the disruption of paleolithic life and education, the new dampness in the air gave the saber-tooth tigers pneumonia, a disease to which these animals were peculiarly susceptible and to which most of them succumbed. A few moth-eaten specimens crept south to the desert, it is true, but they were pitifully few and weak representatives of a once numerous and powerful race.

So there were no more tigers to scare in the paleolithic community, and the best tiger-scaring techniques became only academic exercises, good in themselves, perhaps, but not necessary for tribal security. Yet this danger to the people was lost only to be replaced by another and even greater danger, for with the advancing ice sheet came ferocious glacial bears which were not afraid of fire, which walked the trails by day as well as by night, and which could not be driven away by the most advanced methods developed in the tiger-scaring courses of the schools.

The community was now in a very difficult situation. There was no fish or meat for food, no hides for clothing, and no security from the hairy death that walked the trails day and night. Adjustment to this difficulty had to be made at once if the tribe was not to become extinct.

Fortunately for the tribe, however, there were men in it of the old New-Fist breed, men who had the ability to do and the daring to think. One of them stood by the muddy stream, his stomach contracting with hunger pains, longing for some way to get a fish to eat. Again and again he had tried the old fish-grabbing technique that day, hoping desperately that at last it might work, but now in black despair he finally rejected all that he had learned in the schools and looked about him for some new way to get fish from that stream. There were stout but slender vines hanging from trees along the bank. He pulled them down and began to fasten them together more or less aimlessly. As he worked, the vision of what he might do to satisfy his hunger and that of his crying children back in the cave grew clearer. His black despair lightened a little. He worked more rapidly and intelligently. At last he had it—a net, a crude seine. He called a companion and explained the device. The two men took the net into the water, into pool after pool, and in one hour they caught more fish—intelligent fish in muddy water—than the whole tribe could have caught in a day under the best fish-grabbing conditions.

Another intelligent member of the tribe wandered hungrily through the woods where once the stupid little horses had abounded but where now only the elusive antelope could be seen. He had tried the horse-clubbing technique on the antelope until he was fully convinced of its futility. He knew that one would starve who relied on school learning to get him meat in those woods. Thus it was that he too, like the fish-net inventor, was finally impelled by hunger to new ways. He bent a strong, springy young tree over an antelope trail, hung a noosed vine therefrom, and fastened the whole device in so ingenious a fashion that the passing animal would release a trigger and be snared neatly when the tree jerked upright. By setting a line of these snares, he was able in one night to secure more meat and skins than a dozen horse-clubbers in the old days had secured in a week.

A third tribesman, determined to meet the problem of the ferocious bears, also forgot what he had been taught in school and began to think in direct and radical fashion. Finally, as a result of this thinking, he dug a deep pit in a bear trail, covered it with branches in such a way that a bear would walk out on it unsuspectingly, fall through to the bottom, and remain trapped until the tribesmen could come up and despatch him with sticks and stones at their leisure. The inventor showed his friends how to dig and camouflage other pits until all the trails around the community were furnished with them. Thus the tribe had even more security than before and in addition had the great additional store of meat and skins which they secured from the captured bears.

As the knowledge of these new inventions spread, all the members of the tribe were engaged in familiarizing themselves with the new ways of living. Men worked hard at making fish nets, setting antelope snares, and digging bear pits. The tribe was busy and prosperous.

There were a few thoughtful men who asked questions as they worked. Some of them even criticized the schools.

"These new activities of net-making and operating, snare-setting, and pit-digging are indispensable to modern existence," they said. "Why can't they be taught in school?"

The safe and sober majority had a quick reply to this naive question. "School!" they snorted derisively. "You aren't in school now.

You are out here in the dirt working to preserve the life and happiness of the tribe. What have these practical activities got to do with schools? You're not saying lessons now. You'd better forget your lessons and your academic ideals of fish-grabbing, horse-clubbing, and tiger-scaring if you want to eat, keep warm, and have some measure of security from sudden death."

The radicals persisted a little in their questioning. "Fishnet-making and using, antelope-snare construction and operation, and bear-catching and killing," they pointed out, "require intelligence and skills—things we claim to develop in schools. They are also activities we need to know. Why can't the schools teach them?"

But most of the tribe, and particularly the wise old men who controlled the school, smiled indulgently at this suggestion. "That wouldn't be *education*," they said gently.

"But why wouldn't it be?" asked the radicals.

"Because it would be mere training," explained the old men patiently. "With all the intricate details of fish-grabbing, horse-clubbing, and tiger-scaring—the standard cultural subjects—the school curriculum is too crowded now. We can't add these fads and frills of net-making, antelope-snaring, and—of all things—bear-killing. Why, at the very thought, the body of the great New-Fist, founder of our paleolithic educational system, would turn over in its burial cairn. What we need to do is to give our young people a more thorough grounding in the fundamentals. Even the graduates of the secondary schools don't know the art of fish-grabbing in any complete sense nowadays, they swing their horse clubs awkwardly too, and as for the old science of tiger-scaring—well, even the teachers seem to lack the real flair for the subject which we oldsters got in our teens and never forgot."

"But, damn it," exploded one of the radicals, "how can any person with good sense be interested in such useless activities? What is the point of trying to catch fish with the bare hands when it just can't be done any more. How can a boy learn to club horses when there are no horses left to club? And why in hell should children try to scare tigers with fire when the tigers are dead and gone?"

"Don't be foolish," said the wise old men, smiling smiles. "We don't teach fish-grabbing to grab fish; ₩ develop a generalized agility which can never be develop⌐ training. We don't teach horse-clubbing to club horses; we teach ₁ᴛ develop a generalized strength in the learner which he can never get from so prosaic and specialized a thing as antelope-snare-setting. We don't teach tiger-scaring to scare tigers; we teach it for the purpose of giving that noble courage which carries over into all the affairs of life and which can never come from so base an activity as bear-killing."

All the radicals were silenced by this statement, all except the one who was most radical of all. He felt abashed, it is true, but he was so radical that he made one last protest.

"But—but anyway," he suggested, "you will have to admit that times have changed. Couldn't you please *try* these other more up-to-date activities? Maybe they have *some* educational value after all?"

Even the man's fellow radicals felt that this was going a little too far.

The wise old men were indignant. Their kindly smiles faded. "If you had any education yourself," they said severely, "you would know that the essence of true education is timelessness. It is something that endures through changing conditions like a solid rock standing squarely and firmly in the middle of a raging torrent. You must know that there are some eternal verities, and the saber-tooth curriculum is one of them!"

6

On Real Learning

WILLIAM PLUTTE

Mr. Plutte is the principal of the De Anza High School in Richmond, California.

It is time that a misconception was corrected. First, let us clear the air by stating that we have never coached or taught physical education. This article is not to be construed as a defense of athletics, but a statement of observable concepts.

On what basis are sports and physical education considered frills? So-called experts in education have mouthed this untruth so often that it has been accepted as a cardinal precept. The term may also be related to dramatics, music, assemblies, etc., but we shall confine our statements to sports, the much maligned phase of our educational program. We would like to emphasize again that sports are an integral part of the total educational program.

Extracurricular activities are learning situations in addition to the academic program. It is universally accepted that student government officers must be academically sound, yet this belief is not in general existence for students involved in other areas, even though they are more in the public eye than most elected representatives.

In sports, the general lack of academic achievement has developed the public image of the athlete as one with all brawn and no brains. In some cases this is certainly true, but as an overall picture it is a gross misconception. When an athlete is failing academically, the fault generally lies with the school administration, not the athlete.

High school students will generally come through to the degree of

From *Athletic Journal*, September 1962. Reprinted by permission.

attainment that is expected of them. If school administration policies permit participation in athletics with no regard to academic achievement, there will always be those who are trying to slide by. In addition, there will always be several athletes participating who may actually be failing their grades.

If participants in extracurricular activities are expected to meet their academic obligations, then they are in a worth-while program which gives them abstract knowledge and realistic rewards.

In relating sports to the academic facets of education, in what subject matter course do the individuals have to perform as a team group for the good of the whole? Yet, within this group effort there is ample opportunity for the individual to be recognized for his special efforts.

In what course do we find concrete and evidenced rewards for successful achievement as are present in football, where a youngster is shown the proper way to tackle and minutes later enjoys the satisfaction of applying this knowledge in a practical and satisfying manner? There is constant stress on *learning through doing*, yet, practically speaking, this concept is effected only, with few exceptions, in extracurricular activities.

Possibly much of the malignment of extracurricular activities is due to the fact that no subject enjoys the whole-hearted, voluntary effort on the part of students that they evidence when they participate in sports, plays, etc. It is possible that resentment on the part of academic teachers has tended to minimize or ridicule such activities to the point where it is universally accepted by some people, that frills have no place in a school program.

A further examination of the total program in schools would indicate a need for humanizing our offerings. Techniques and sound and immediate goals can be improved and devised to afford students sound learning in all areas.

Pedagogical ivory towers should be demolished and a real-life approach to education must be developed and used—not merely phrased in course outlines. When youngsters are finally striving in courses, not just to earn a grade, but because they have a true understanding of why they are learning, then school administrators will find it quite unnecessary to downgrade activities as frills. Then the true value of sports, dramatics, marching bands, rallies, and assemblies will have been recognized for what they were all the time—learning situations outside the cubicles known as classrooms.

7

Athletics in High School

JAMES S. COLEMAN

Mr. Coleman is professor of sociology at the Johns Hopkins University. He is the author of The Adolescent Society *(1961).*

The role of interscholastic athletics in high schools is a controversial one. Athletics is castigated as the antithesis of scholastic activity by intellectuals—many of whom have never taken part in interscholastic sports. It is defended and praised as the builder of men by coaches and athletes—most of whom have a vested interest in this proposition.

It is characteristic of athletics to provoke violent and lasting controversies, for it occupies a very special position in high schools. The amount of attention devoted to athletics would be most striking to an innocent visitor to a high school. A visitor entering a school would likely be confronted, first of all, with a trophy case. His examination of the trophies would reveal a curious fact: The gold and silver cups, with rare exception, symbolize victory in athletic contests, not scholastic ones. The figures adorning these trophies represent men passing footballs, shooting basketballs, holding out batons; they are not replicas of "The Thinker." The concrete symbols of victory are old footballs, basketballs, and baseballs, not works of art or first editions of books won as literary prizes. Altogether, the trophy case would suggest to the innocent visitor that he was entering an athletic club, not an educational institution.

Walking further, this visitor would encounter teen-agers bursting from classrooms. Listening to their conversations, he would hear both casual and serious discussions of the Friday football game, confirming

From *The Annals of the American Academy of Political and Social Science*, November 1961. Reprinted by permission of the publisher and the author.

his initial impression. Attending a school assembly that morning, he would probably find a large segment of the program devoted to a practice of school yells for the athletic game and the announcement of a pep rally before the game. At lunch hour, he would be likely to find more boys shooting baskets in the gymnasium than reading in the library. Browsing through a school yearbook, he would be impressed, in his innocence, with the number of pages devoted to athletics.

Altogether, this visitor would find, wherever he turned, a great deal of attention devoted to athletics. As an impressionable stranger, this visitor might well suppose that more attention is paid to athletics by teen-agers, both as athletes and as spectators, than to scholastic matters. He might even conclude, with good reason, that the school was essentially organized around athletic contests and that scholastic matters were of lesser importance to all involved.

To be sure, his impression would vary from school to school—but, perhaps surprising to him, it would vary little by the social origins and destinations of the adolescents served by the schools. In ten schools recently studied by the author, athletics was about as dominant, by any of several criteria, in middle class schools with a high proportion of their graduates going to college as in working class schools.

Considering his impressions, such a visitor to American high schools might ask himself two questions: First of all, why is it this way? He had assumed, naively, that schools were for learning, yet his impressions led to a different conclusion. He had talked with educators about curriculum, new academic programs, and scholastic standards. Yet, upon visiting the schools, he found the adolescents' attention on athletics, and all the excitement and enthusiasm he found was focused around athletic contests. Why the discrepancy?

The visitor might ask another question: What are the consequences of the attention devoted to athletics? What are the consequences within the school itself, and what are the long-term consequences for these adolescents when they have become adults?

It is indisputable that the interscholastic sports function to give the school and the community a collective identity. Few principals would seriously consider dispensing with these games. Yet, it is also indisputable that athletic contests create serious problems for schools. Perhaps the most serious problem is the change they engender in the institution itself. Their very importance to the life of the school transforms the school from an institution devoted to learning into an institution focused, at least partly, on athletics.

It is useful to wonder whether another mechanism might not give the school collective goals without effecting this transformation. Completely to replace athletic contests between schools with something else would possibly have ill effects. To reduce the dominance of athletics in high schools, however, clearly would be desirable. The most obvious course is to keep the game but to change the content in the direction of educational goals. Although it is true that athletics fits especially well with the interests and energies of adolescents, other games could fit equally well.

There is some experience with games and contests other than athletics, the most extensive being with debate. In a number of areas where debate leagues have flourished, these contests have generated some of the same community and school enthusiasm and involvement that is evident with athletic games. In a few states, interscholastic leagues promote competition in other fields than athletics: music, drama, mathematics. Although the effects of these contests have not been adequately evaluated, they do provide examples of what might be done.

There has very recently been another development which promises to make games truly educational in many areas. These are social and economic games which use a complex environment provided by electronic computers. The first to be developed were management games which involve teams of decision-makers representing competing firms. These games have been used by business and are coming to be used in graduate business schools. A political game, with teams representing political candidates in competition for votes, has been programed for a computer and is used in a college course at Johns Hopkins. At least one economic game has been developed—at Washington University in St. Louis—for teaching the course in principles of economics. Experience with these games shows that they generate a high degree of involvement and interest among players and spectators. It is possible that the most valuable use of machines in education will come to be their use for games, rather than programed learning.

These examples indicate that it is possible to change the content of games in an educational direction yet to maintain some of the values athletics provides for school. To do this, however, would require more than sporadic contests. To gain attention and involvement, leagues, schedules, and tournaments would be necessary. Through such means, it might be possible to transform schools back into the educational institutions they were intended to be. An innocent visitor to such an institution, upon examining the trophy case, listening to student conversation, and examining a yearbook, might well conclude that the institution was one devoted to learning.

8

The Comprehensive High School

JAMES B. CONANT

Mr. Conant is the former president of Harvard University. In 1963 he was completing a two-year study on the education of American teachers under the auspices of the Carnegie Corporation in New York. The American High School Today, *from which this extract is taken, is the first in a series entitled the Carnegie Series in American Education. Other books by Mr. Conant include* The Child, the Parent and the State *(1959) and* Slums and Suburbs *(1961).*

. . . the comprehensive high school is an American development of this century. It has no equivalent, so far as I am aware, in any European country. If the high school is of sufficient size and located in a community where parental pressure for preparing for college is not overriding, those boys and girls who desire to pursue education beyond the high school level will be in a minority. The question arises whether, being in a minority, such students can obtain an adequate education. Stating it another way, one can raise the question whether, under one roof and under the same management, it is possible for a school to fulfill satisfactorily three functions: Can a school at one and the same time provide a good general education for *all* the pupils as future citizens of a democracy, provide elective programs for the majority to develop useful skills, and educate adequately those with a talent for handling advanced academic subjects—particularly foreign languages and advanced mathematics? The answer to this question would seem to be of considerable importance for the future of American education. If the answer were clearly in the negative, then a radical change in the structure of American public secondary education would be

From *The American High School Today* by James B. Conant (New York: McGraw-Hill, 1959). Copyright © by James Bryant Conant and reprinted with his permission.

in order. If the students in a given geographic area who have the ability to profit from the study of foreign languages and advanced mathematics on the high school level cannot obtain an adequate education in a comprehensive high school, then one can argue that separate high schools for these students should be maintained, as is now the case in some of the large eastern cities. On the other hand, if the answer is in the affirmative, then no radical change in the basic pattern of American education would seem to be required.

The problem of protecting the interest, so to speak, of a minority in an institution arises not only in connection with the pupils who are scholastically able, but also in many schools in connection with the education of those boys who desire to make progress in learning a skilled trade during the high school years. A generation and more ago, in certain states those who were urging the expansion of vocational education with the aid of federal funds decided that it was impossible to do justice to the needs of boys desiring a vocational education within the framework of a general high school. In these states the administrators of the vocational funds insisted on setting up separate vocational schools or, at least, were lukewarm in their enthusiasm for vocational programs in the comprehensive high school. Knowing of this situation, I was curious to discover not only whether in a comprehensive high school the interests of the minority who are academically able were well protected, but also whether it was possible for such a school to provide a satisfactory program for developing certain vocational skills through shopwork if the state permitted the use of federal funds in the comprehensive high school.

A CAUTIONARY NOTE

It is important to point out that this report is in no sense a survey of the comprehensive high school. The study has made no attempt to answer such questions as "How satisfactory is the typical American high school?" Indeed, I am now convinced that it is impossible to obtain information on which one could generalize about the success or failure of the American high school in regard to the education of any group of children. There are too many high schools of too many different types, and I doubt if any procedure can be worked out by which a meaningful sample can be drawn from the 21,000 public high schools. Unless some sort of valid sampling procedure were developed or one had large resources, it would be impossible even to pass judgment on the thousands of high schools of sufficient size in the twenty-six states which have been included in this study. As will be made evident by this report, however, it is possible to make valid judgments about American secondary education, but only *school by school*.

AN EXAMINATION OF COMPREHENSIVE HIGH SCHOOLS IN EIGHTEEN STATES

To repeat, the three main objectives of a comprehensive high school are: *first*, to provide a general education for all the future citizens; *second*, to provide good elective programs for those who wish to use their acquired skills immediately on graduation; *third*, to provide satisfactory programs for those whose vocations will depend on their subsequent education in a college or university. If one could find a single comprehensive high school in the United States in which all three objectives were reached in a highly satisfactory manner, such a school might be taken as a model or pattern. Furthermore, unless there were some especially favorable local features which enabled such a school to attain these three objectives, the characteristics found might be developed in all the other schools of sufficient size in the United States. . . .

CRITERIA FOR EVALUATING A COMPREHENSIVE HIGH SCHOOL

After visiting a number of schools, with the assistance of my staff I drew up a tentative list of criteria which would be useful in passing judgment on whether or not a given school was performing satisfactorily the three main functions of a comprehensive high school. In addition, I noted several features of school organization, the absence or presence of which seemed to me significant. A tentative list thus prepared was subjected to scrutiny by a number of experienced public school administrators, who made certain suggestions for improvement. As finally adopted, the list was as follows, and in all my reports I attempted to answer with a *yes* or *no* the questions implicit in the points listed:

A CHECK LIST TO ASSIST IN
EVALUATING A COMPEHENSIVE HIGH SCHOOL

A. Adequacy of general education for all as judged by:
  1. Offerings in English and American literature and composition
  2. Social studies, including American history
  3. Ability grouping in required courses
B. Adequacy of nonacademic elective program as judged by:
  4. The vocational programs for boys and commercial programs for girls
  5. Opportunities for supervised work experience
  6. Special provisions for very slow readers
C. Special arrangements for the academically talented students:
  7. Special provisions for challenging the highly gifted
  8. Special instruction in developing reading skills
  9. Summer sessions from which able students may profit
  10. Individualized programs (absence of tracks or rigid programs)
  11. School day organized into seven or more instructional periods
D. Other features:
  12. Adequacy of the guidance service
  13. Student morale
  14. Well-organized homerooms
  15. The success of the school in promoting an understanding be-

tween students with widely different academic abilities and vocational goals (effective social interaction among students). . . .

In addition to attempting to evaluate each school in terms of the fifteen points listed above, I was concerned with the instruction in mathematics, science, and foreign languages. Discussions with teachers of these subjects, visits to classrooms, and the comments of students threw light on the adequacy of the offerings and often on the effectiveness of the teaching. It was clear from what the teachers said that only a fraction of the boys and girls in the school in question were able to study effectively and rewardingly a wide program of advanced mathematics, science, and foreign languages. I refer to these students as the "academically talented." In a school in which the distribution of academic talent corresponded roughly to the national norm, only about 15 to 20 per cent of the student body in the ninth grade seemed to be in this group. And it was evident that, in schools with an adequate counseling staff, a majority of the more able students could usually be spotted at least by the end of the eighth grade on the basis of aptitude tests of one sort or another, the records of their work in the lower grades, and teacher evaluations. There are undoubtedly some in the next 10 or 15 per cent who also have the ability to study effectively and rewardingly both foreign languages and mathematics, but the number of those who have real difficulty with either languages or mathematics seems to increase as over-all scholastic aptitude diminishes.

As I discussed with teachers and guidance officers the work of the more able students, I became more and more interested in the programs of the academically talented. Yet, in no school which I visited was it possible for the administrator or the counseling officer to answer with assurance the following question: Are all the able students (say the top 15 or 20 per cent) in this high school electing the twelfth-grade mathematics course (often trigonometry) and the physics course, usually offered in the twelfth grade? Questions of this type which could also be asked about the foreign language program could only be answered in general terms based on an opinion formed by the counselors, the administrators, and the teachers. Information of this sort is obviously of the greatest importance in judging the school under investigation; it might easily happen that the vocational programs leading to the development of skills marketable on graduation would be so attractive as to draw into the programs students who had very high aptitude for academic work. Or even if these programs were not attractive, it might be that the bright-but-lazy boy or girl would concentrate attention on subjects which do not require homework, such as art and music, or typing, or shopwork, rather than elect a stiff academic program.

Because I was unable to obtain from my visits even an approximate answer to the questions about the programs of the more able students, I decided to ask the principals of twenty-two of the schools if they would provide me with what I called an "academic inventory."

I wish to record here my indebtedness to those who cooperated in providing this information at no inconsiderable trouble to themselves. What I asked was to have a list prepared of the students graduated in 1957 whose academic abilities would have placed them in the top 25 per cent of their class prior to the ninth grade. The selection, I suggested, should be made on the basis of a scholastic aptitude test or series of tests. I asked for the full four-year program of each of the students on such a list, omitting the student's name, of course, and indicating whether the student was a boy or girl. From these programs it was then possible for me to answer a variety of questions concerning what courses were being elected by those who were the most able from the point of view of handling academic subjects. In working over the information supplied by the schools, I decided to summarize the programs of the 15 per cent of the most academically able on a national basis as measured by the test scores given us by the school; I would thus have at hand information about the programs of the academically talented. It was evident that the programs of the boys and girls should be treated separately, as there was a clear difference in most schools between programs chosen by boys and those elected by girls.

PRINCIPAL FINDINGS OF MY STUDY

The question I set out to answer I can now answer in the affirmative. *I found eight schools which, in my judgment, were satisfactorily fulfilling the three main objectives of a comprehensive high school.* They were offering adequate instruction in English and social studies as part of general education required of all. These schools were providing significant nonacademic programs which were elected by a substantial number of students. In these same schools, the academic inventory showed that more than half the academically talented boys had studied at least seven years of mathematics and science as well as seven years of English and social studies. This fact is interesting in view of the recent stress on mathematics and science. . . . On the other hand, in no school had a majority of the academically talented girls studied as much as seven years of mathematics and science.

The situation with regard to the study of foreign languages in these eight schools was, in most cases, not satisfactory. In only two schools had a majority of the academically talented boys studied foreign language for as long as three years. In most schools, even the few who had elected to study foreign languages for three or four years had to be content with two years of one language and one or two of another. The academic inventory showed a somewhat better picture so far as the academically talented girls were concerned: in five schools a majority of these girls had studied foreign language for three or more years.

A little arithmetic makes it clear that in those schools in which a majority of the academically talented boys had studied seven years of English and social studies, as well as three years of foreign languages and seven years of mathematics and science, a total of seventeen academic courses with homework had been taken in four years. In only one of the eight schools was this the case for the academically talented boys, and in no school was it the case for the girls.

In all but a few of the schools I have visited, the majority of bright boys and girls were not working hard enough. Academic studies did not cover a wide enough range. Both these deficiencies in the majority of schools on which I have information can be readily corrected by a

Table 1: *School Summary Chart*

School* Size of Graduating Class	A 95	B 373	C 760	D 407	E 273
SCHOOL SUMMARY					
▶ Adequacy of General Education for all as judged by:					
1. Adequate Instruction in English Composition	X	X		X	X
2. Adequate Instruction in Social Studies	X			X	X
3. In required subjects, students grouped by ability	X	X	X	X	X
▶ Adequacy of Nonacademic Elective Program as judged by:					
4. Adequate Nonacademic Elective Programs	X		X	X	
5. Adequate opportunities for supervised Work Experience	X		X	X	
6. Special Provision for Slow Readers	X		X	X	X
▶ Special Arrangements for the academically talented student:					
7. Special provisions for challenging the highly gifted		X	X	X	X
8. Special Instruction in developing Reading Skills	X			X	
9. Regular Summer Session				X	
10. Individualized Programs	X	X		X	X
11. School day organized into 7 or more instruction periods	X	X	X	X	X
▶ Other Features					
12. Guidance Service	X	X	X	X	X
13. Good Student Morale	X	X	X	X	X
14. Well-organized Homerooms		X			
15. Effective Social Interaction among students		X		X	X
ACADEMIC INVENTORY					
16. A majority of the academically talented boys in their four high school years took at least:					
a. 7 years of Math and Science	X	X	X	X	X
b. 7 years of English and Social Studies	X	X	X	X	
c. 3 years of Foreign Languages	X	X	X		X
d. 17 full academic subjects	X	X	X	X	X
17. A majority of the academically talented girls in their four high school years took at least:					
a. 7 years of Math and Science					
b. 7 years of English and Social Studies	X		X	X	
c. 3 years of Foreign Languages	X	X	X	X	X
d. 17 full academic subjects	X	X	X		X

* These 22 high schools are located in the East, Middle West, Southwest, and Far West.

shift of emphasis on the part of those in charge. Improvement would come about almost automatically in most schools if seven years of English and social studies were required and if, instead of a two-year course in a foreign language, a sequence of four years of at least one foreign language were offered, provided the counselors emphasized the importance of foreign language for the academically talented boys and mathematics and science for the academically talented girls.

(X indicates fulfillment of the criterion)

F	G	H	I	J	K	L	M	N	O	P	Q	R	S	T	U	V
596	175	443	422	350	378	400	312	550	73	100	382	440	310	502	360	787
X		X	X	X			X	X		X	X		X			
X	X	X	X	X	X		X	X		X			X	X	X	
X		X		X		X					X		X	X	X	X
X	X	X	X	X		X	X	X	X**	X**		X		X	X	X
X		X	X			X	X								X	
X		X			X	X	X				X		X			X
X	X	X	X			X	X	X	X					X	X	X
		X	X	X					X					X		X
		X			X		X					X				X
X	X	X	X	X	X		X	X	X			X	X		X	X
X	X		X	X					X							
	X	X	X	X	X	X		X	X		X	X	X	X		X
X	X	X		X	X	X	X	X	X	X			X	X		X
X					X				X							
	X	X						X				X				
X	X	X	X	X	X	X	X	X	X	X	X	X	X		X	
X					X		X	X					X	X		

**Schools *O* and *P* are Rural Consolidated High Schools. They have limited vocational trade and industrial programs but have strong programs in agriculture.

One matter on which I should also like to report is the extent to which I found the nonacademic elective programs to be composed of meaningful sequences of courses leading to the development of marketable skills, rather than a hodgepodge of miscellaneous subjects. I venture to take some space to consider this point, because a considerable body of criticism of our public schools has been directed to it. There are those who believe the work in the shops for boys and the courses in stenography, clerical machines, typing, and home economics for girls have no place in a high school in which academic subjects are studied by any considerable fraction of the student body. My conclusion after visiting the shops and talking with the vocational directors in many schools is quite the contrary. There is a false antithesis sometimes drawn between vocational work and an academic program. Even those who elect a vocational program are devoting half their time to academic work in English, social studies, mathematics, and science.

Not only have I found adequate nonacademic elective programs . . . but I have been surprised to see in a number of schools to what a high degree the students in these programs are committed to an elective sequence which is aimed toward developing a particular skill which may be useful to them directly on graduation. . . .

ELIMINATION OF THE SMALL HIGH SCHOOL— A TOP PRIORITY

Most of the schools visited by me and my staff during this past year have had graduating classes of one hundred or more. From what I observed in these schools, in the two schools noted in Table 1 with graduating classes of less than one hundred, and in a much smaller school I visited, I am convinced small high schools can be satisfactory only at exorbitant expense. The truth of this statement is evident if one considers the distribution of academic talent in the school which serves all the youth of the community. It will be a rare district where more than 25 per cent of a high school class can study with profit twelfth-grade mathematics, physics, and a foreign language for four years (assuming that standards are maintained). If a school has a twelfth grade of only forty and if indeed only a quarter of the group can handle the advanced subjects effectively, instruction in mathematics, science, and foreign languages would have to be provided for a maximum of ten students. If the girls shy away from the mathematics and science as they do in most of the schools I visited, the twelfth-grade mathematics classes may be as small as six or seven. To provide adequate teachers for specialized subjects is extremely expensive. Furthermore, to maintain an interest in academic subjects among a small number is not always easy. Wide academic programs are not likely to be offered when the academically talented in a school are so few in number. The situation in regard to the nonacademic elective programs in a small high school is even worse. The capital outlay for equipment as well as the salaries of the special vocational instructors adds up to such a large figure in terms of the few enrolled as to make vocational programs almost prohibitively expensive in schools with a graduating class of less than one hundred.

For the reasons given in the preceding paragraph . . . the district which supports a comprehensive high school must be large enough to provide a school of sufficient size. *I should like to record at this point my conviction that in many states the number one problem is the elimination of the small high school by district reorganization.* Such reorganization has been virtually accomplished by leadership at the state level, legislative action, and subsequent decisions of the electorate in a few states. In all others, citizens who wish to improve public education might well devote their energies to mobilizing opinion in behalf of district reorganization directed toward the reduction of the number of small high schools.

9

A Dilemma of the American Comprehensive High School

FRANK B. LINDSAY

Mr. Lindsay is Chief, Bureau of Secondary Education, California State Department of Education.

"A great tragedy of recent high school education is that so many of our most able young people have learned to express themselves in only one medium—words," stated Professor Herbert J. Klausmeier of the University of Wisconsin, in concluding his extensive study of programs for superior students in Milwaukee and Racine. "Five years of research have shown that superior students are very different in interests, values, types of abilities, and career plans. Such students should not be forced into the same mold. What is needed in high schools is a sense of balance."

These remarks by Professor Klausmeier point out a fundamental dilemma of the American public high school. The high school is a youthful institution, just 142 years of age. Throughout its history, its curriculum has changed in response to demands of the people of the United States for the education of boys and girls. In California, for instance, the first high schools—at San Francisco and Sacramento—were established in August, 1856. At that time the only requirements for admission to Ivy League colleges, in addition to Greek and Latin, were algebra to quadratics and the first two books of Euclid's geometry. The fact is that a century ago the undergraduate curriculum at

From *Journal of Secondary Education*, February 1963. Reprinted by permission of the publisher and the author. (Footnotes that appear in the original source have been omitted.)

Harvard, Yale, and Princeton was not as advanced as the course of study any high school graduate completes today. Then trigonometry was a college sophomore course. Today it is regularly offered in senior high school and tends to be disappearing altogether as a separate course as its elements rapidly enter the mathematics ordinarily studied by junior high school students.

THE DILEMMA: TWO FACTORS

The foregoing references to mathematics highlight two factors which contribute to the high school's dilemma. The first is the stereotype which afflicts both the public and educators: a tendency to assume that the same conditions hold which they experienced in their formative years. The real business of teachers is to direct the learning of today's youngsters toward *their* tomorrows instead of repeating lessons that only extend to the precarious present. A second factor abetting the high school's dilemma is the hidden expectation that the high school population today is or should be like the student bodies of a generation or so ago. The self-satisfaction of educators over enrolling all youth in high school has been marred for some by the dismaying discovery that many students vigorously reject the values and career goals held by the middle-class segment that formerly composed almost the entire student body.

It is a myth that a high school may claim comprehensiveness when it offers a variety of courses in academic and occupational subjects. A high school is not primarily a collection of courses of study. Before a proper curriculum can be established or a faculty of teachers employed, it is essential that a high school face the facts of its community and recognize the genuine range of its prospective students. The entire spectrum of family backgrounds and student abilities must be taken fully into account. The slow learners or "indifferent" pupils are as properly a concern of high schools as the more able and average. The strategic questions are, "slow learners at what, and able to achieve what?" A state or nation whose schools graduate only glib manipulators of words is plunging headlong toward destruction. The vaunted graduates of a narrow academic curriculum will prove helpless to save civilization or themselves.

RELEVANCE OF DISCOVERY

Academic myopia has already been recognized by leading scientists and mathematicians, as recent nationwide efforts to modernize high school and college instruction witness. Too frequently high school and undergraduate college courses have been studies *about* science or mathematics. Students have not had opportunity to learn or practice how a biologist, chemist, or physicist thinks and works; what queries each must put to the world of phenomena to obtain intelligible answers. The new approaches urged by the Biological Sciences Curriculum Study, the Chemical Education Material Study, and the Physical Science Study Committee intend to shift the learner from passive recipient of knowledge to practitioner along with experienced scientists. In similar fashion the School Mathematics Study Group and the University of Illinois Committee on School Mathematics have made *discovery* an important element in learning. Laboratories today are no ivory towers for recluses from the real world. The Third Edition (1961) of Webster's *New International Dictionary* testifies that even students of English language are in touch with the usage of daily intercourse.

As the American high school becomes less a cafeteria of canned knowledge and truly "a college of learners" in the original sense of college, not misconceived as a dispenser of erudite bookishness, its potential for comprehensive service to students will appear. The demand for professional and technical personnel over the past decade has tended to obscure the need for a very much enlarged corps of technical aides and skilled workmen to support the professions and man the machines of industrial technology. The ultimate effects of automation, new processes, and new labor-saving devices will be immense increase in installations for production of essential goods. It is a delusion to suppose that the nation faces a surplus of workers even though a particular group in the labor force, as agricultural workers, may further decline in numbers. Employment opportunities in trade, finance, and service industries are growing. Unless the high school doggedly refuses to fulfill its historic mission of educating Americans, it cannot help but shake off its longtime allegiance to Carnegie units and courses couched in a stilted academic mold. Scientists and mathematicians engaged in the reformation of the learning of their disciplines have discovered that the ideas and principles central to these fields, when divested of shackling verbiage and employed in lifelike situations, may be mastered by many students formerly screened away from these studies. Not only can countless additional students do well in reorganized courses; they see sense to knowledge which they may immediately utilize in training for their chosen occupations.

EXCITING NEW PROGRAMS

The high school of the next decade promises to be an exciting institution. Americans have been proud that their educational system has kept open access at many levels to young people and adults who want training or retraining. Access has been in effect denied, however, when regimentation into grades, semesters, and ability groups has confined learning in rigid compartments. Faint forerunners of the high school to come are evidenced by the Trump Plan, Melbourne, Florida's ungraded high school, and the Middletown, Rhode Island, "six-year" school.

Central features of all these plans have been (1) organization of learnings in a given study into a logical sequence of short units, programmed in advance; (2) opportunity for students to proceed as rapidly or slowly as their capacities dictate; and (3) emphasis upon independent mastery without the nagging spur of marks and credits. Teachers thus become directors of learning rather than reservoirs of facts to be sprayed indiscriminately classwide. The individual is put on his own; the mentally gifted, for example, are not singled out but proceed at their normal, accelerated rates; the slow learner is not cut off at the close of a predetermined number of weeks with a mark of incomplete or failure. The contract plan of Winnetka several decades ago, and still utilized successfully in continuation education classes, anticipated this procedure of a student competing with himself.

In the academic fields the sequence of essential learnings has a ready reference in College Entrance Examination Board tests and college admission requirements. In vocational subjects the task is more difficult. Representatives of management and labor, through advisory committees, grope to define the skills and background prerequisite for entrance into occupations. Curriculum directors and coordinators ordinarily develop the usual standard courses in English and the like without too much difficulty. Less often does a school district devote its time of staff and funds to perform the much harder task of outlining, in precise steps, occupational learnings with their requisite foundations drawn from the contributing academic areas. Yet high school cannot realize its possibilities for educating youth until this has been achieved.

COSTS

The situation naturally leads to considerations of costs. If the public has rested content to maintain only a superficial college-oriented high school curriculum, the fault lies with educators who have not demonstrated at the local level the superiority of studies in depth which challenge numbers of pupils rarely touched. The wastelands of American education are grades seven through fourteen. Elementary schools know pretty well what they are about in teaching arithmetic, spelling, and how to learn to read—for reading is not a single skill mastered once and for always, but a whole series of proficiencies achieved during a lifetime of study and work. In comparison secondary schools and lower divisions of colleges present a sorry picture. Teachers have been bemused by the false counsels of college professors who are only now discovering how wretched have long been their own introductory offerings. The reformed and reorganized courses high schools are beginning to introduce will fall short of the mark if left disjointed and piecemeal. Unless they become woven into a coherent curriculum, broadened by industrial arts and fine arts, students will not discern the pattern in which every part reinforces the whole, and all together build insight into the world of work. Psychologists Jacob W. Getzels and Philip W. Jackson, University of Chicago, and Liam Hudson of Cambridge have lately demonstrated that high IQ too often conceals tendencies to conformance—the grey-flannel syndrome—and that "divergent" types sometimes represent potential for imaginative and creative thinking.

In passing, Admiral Rickover and Professor Bestor have said little to clarify the situation, except to stimulate second glances at some of the nonsense pervading customary classwork in high school and college. Reference to European or Soviet education affords small insight for American problems. As a matter of fact, the nations of the Atlantic basin seek guidance from the United States in recasting their own school systems. The reason that so many mute, inglorious Miltons and guiltless Cromwells repose in the country churchyards of England is that they never had a chance to learn anything. How many youngsters at age eleven can demonstrate with certainty aptitude for professional education? Early separation by examination works ill upon all. The waste of undiscovered intellectual potential of adolescents would be intolerable to Americans.

Every drop-out from high school represents not only a waste of tax-funds expended upon his previous instruction but a missed opportunity which the nation cannot afford. A dominantly verbal education puts a premium upon passivity and glibness in mouthing phrases cherished by teachers. On the other hand, high school courses that link thinking with doing effect change in human behavior which alone means education. A high school graduate stuffed with fragments of knowledge like a Strasbourg goose is almost useless to himself as a citizen or to the nation as a productive member of the labor force. It may be that the high school has been eliminating the wrong end of the student spectrum. A high school program can be reliably appraised only in terms of the changes in behavior it makes in its students.

Expenses for facilities that really train for manual dexterity to accompany development of understanding and imagination will be borne by a public that *sees* the superiority of a new kind of high school graduate. The applied arts have grievously been misapplied to high school students. In the first place, vocations today demand skills as much intellectual as manual. Again, instead of a convenient dumping ground for academically unsuccessful pupils, the industrial arts should be an accompaniment of any academic curriculum. A chemist or physicist who cannot devise apparatus from materials must forever be a spectator in his discipline as the frontiers of science leave him behind. Likewise a student with a pair of skillful hands can surmount occupational obsolescence many times over.

LEARNING TO LEARN

In a sense the dilemma of the American high school has no reason to exist. Blueprints to achieve the historic mission of secondary education have long existed. Since 1918 the Cardinal Principles have directed attention to the many-sidedness of secondary education with their recognition of education for vocations, family membership, health, citizenship and worthy use of leisure as well as the traditional obeisance to basic education and development of ethical character. Conant's investigations of the last decade rightfully re-emphasized the rights of students to receive thorough grounding in English, foreign languages, science, and social sciences. Unfortunately he overlooked the contributions of the fine and applied arts to a well-rounded liberal education. The challenge and the opportunity to achieve the optimum education exist in the same spectrum: the wide range of students in high school at any one time. As President John H. Fischer of Teachers College, Columbia University, told the superintendents of California at their 1962 conference: "The vast majority of all our people must now become educated not only in order to acquire certain knowledge and skill, and the ability to apply their minds to their work, but because they must be prepared to continue to learn throughout their lives. The men and women who are suffering most as the result of industrial automation are not those who must take time out to learn new skills, but those who find it discouragingly difficult to learn new ways of working. The tragedy is that many of them have never been taught how to approach a new learning task."

10

Citizenship and the High School:
Representative Current Practices

FRANKLIN PATTERSON

Mr. Patterson is professor of education at Tufts University in Massachusetts.

. . . Curriculum patterns, whether one stands at a distance or up close, appear to have a certain similarity. If one is looking at a traditional private school or at a public high school, certain differences are identifiable, but there are likely to be similarities, too. Here, for example, are descriptions of their respective programs by the headmaster of Phillips Academy at Andover, Massachusetts, and the principal of Central High School in Omaha, Nebraska:

> Ours is a college preparatory curriculum. Sixteen courses are required for graduation and among these every boy must have four years of English, three years of mathematics, three years of a foreign language, one laboratory science, and one year of American history, the last being a requirement of the Senior year. There are minor required courses in the Bible and in art and music appreciation. So far as the program educates for citizenship, it does so in the sense that a college liberal arts program does. We offer a few elective courses, some of which might apply more specifically, as, for example, a minor course open to seniors called Social Problems.

> Most of the citizenship education that we have at Central High School is somewhat indirect. We spend a semester studying American government and attempt to draw what lessons we can in sound citizenship practice from that course. We have a course in Modern Problems which quite frequently touches upon good citizenship. A great deal of our literature is meant to deal with analyses that will lead to more intelligent citizenship.

As one visits high schools from one part of the country to another, however, one finds similarities other than those just mentioned. The principal of Newton High School in Massachusetts comments that

we believe that youngsters have to know something before they can be intelligent participators in group privileges, which I take it, is what we mean by citizenship. Most of our students take the Problems of Democracy course in Grade XII, and this emphasizes detailed analysis of real problems in their historical contexts about as much as any course we have. Together with American history in Grade XI and world history in Grade X, this twelfth-grade course helps us to graduate students who understand that there are some basic problems men live with and don't necessarily solve, but who also believe that honest men of good will can live with these problems successfully if they are free. I suppose I make a mistake to restrict the inculcation of these attitudes to our Social Studies curriculum, for my guess is that our English program is as much along these lines as any other. After all, it is in discussing plays, poetry, and novels that youngsters come up against difficult questions of right and wrong which help them form their opinions and character. This is the essence of citizenship education.

Or consider the description of curriculum offered by the principal of Bethesda-Chevy Chase High School in Maryland:

Citizenship education begins with Civics in the ninth grade, followed by Economic Geography or World History in the tenth grade, United States History in the eleventh grade, and Economics-Sociology, Senior Problems, or Far Eastern Affairs-Pan American History in the twelfth.

Similarities continue to show up when one looks at the New York City course of study which provides for a ninth-grade course in "World History and Our Economic World," a tenth-grade course in "Modern World History," an eleventh-grade American history course, and a twelfth-grade semester course in economics.

While it is true that there are pronounced similarities in curriculum structure and sequence in high schools in all parts of the country, this is by no means the whole story. Labels can be the same without meaning that the same kinds of learning are proposed or accomplished. Let me cite two extremely different examples.

Both Orangeville* High School in California and Phillips Academy

---

* The name of the community and school has been replaced by this designation for the present report.

in Exeter, New Hampshire, offer American history in the eleventh grade. The first is a public comprehensive high school in a modest suburban area outside of Los Angeles. Some two thousand students attend Orangeville High. It has a new plant with very modern classrooms. The faculty at Orangeville are young, and the intention of the school leadership is to provide a comprehensive program suited to the needs of the boys and girls of the community.

The eleventh-grade course in American history is described in the bulletin of Orangeville High as having an emphasis on the events of the twentieth century. In the fall of 1958 there were five sections of United States history (college preparatory) and ten sections of "American Institutions" (noncollege) at Orangeville. These fifteen sections of students involved more than 400 boys and girls and were taught by four teachers. Students were told by teachers that their performance on homework would count for one half of the final grade in the course, with tests making the other half. Homework involved weekly assignments set forth on dittoed sheets requiring students to define terms and identify names, to answer such questions as "Why are many different kinds of fish caught in the waters along the New England coast?," and to perform such exercises as drawing a map of western Pennsylvania showing the routes of George Washington in 1753–54 and General Edward Braddock in 1755, marking all forts and rivers in the vicinity. At the outset of the year, a special mimeographed bulletin was given to all eleventh-grade history students on the subject of "class participation":

If it is necessary for the instructor to correct a student because he is interfering with the learning effort of other students, that student will have a choice of two possible correction devices: a reduction in points or detention. The instructor will assign the amount of detention commensurate with the offense. The student will then indicate whether he will serve the detention or lose 50 points for every half hour of detention assigned. If the student chooses to serve detention and fails to do so, he will be referred to the counselor and possibly be placed on the first step of the three-step probation system set up by the 11th-grade unit office.

Somewhat different conditions of eleventh-grade history instruction are encountered at Phillips Academy, Exeter, New Hampshire. Course titles are the same and the grade placement approximately the same, but what is proposed and accomplished under the label differs rather substantially at Phillips Exeter. A comparison here is intended only to suggest how instructional practices can vary under a common label and how different an approach to adolescent education for social understanding can be when, as at Exeter, teaching is more adequately supported than at most public high schools.

The Phillips Exeter Academy has a present enrollment of just over 760 boys from all parts of the United States and from several foreign countries. The school has a book-value endowment of more than twenty million dollars, a campus of 400 acres, and a well-paid and well-trained faculty. At the beginning of the 1930's, a gift from Edward S. Harkness doubled the size of the faculty and reduced the average class size from approximately thirty to twelve. The Harkness gift also provided the school with classrooms equipped with round or oval tables to promote discussion. Each of the nine members of the history department at Exeter has his own such room in which he meets his classes of twelve students. In addition to a seminar table, a faculty member's room includes ample space for a working library, for files of materials, and for his own desk. The required course in American history meets for four class periods of fifty minutes each per week, with an expectation of an hour and a half of preparation for each class. Because classes are small enough to be seated around a table, a great deal of class time is devoted to discussion and controversy. From time to time the several classes meeting at a given hour attend a formal lecture given by a member of the department. Homework in the American history course involves extensive reading. It also requires the student to prepare a research paper. These research papers are a major feature of the program. Topics are chosen by mid-November of the year, but the final deadline is not until the following March. Students are encouraged to tackle original research, often relating to the history of their own home localities. A good deal of their research, therefore, is of a field nature, accomplished during visits to their homes. Some sample titles of research papers accomplished by Exeter students in the recent past are: "The Negro Situation in Sanford, Florida"; "Some Aspects of

Early Milwaukee History"; "Salem Privateering in the War of 1812"; "The Socialist Community of Zoar, Illinois"; "*The Chicago Tribune*"; and "General Frémont in the Civil War."

Topics are chosen with the intention of letting a boy follow his own interests if they can be related to the historical background of our country, of encouraging him to do original research, and of having him dig into the record of the human past in his own home area. Tests in American history used at Exeter, as one might expect, tend to be of the essay or "thought" type. Here is an example of a thirty-minute question recently used:

"The history of the present King of Great Britain is a history of repeated injuries and usurpations, all having in direct object the establishment of an Absolute Tyranny over these states."
Write an essay explaining how far you consider this an accurate statement of the causes of the American Revolution.

Comparison of what lies beneath the curriculum label at Orangeville High School and at Phillips Exeter Academy may seem unprofitable, since the situations of the two schools are so different. Some might argue that the capabilities of the boys fortunate enough to attend Exeter are so much higher than those of students ordinarily found in public high schools that comparison of curriculum practices does not make sense. It seems to me, instead, that Phillips Exeter performs a very real service for public high school education by demonstrating that teaching can have added quality and creativity if it has added financial support of real size. While Exeter's curriculum might be improved in terms of civic education, the conditions of classroom instruction there could be coveted for all American boys and girls.

In passing, there is another label under which it is well to look. "Problems of Democracy," or "Modern Problems," is a course commonly found in the twelfth grade in American high schools. Arthur William Dunn and many others have hoped that this course would open up critical issues and problems of our times for study by boys and girls at the point when they are leaving high school for adult employment or for college. What actually takes place in classrooms where this course is offered is likely to deviate from Mr. Dunn's expectations, to judge both from observation and research. Truman Hall, for example, in a research reported in 1953 found that secondary school teachers in Ohio were typically cautious about dealing with controversial issues in the classroom.

Several points can be made concerning curriculum patterns and subject-matter sequences in secondary schools. First, there is a remarkable uniformity of curriculum structure, course designations, and grade-level placements in the patterns of social studies-civic education to be found in American high schools, whether public or private. Second, history and the study of government are consistently the main threads in the announced program of studies for citizenship. Third, what actually happens under a given curriculum label depends on the school, on the creativity and quality of its faculty, on the adequacy of educational support in the community, and on other variable factors. Fourth, studies derived from other disciplines than history and government are limited largely to peripheral courses or units dealing with economics and to some extent to something generously labeled as "sociology." There is no significant evidence of social studies-civic education utilizing the insights and data of anthropology, social psychology, mental hygiene, or other social science disciplines.* Fifth, one finds a certain amount of proliferation of units and courses dealing with a wide variety of things placed for convenience under the heading of citizenship learnings. This proliferation has included such matters as orientation to the school, driver education, alcohol education, safety education, and other concerns. Sixth, while most high schools approach the study of "modern problems" in a manner that can be described most charitably as limited and gingerly, some secondary schools try to engage boys and girls in studying genuinely critical issues of our society.

---

* Exceptions, such as the ninth-grade course in anthropology at Germantown Friends School in Philadelphia and the humanities course at the Verde Valley School in Arizona, are notable for their rarity.

11

Innovations in the High School Curriculum

ROBERT S. GILCHRIST

Mr. Gilchrist is superintendent of schools in University City, Missouri.

Some schools are beginning to recognize that there must be school-wide objectives toward which every teacher is striving if the secondary school is to serve its role effectively. The University School at Ohio State University has identified sixteen continuous curriculum experiences which are directly related to, or implied by, democratic values and which it tries to emphasize throughout the school environment. These "threads of continuity" or all-school outcomes give direction to the selection and evaluation of learning experiences in all areas of the program.

Many other schools described their efforts to define school-wide objectives and their attempts to set up environments in which these goals can be achieved. The Phoenix Union High School emphasizes mental health as a goal in all subject fields. The University of Illinois is working with several high schools in Illinois to improve the teaching of critical thinking. Evanston, Niles, and New Trier are three of the high schools engaged in this project. The aim is to develop critical thinking through instruction in logic, semantics, and scientific method in connection with four of the subject-matter areas. . . .

Several promising practices in the various subject fields suggest ways in which curriculum content may be more effectively organized

---

for achieving avowed objectives. I shall cite illustrations in only a few of the subject areas.

Increased attention to science and mathematics reflects the country's growing concern about the shortage of scientists and about the role which science is playing in modern life. Many schools and some national organizations and agencies are making concentrated efforts to improve the curriculum in these areas. The science program of the Evanston (Illinois) Township High School illustrates the efforts of a number of major high schools.

> Science at Evanston Township High School is for everyone—the most strongly academic student and the pupil of low ability. . . .
> To provide for students planning a career in science or engineering, ETHS offers strong mathematics and science curriculums. Mathematics courses and science courses through college-level physics, analytical geometry and differential and integral calculus, opportunity for original study and research in a science seminar, and rigorous laboratory experience—all contribute toward giving students an excellent opportunity to prepare for subsequent work in any college program but especially for a major in science.
> To provide for the non-college bound and low-ability pupil, whose only formal study of science will be that in high school, ETHS offers non-laboratory courses which emphasize practical aspects of science, aim to acquaint pupils with the "method of science," develop skills that may prove useful, and provide general cultural and educational values. . . .
> Science enrolment at ETHS is on the increase.

A physical-science study project sponsored by the National Science Foundation has definite implications for the science curriculum. Under a grant from the Foundation, the Massachusetts Institute of Technology has undertaken a project to improve the teaching of physics in secondary schools. A Physical Science Study Committee, made up of scientists from colleges and universities and industrial laboratories as well as of high-school teachers and educators, is directing the project. The purpose of the project is expressed in the following quotation:

> [The committee's] point of view is expressed in three fundamental and interrelated aims: (1) to plan a course of study in which the major developments of physics, up to the present time, are presented as a logical and an integrated whole; (2) to present physics as an intellectual and cultural pursuit which is part of present-day human activity and achievement; and (3) to assist existing physics teachers, by means of various teaching aids, to carry out the proposed program.

As a first step, the committee will prepare a physics course for high-school Juniors and Seniors, including the fundamental chemistry that enters naturally. In presenting their plans, the committee goes on to say:

The new physics course will not be aimed specifically at preparing students for college physics, nor does the committee expect that all high-school students will take it. At present about one-quarter of them take physical science, and the new course will address itself to the same fraction. From this group come most of our lawyers, businessmen, statesmen, and other professionals who will not take science in college. The committee hopes that the new course will build a sound scientific background in this section of the population; that the resulting greater interest in science and better teaching methods will encourage more children to take science in high school and more young people with scientific aptitudes to elect science as their career.

Many educators are also observing with interest a project to strengthen high-school mathematics which is being sponsored by the University of Illinois. At that institution the Colleges of Education, Engineering, and Liberal Arts and Sciences have been collaborating for a number of years in efforts to improve the teaching of high-school mathematics. The Illinois project aims, among other things, to achieve these objectives:

1. To vitalize the high-school mathematics curriculum by giving the student opportunities to approach his mathematics from the creative point of view of the contemporary mathematician and by including certain topics which are new to the high-school curriculum.

2. To develop student and teacher materials which present mathematics as an integrated subject rather than as a group of isolated courses.

3. To enable teachers to teach the program's mathematics by providing classroom text materials, by demonstrating teaching techniques for the teachers in their own classrooms, by writing guides to accompany student materials, by holding training conferences, and by bringing experienced teachers and teacher trainers to the University of Illinois Campus for a year of study. . . .

MODIFYING TEACHING METHODS AND
UTILIZING AIDS TO LEARNING

More effective learning occurs as teachers discover teaching methods consistent with learning processes and adolescent development. Several practices along this line deserve mention.

Many secondary-school classrooms are becoming laboratories which encourage particular kinds of learning. A social-studies laboratory in the Kokomo (Indiana) High School, as an illustration, contains conference tables and chairs, work tables and chairs, maps of all types, reference books, and parliamentary equipment.

A phase of the Massachusetts Institute of Technology program sponsored by the National Science Foundation is concerned with the development of simple, readily available equipment for physical-science courses. Baling wire, razor blades, and copper foil are examples of the cheap and available materials that are proposed for use by students. According to Director Jerrold Zacharias, such materials are used "to inspire students to devise equipment, just as working scientists do. Instead of merely reading about past discoveries—often in outmoded textbooks—they will to some extent participate in making those discoveries for themselves, and thereby learn how it feels to work on the frontier of science."

The possibility of using television to enrich classroom learning is now the subject of much discussion and study. More than twenty educational television stations are now in operation. It seems clear that television, used in an intelligent manner, can improve classroom teaching. The camera's ability to enlarge subjects to any size can give every student a closer and clearer view in science demonstrations. In fact, the relationship between the viewer and the person who is speaking on television seems to take on a certain intimacy. . . .

Significant developments are occurring in the use of community resources to enrich the high-school curriculum. These practices include bringing persons from the community into school classrooms and taking pupils out into the community for experiences which cannot be provided in the classroom. In Tulsa, Oklahoma, a committee of the Chamber of Commerce and of school administrators have worked out a plan in which several kinds of help have been made available to science teachers in junior and senior high schools. Personnel from industry speak to classes on various topics and conduct individual conferences for guidance purposes. Teachers and pupils are invited to community meetings where the subject under discussion is of interest to them. Technical literature, bulletins, magazines, films, filmstrips, and exhibits, if relatively free of advertising, are made available to schools. Tours of industrial laboratories and plants are arranged. Science teachers are employed in summer jobs related to their teaching fields. More than twenty firms have already volunteered to take part in the project, and a "Thirty Hour Club," composed of engineers, geologists, geophysicists, mathematicians, chemists, physicists, and other research personnel, has been formed. Each member has agreed to give a total of thirty hours a year to school service.

Work-experience programs in which adolescents have an opportunity to perform significant work under good supervision is a promising practice. Many co-operative work programs are designed to lead directly into vocations, and a few school systems have programs which are integral parts of the general-education program. The program of the Santa Barbara County high schools, with an annual participation of approximately five hundred Senior students, is outstanding.

PROVISION OF TEAM TEACHING AND INTEGRATED COURSES

Teachers often find that working with colleagues in joint projects helps them do more effective teaching. In some instances the provision of a longer block of time and the opportunity to use an approach in which the subject matter of more than one field is utilized represents a promising area for experimentation. The Tulsa (Oklahoma) senior high schools use a block program which includes English, social studies, and science. The same students are scheduled to the three teachers of these areas, and these three teachers are scheduled together daily in a joint planning period. Through co-operative planning, units of work in the three areas are correlated; strengths, weaknesses, and common needs of the classes are determined; individual students with problems are identified; and a concerted effort is made to meet individual and common needs that have been discovered. . . .

Examples of integrated courses are provided by Whittier (California) High School and by the Edsel Ford High School of Dearborn, Michigan. A course offered at the Whittier High School is the equivalent of the second year of algebra, and the regular course in college-preparatory physics, plus theory and practice in an advanced shop-type course in electronics. The mathematics taught is related both to the general physics field and to the electronic field.

The Edsel Ford High School offers an integrated humanities course which covers various cultures of the world. The course is under the supervision of a regular teacher who acts as a co-ordinator, working with a music teacher, an art teacher, and a teacher of literature. Also, the staff in the same school has written its own textbooks for a course entitled "High-School Social Science," which presents an integrated approach to the social-science field, covering the broad fields of history, philosophy, anthropology, economics, and civics. . . .

12

Cure for English

FRED M. HECHINGER

Mr. Hechinger is the education editor of The New York Times. *He is the author of* The Big Red Schoolhouse *(1959) and, with Grace Hechinger,* Teen-Age Tyranny *(1963). Mr. Hechinger has contributed articles on education to* Harper's *and* Saturday Review.

For the past five years the mathematics and science reform appeared to be outrunning the improvement of English teaching so rapidly that the new student generation might have been expected to "say it with numbers" instead of words. But the English reform movement is stripping for action at last.

With the College Entrance Examination Board's Commission on English ready to "re-train" the first wave of 900 high school English teachers on twenty university campuses this summer and the United States Office of Education making it known last week that it has launched a nationwide Project English for curriculum reform, first aid appears on the way.

The seriousness of the problem has been described by the National Council of Teachers of English. In 1960, about 150,000 students flunked the college entrance test in English. Approximately 70 per cent of all colleges in the country must offer remedial work in English at a cost of about $10 million annually and some graduate schools complain that the efforts of even their more brilliant students are hampered by inability to put their ideas into words. . . .

The work for the Commission on English and for the government's Project English, which plans to establish its first three Curriculum

Study Centers this spring, is clearly cut out: to improve the elementary and high-school curriculum, re-train as many teachers as possible and improve the education of new teachers.

But the reform will lead to disaster in college, unless the colleges keep, not only in step with the reforms, but one step ahead. Dr. Kitzhaber* reports encouraging signs: remedial courses are declining and those offered for credit disappearing; the "Review of Fundamentals" freshman course is being dropped by many colleges; more scholarly books, which four years ago were confined to honors sections, are being substituted for the routine texts; English departments, instead of having to nurse along masses of semi-literate students, have more time for those ready for advanced study.

The next five years will probably seem like the answer to a long and fervent prayer to the better colleges. They may also be humiliating to those who underestimate the potential literacy of post-reform freshmen.

---

* *Editors' Note:* Dr. Kitzhaber is a professor of English at the University of Oregon and is 1st vice president of the National Council of Teachers of English.

13

The Non-Graded High School

B. FRANK BROWN

Mr. Brown is the principal of the Melbourne High School, Melbourne, Florida.

What the space age needs educationally is a crack public school system designed to educate more youngsters than ever before and do the job faster and better. The components for the kind of school needed are inventiveness, flexibility, and quality.

These qualities are prominent in the non-graded high school, an innovation now beyond the hothouse stage. But the non-graded high school is an iconoclasm, and the conventional school administrator fears it. When he considers it at all, he thinks of it as involving an esoteric organization suitable only to unique situations. In reality there is nothing mysterious nor singular about it. It is a clear, crisp, logical arrangement by which schools can take off the academic bridle which restrains youngsters intellectually.

If the public schools in America are ever to achieve the ideal of having each youngster progress at his best rate of learning, then some form of non-grading must be instituted. This leads to the shattering implication that within the next five years every intellectually respectable high school will have some degree of non-gradedness. For the grade is a trapping of the outworn past. It was first conceived during the Middle Ages in a *gymnasium* at Stuttgart, Germany, and has grown sterile in the age of universal education and the hydrogen bomb.

The durable attractiveness of the grade lies in its administrative convenience. It serves as a comfortable holding pool in which school administrators can and do throw youngsters for custodial purposes and

From *Phi Delta Kappan*, February 1963. Reprinted by permission.

forget them for a year. By comparison, non-grading is an administrative prickly pear constantly needling for attention to the learning needs of youngsters.

The schools have been both the inheritors and the prisoners of the grade tradition. In an era of invention and change, educators must overcome inhibitions against breaking the grade lockstep. With it will go some of the obsolescence which has been built into the curriculum with the grade.

The logical basis for non-graded education was clearly stated recently by Henry Dyer, vice president of the Educational Testing Service. In an address before the tenth College Board Colloquium, Dyer reported that the practice of measuring students intellectually by the grade they have reached is not even remotely reliable. He asserted that the grade average is only an event at best and no measure of achievement at all.

The academic design should be reduced from the current seventeen fragmented divisions of learning (K-12 plus four) to five general areas with learning continuous within each. Trends today suggest that the school of the future will be composed of the non-graded primary curriculum, the non-graded intermediate curriculum, the non-graded junior high curriculum, the non-graded senior high curriculum, and the non-graded college curriculum.

Space limitations prohibit treatment of the entire non-graded spectrum. Consequently, this article will deal only with the non-graded innovation of the secondary school, with the exception of a brief word about the implications for colleges.

We realize that bringing about change in the college curriculum is somewhat like moving a graveyard, but the impact of students educated without the academic bridle is already bringing a new respect for change in higher education. Spurred by the increased intellectual excitement of their students from non-graded high schools, colleges too will turn to the non-graded system. One result will be that college students in far greater numbers will enter graduate school.

TO RECOVER FROM DISASTER

The first step in recovering from decades of intellectual disaster wrought by the grade must be to reclassify youngsters for learning on the basis of their achievement rather than the grade to which they have been chronologically promoted. They must be fanned out in a new design. This is accomplished by clustering students intellectually on the basis of their performance on nationally standardized achievement tests. The intelligence quotient, which has been a primary measure in the past, is of little or no value in the non-graded school.

The results of standardized achievement tests dramatically reveal the fallacy of continuing to group students into grades. In the average grade in high school, only half the youngsters have the required knowledge to be in that particular grade. For example, the dispersal of achievement among students in a tenth-grade class in English will range from grade three through grade thirteen, which is the first year of college. The scatter is equally great in most other subjects. It is even greater in mathematics.

Youngsters at Melbourne High School have been reclassified in line with their level of achievement and assigned to fluid learning situations in each subject on the basis of their needs. Through selective acceleration, some students begin college level work when they arrive as tenth-graders. By the same token, some students in the twelfth grade receive greater amounts of remedial work in areas in which their achievement is below standard.

The plan for continuous learning at Melbourne accommodates youngsters by placing them in temporary learning situations from which they can move at any time. These *ad hoc* learning arrangements are called phases. A phase is a stage of development with a varying time element. One student may remain in a low phase indefinitely; another may progress rapidly into higher phases.

When students enter Melbourne High School they are sorted on the basis of nationally standardized achievement tests. They are then clustered into a new spectrum in line with their various aptitudes and abilities.

Phase 1—Subjects are centered around remedial work.

Phase 2—Subjects are concerned with basic skills.

Phase 3—Subjects are designed for students seeking an average education.

Phase 4—Subjects are available for students desiring education in considerable depth.

Phase 5—Subjects are open to students who are willing to assume responsibility for their own learning and plan to go far beyond the boundaries of a single course.

Phase Q—Students whose creative talents are well developed in special areas should give consideration to this "Quest" phase of the curriculum. This is an important dimension of the phased organization designed to give thrust in the direction of individual fulfillment. In this phase a student may research an area in which he is deeply and broadly curious, either to develop creative powers or in quest of knowledge. A student may spend from one to three hours a day in Quest.

Phase X—Non-academic subjects which do not accommodate student mobility; e.g., typing, physical education. These subjects are ungraded but unphased.

This realignment of students brings about a major difference in course content between the non-graded and conventionally graded school. The motion of the non-graded curriculum compels the school to resort to a much wider range of materials. No standard textbooks are used in any phase. A multiplicity of material has replaced them. A gradeless curriculum designed for student mobility must be saturated with variegated materials.

The effect of non-grading is to change the educational process so that students are accelerated through subject matter on a continuing rather than yearly basis. Learning is both more appropriate and more viable when children of comparable academic accomplishment and pace are grouped together.

There are no study halls in the Melbourne plan for a non-graded school. The study hall, like the grade, belongs to the remote past. In a non-graded curriculum students are expected to take responsibility for their own learning and the monitored type of study hall becomes a useless appendage.

All students at Melbourne High are registered for six subjects. Subjects do, however, vary greatly in depth. For example, in a phase one mathematics class the concepts studied are fundamentals which the student should have been required to learn in the elementary school. At the other end of the scale is phase five, which encompasses calculus during the third high-school year. This kind of flexible and mobile curriculum is rewarding to both the untalented and the multi-talented. Equalitarianism wrongly conceived ignores differences in both achievement and native talent.

The following are typical schedules of three students of the same age but of widely varying abilities.

Student A		Student B		Student C	
	Phase		Phase		Phase
English	1	English	3	English	4
Mathematics	3	Mathematics	2	Differential Equations	5
World History	2	Amer. History	4	History of Asia	3
Biology	3	Chemistry	3	Physics	5
Phys. Ed.	X	Band	X	Spanish	4
Typing	X	Art	4	Probability & Statistics	Q

CHANGES WROUGHT BY THE GRADELESS PLAN

What are some of the changes that have taken place at Melbourne High School after three years of gradeless learning?

First, it is evident that a non-graded school is different from a graded school in more ways than just a re-ranking of students. Some classes must be smaller; others must be larger.

A subject in which class size has been dramatically increased is typing. Typing classes have been expanded to 125 students per class. The surprising thing is that we never thought of this before. The typewriter is a gadget and students attempting to master a mechanical device can be taught in classes of almost unlimited capacity. Space and administration are the only considerations. The teacher needs merely to be equipped with a first-rate public address system and a transistorized neck microphone without wires, so she can move freely about the room. One typing teacher at Melbourne easily instructs 625 typing students a day in five classes of 125 students each.

Since we have found that students can be taught typing in classes of 125 as well as in classes of thirty, three teachers are released for assignment elsewhere in the school program.

Typing and similar subjects at Melbourne High School which are ungraded but do not permit student mobility are scheduled as phase X. The student remains for a semester or even a year in phase X classes.

The non-graded high school as developed at Melbourne stands squarely on the concept of basic education first. This requires that youngsters coming into the high school who are weak in the basic subjects of English and mathematics devote double time—two periods a day—to each of these subjects until such time as they are up to the standard we set. The non-graded innovation, while embracing flexibility, is centered on a tightening and toughening of the academic sinews.

The gradeless curriculum at Melbourne High is also founded on an awareness that each of the school's students is different. The program of studies is designed to accommodate these variances in individuals.

The curriculum, which has a degree of flamboyance and at first seems complex, is merely unrestrained. It is designed to offer a bountiful academic fare on a wider range than is conventionally permitted when students are chronologically grouped in grades ten, eleven, and twelve.

Since English is the most widely studied subject in any school, perhaps the strategy of the Melbourne curriculum is best understood through this subject and what happens to a student who enters Melbourne High in the tenth grade.

Many tenth-grade students are hampered by an inability to read at what is called the tenth-grade level. These handicapped students rarely finish school. Truancy to them is a matter of self-preservation. In an effort to meet this problem, the teacher time gained from consolidating typing classes is used to reduce loads in classes for students in need of remedial work (phase one). These classes contain a maximum of fifteen students. They are designed so that each student may be involved in a personal engagement with learning.

Remedial students are taught to read through phonics. Students who have not learned basic skills are vigorously confronted with basic education and each phase increases in depth. At the other end of the spectrum is phase five English, which is an open-ended advanced placement college program in which the student can study and learn for three years. The intent here is to do something for students who can "run a faster mile."

In order to avoid repetition in literature and accommodate up-phasing of students, all phases of English study the same literature in a given year. One year all phases study American literature, the next year English literature, and the third year world literature.

Another reform which is spurred by non-graded education is a change in the function of the teacher. Students who are unbridled intellectually are no longer content with a passive "telling" kind of education. Teachers must throw out the old kit bag.

Gradeless schools are moving from memorized learning and simplified explanations to the process of inquiry for each individual. What is inquiry? In its simplest form, inquiry is curiosity linked to action. It means newer and deeper perceptions for the individual. In its ultimate form, it leads to the development of traits of imagination and creativity and eventually to new discoveries for science and the humanities.

In the non-graded school, the intellectual pace of various students is more separate and unequal than in graded education. As the curriculum is expanded and becomes variegated, achievement becomes a hallmark of the school. The illusory aim of evenness in achievement which is characteristic of graded schools is not evident here.

Rebellion against the grade lockstep is one of the missed revolutions of our time. Still poised and full of ferment, it may never occur, although the grade curtain which was rung down around learning has been pierced by a new system of learning where the flashpoints are phases instead of annual promotion.

As Philip Coombs said when he was executive secretary of the Fund for the Advancement of Education, "What the schools need is not simply more money from the outside but sweeping changes on the inside." Sweeping changes do take place in a non-graded school, and without an increase in the budget.

14

From Skinner to Crowder to Chance:
A Primer on Teaching Machines

WILLIAM E. HOTH

Mr. Hoth is associate professor of English Education at Wayne State University, Detroit, Michigan. He is also Chairman of the Committee on Technological Change of the National Council of Teachers of English.

Teaching machines, feared, jeered and not widely understood, stand ready in the on-deck circle about to come to bat with team teachers, accordion-partitioned gyms, language labs, driver training fleets, congenial administrators, and air-conditioned school buses as members of the home team in the secondary school ball game. Their use is basic to the Trump plan[1] and their "programmed" materials fill a full day in the Diederich plan.[2] Their debut causes a dean of English teachers to compose a delightful parody.[3] Quite clearly all of us in the profession need to get acquainted with them. Let's begin our lesson.

First, to be very sure, these electronic devices are not yet *teaching* machines. Better to call them *training*, *tutoring*, or to be more flattering to their proponents, *learning* machines. For machines they are, capable of controlling what is presented, how much, when, for how

---

From *The English Journal*, September 1961. Reprinted with the permission of the National Council of Teachers of English and William E. Hoth.

[1] J. Lloyd Trump, *Images of the Future* (NASSP: 1201 Sixteenth Street, Washington D.C., 1959).

[2] Paul Diederich, "The Rutgers Plan for Cutting Class Size in Two," *The English Journal*, XLIX (April 1960), pp. 229–236ff., and Ralph R. Shaw, "To the Editor," *The English Journal*, L (February 1961), pp. 137–38.

[3] Robert C. Pooley, "Automatons or English Teachers," *The English Journal*, L (March 1961), pp. 169–73.

long, and how often; but incapable of performing any act which their "programmer" has not anticipated, and completely insensitive to the quizzical look of an eager but confused mind. Given these limitations, what makes these contrivances different enough from a phonograph, or a motion picture or slide projector, to justify the special label; why not just refer to them as a new audio-visual device? Let's look at a definition:

". . . teaching machines [are] devices which (1) present a unit of verbal or symbolic information visually, usually in question form; (2) provide the student with some means of responding to each unit; and (3) inform the student as to the correctness of each response."[4]

The distinctive feature seems to be the presentation of information to the learner in predetermined increments. As the learner masters each of these increments, he moves or is moved on to the next unit. These increments and the sequence in which they are presented make up the *program*, a term without which you cannot talk about teaching machines for long. If these automated lectures had been developed by classroom teachers, then something like *text* or *learning materials* might have been used for *program*; and *planning* for *programming*; and *teacher-author* for *programmer*. For *programmers* are writers whose programming consists of organizing information into sequential increments according to the rationale of the particular machine with which they are working.

RATIONALES

For beginning students, it's fair to say there are two major rationales. The first is identified primarily with Skinner. In his work, Skinner underscores the necessity of small bits of information which are readily acquired by the learner. Written so that it is very hard not to get the right answers to questions, Skinner material (or *programming*,

---

[4] Edward B. Fry, Glenn L. Bryan, and Joseph W. Rigney, "Teaching Machines: An Annotated Bibliography," *Audio Visual Communication Review*, VIII (1960), p. 5.

remember) leads the learner through a series of successes and this insistence on immediate reward is fundamental to the rationale.

Quite the contrary is the rationale of Crowder. In his Auto Tutor, the information is accompanied by multiple-choice questions. Here the learner is confronted with four choices, three of which are wrong. If the learner chooses correctly, he gets the next increment of information and the next set of choices. If he chooses incorrectly, the machine presents review material, characteristically by taking the learner through a more simplified series of steps leading up to the question he originally missed. In a device called a "scrambled book," the method works like this, for example: the learner is given some information and then confronted with a multiple-choice question. If he chooses A (an incorrect response), he is directed to read page 28; if B (also wrong), p. 19; if C (right), the next page; if D (wrong), p. 81. On pages 28, 19, and 81 are presented explanatory information, clarification of terms, simplified breakdowns of complex elements in the question, etc. The trick in this method is to predict the kind and source of error and then "teach" to it. Programming in a Crowder program is always dependent on *branching* or rerouting the learner.

Now it is apparent that the rate at which any learner moves along is completely dependent on the individual; or in more technical terms, both Skinner and Crowder programs are self-pacing. Each step confronts the learner only as he responds to the one preceding. The informed student moves through both types of programming quickly. The slower student pursues detours in Crowder programs and is led hesitantly along in Skinner programs. In both, while the program put into the machine can be standardized (the same for all students), the way in which it becomes "learned" is more individualized than in many classroom practices today.

THE PROS AND CONS

That is just one argument of machine enthusiasts. Further, they point to the release of teachers from routine question-and-answer sessions, from drill, from routine testing, and from some kinds of lecturing and other schemes for presenting information. They stress that students do not have to be graded on responses to programmed materials. Tests can be conducted quite separately so that the machines are simply for "learning," and cheating becomes impossible. Any student who paces himself through the program falsely doesn't do well on the test, it is alleged.

In fairness to enthusiasts it should be pointed out that educators who favor the machines see them as real helpers whose widespread use will enable good teachers to impart spiritual and moral values through better teaching and the guidance made possible by the time gained in release from routine tasks. Some, too, are almost poetic in their talk of the dialogue between machines and students.

Detractors, to date, come from many camps. Some are generally suspicious of machinery in the classroom. Others fear a lock-step curriculum that shows little regard for the individualized nature of growth and development. They sense an emphasis on mastering facts and concepts without accompanying insight, the illumination without which the learning of any content is a hollow reward. Some critics are afraid that teachers who now rely exclusively on workbooks, true-false tests, teacher asks-student answers, and other mechanical methods will be armed with a superior weapon to abuse young minds. A real controversy abides.

What of English? To date there have been efforts to program English materials along Skinner lines. Blumenthal, for example, uses small step-by-step methods to take the learner through fairly traditional textbook information about usage and what most of us had grown accustomed to calling grammar, before we heard of descriptive linguistics.[5] To illustrate his plan, Diederich has prepared some mimeographed material that leads a student through the disciplined reading of a lyric poem. In an advanced curriculum course in English Education at Wayne State University in winter, 1960, two young teachers developed a program for introducing students to elementary concepts in the study of poetry. In Denver, programming on the mechanics of writing is being tested this year.

---

[5] Joseph Blumenthal, *2600* (New York: Harcourt, Brace, 1960).

In fact it is in this realm of inexpensively reproduced materials, prepared according to the rationale of the machine psychologists, that teachers are most likely to encounter the "modern" point of view initially. The machines can be expensive and school administrators may be reluctant to install rows of them (although as language lab experience shows, Federal matching funds work wonders). Yet it is relatively simple to allow a class to pace themselves individually through a printed program. The task for the profession is (1) to supervise the preparation of materials so that the best of what is known about any body of content (literature, language, composition, etc.) gets written in, (2) be informed on details of rationale so as to advise school administrators intelligently, (3) create curriculum designs that capitalize on the released time to provide better face-to-face contacts between teachers as mentors and students as inquirers.

So the keystone combination may be from Skinner to Crowder to an informed profession that knows a truth of modern life. Automatic wash machines do not "free" a housewife. They allow and almost compel her to maintain a cleaner supply of clothes. Language labs do not "release" a modern language teacher for rest nor personal pleasure. They make it more difficult for him to apologize for students who cannot speak a word after a year's study, and they compel him to find a substitute for routines which the machine has usurped.

Among us English teachers are many, and some in high places, who suspect the machine because it is not a book. They should not fear. For the machines present an exciting challenge. At last, good teachers can demonstrate their unique skills and their specific usefulness. In the not too distant future we may hear no longer of the wonderful senior English teacher whose students remember how sternly she drilled them on diagramming and mechanics. If the machines take over that which can be learned mechanically, what a fine chance for the really competent English teacher to contribute what is distinctly human.

15

Taps for Teaching Machines

JOHN F. FELDHUSEN

Mr. Feldhusen is associate professor of educational psychology at Purdue University. He holds a joint appointment in the departments of education and psychology.

The logical questions to ask now are these: Is the teaching machine movement a failure? Is programed learning material in any way more effective than simpler narrative presentations by text, teacher, or television? A growing tide of research evidence, classroom experience, and personal sentiment suggests a "yes" to the first question, a "no" to the second.

The demise of the machine came first. A number of researchers reported that learning proceeded as well with programed texts or with other substitute devices as with mechanical teaching machines. Although the programed text and other substitutes did not incorporate the cheat-proof features of the mechanical machines, it appeared that the essence of the whole business, *i.e.*, the program, could still be presented effectively without a machine.

The need for active, overt participation through questions, blanks to be filled, or responses to be selected was asserted strongly by Skinner. But a number of researchers produced evidence to indicate that covert or mental responses or presentation of a program with no direction or opportunity to respond were just as effective. In several projects the opportunity for overt response was removed by filling in the blanks of the linear program and requiring the student merely to read the statements. One researcher reported a decrement in learning under this condition but several others reported that students learned as well when they merely read the narrative statements. It was also

From *Phi Delta Kappan*, March 1963. Reprinted by permission. (Footnotes that appear in the original source have been omitted.)

reported in a number of studies that the condition of covert response yielded a considerable saving in time to work through the program, and this advantage was apparently secured without reduction in the amount learned.

Attention was also directed to the size of step or amount of information packed into each frame. Could the learner handle a paragraph? Or must we stick to the very small step containing only a bit of information in each frame, as Skinner proposed? The answer seemed to be that a frame or step of the program could be larger, sometimes as large as a paragraph, and effective learning would still occur. But evidence favoring the small step was also forthcoming.

What of the feedback system in programed learning? Is it indispensable? Pressey's background work seemed to support the underlying principle. But Pressey's work was not done with programed learning material. Pressey demonstrated the instructional value of immediate feedback of right answers in a testing situation. Would the principle hold good for the linear program? The answer now seems to be no. First, several of the studies cited above showed that even though the researcher filled the blanks with the right responses and merely asked the student to read the frames, the amount of learning was not reduced. Here there could be no formal feedback, since no observable performance was required of the learner. Still other researchers removed or reduced the feedback of right answers while requiring active participation in the form of blanks to be filled or questions to be answered. They found no decrement in learning. In general, it seems that a linear program written to assure correct response 90 or 95 per cent of the time is inherently so easy for most learners that they know they are giving right answers without having to check with a feedback system.

Perhaps most sacred of all was the reinforcement principle in teaching machines and programed learning. Frame by frame and program by program, the learner should find his correct answers, his successful performance, reinforcing his learning. But instead of reinforcement, some researchers found disturbing signs of boredom, or the "pall effect," among students after longer regimens of programed instruction. Although affective responses of students were often noted as highly favorable to selected aspects of programed instruction, the signs of boredom and dissatisfaction were sufficiently great to indicate that the program would not be a uniformly reinforcing experience for all youngsters. However, in a previously unreported study I found that among ten youngsters who expressed predominantly negative attitudes toward programed learning after seven weeks of programed instruction in arithmetic, the average gain in arithmetic achievement was not significantly less than the gain for sixteen youngsters who expressed predominantly positive attitudes.

We had also been told that a great new advantage of teaching machines and programed learning was that differences in aptitude or intelligence would be reduced or eliminated as factors in learning. Children at various levels of mental ability would learn equally well from the program. However, recent research evidence indicates that this is not true. As is true with most learning materials, more able youngsters learned more and learned more rapidly with the programed material. Of course, the highly verbal nature of most programed learning material naturally makes it more suitable for bright and more verbally able youngsters. The task with the program is to read and write or select correct answers—essentially verbal activities.

The advantage of individual rates in learning was also offered as a factor in programed learning material. However, in two projects it was found that there was no decrement in learning when the program was presented at a uniform rate for a group rather than at individual rates. This suggests that even though individual rates in programed learning are waived in order to facilitate presentation by some audio or visual media which necessitates a group rate, learning may still be produced. . . .

Stolurow has suggested recently that a problem facing enthusiasts in the field of programed learning is getting teachers to accept and use programed materials and teaching machines. The evidence reviewed in this paper indicates that rather than get teachers to accept or use programed material we should caution them to proceed slowly. They ought to be urged to question the excessive claims of some publishers and researchers. . . .

Pressey said recently, " . . . enthusiasts carry an idea to extremes." This has certainly been true of programed learning.

16

What Good High Schools Are Doing

LEE A. DuBRIDGE

Mr. DuBridge is president of California Institute of Technology.

A strong and rapidly growing movement has been under way in many of the best American high schools during the past ten years, aimed toward preparing those students who expect to attend a college or university with a much stronger academic base for their higher educational experience. Students now entering as freshmen in dozens of the best colleges and universities throughout the United States come with a far better preparation than formerly in mathematics, science, English, foreign languages, and other subjects.

There are many factors which have produced this situation. Better counseling of the more able high school students is one. Better, more modern, and more advanced course materials, especially in mathematics and science, have been introduced. Advanced placement courses are now given in nearly 1,500 high schools throughout the country, and thousands of students are able to pass the advanced placement tests which enable them to go directly into more advanced college and university courses. Something like one-half of the entering students at such institutions as Harvard and Princeton enter with advanced standing in at least one subject, and many in two, three, or four subjects.

A few years ago it would have been unthinkable that high school seniors would be taking a college-level course in calculus. Today, however, nearly half of the freshmen entering such institutions as Caltech and M.I.T. have had an introductory calculus course, and many of

From *Your Schools* supplement, *Los Angeles Times*, May 5, 1963. Reprinted by permission.

them had a sufficiently advanced course to be able to skip part or all of the normal freshman course in calculus. The old remedial courses in mathematics, elementary science, English and other subjects have been discontinued in many of our better colleges because they are no longer required.

The better preparation of the incoming freshmen at many institutions has stimulated a very thorough revision of the entire undergraduate curricula at these institutions. The freshman courses in mathematics, physics, and chemistry have been thoroughly revised to start at a more advanced level and take the student much further into the respective subjects. The old freshman English courses have often been abolished, allowing the freshman to start directly with a mature course in English literature. Where formerly a large number of college applicants had not had the desired two years of a foreign language, now most college applicants have had two years and many of them four years.

The fact that time can now be saved in eliminating the review of high school level courses enables the student to proceed further in his special field of interest, as well as to broaden his college curricula and take more courses outside of his specialty. Thus, today's college graduate is a richer, broader individual by virtue of the fact that he got a head start in his better high school preparation.

That not all high schools in the country have improved their course offerings, their teaching, and their counseling in the same degree goes without saying. Many schools still lag far behind. But, 1,500 high schools—most of them with fairly large enrollments—have gone as far as participating in the advanced placement program. At least that many more have substantially improved their regular high school offerings. They have shown the way and they have shown it can be done. The movement is rapidly spreading to other schools, and the problem now is not to start something new but to spread to all high schools of the country the quality of education which many have shown can be provided.

WHO ARE THE TEACHERS? | III

1

Here Lies Miss Groby

JAMES THURBER

*James Thurber (1894–1961) contributed both humorous essays and cartoons to the
New Yorker from 1926 until his death. Among his books are My Life and Hard
Times, Fables for Our Time, The Male Animal, The Thurber Album.*

Miss Groby taught me English composition thirty years ago. It
wasn't what prose said that interested Miss Groby; it was the way
prose said it. The shape of a sentence crucified on a blackboard
(parsed, she called it) brought a light to her eye. She hunted for Topic
Sentences and Transitional Sentences the way little girls hunt for
white violets in springtime. What she loved most of all were Figures
of Speech. You remember her. You must have had her, too. Her influence will never die out of the land. A small schoolgirl asked me the
other day if I could give her an example of metonymy. (There are
several kinds of metonymies, you may recall, but the one that will
come to mind most easily, I think, is Container for the Thing Contained.) The vision of Miss Groby came clearly before me when the
little girl mentioned the old, familiar word. I saw her sitting at her
desk, taking the rubber band off the roll-call cards, running it back
upon the fingers of her right hand, and surveying us all separately with
quick little henlike turns of her head.

Here lies Miss Groby, not dead, I think, but put away on a shelf
with the other T squares and rulers whose edges had lost their certainty. The fierce light that Miss Groby brought to English literature
was the light of Identification. Perhaps, at the end, she could no longer
retain the dates of the birth and death of one of the Lake poets. That

From the *New Yorker*, March 21, 1942. Reprinted by permission; Copr. © 1942
The New Yorker Magazine, Inc.

would have sent her to the principal of the school with her resignation. Or perhaps she could not remember, finally, exactly how many Cornishmen there were who had sworn that Trelawny should not die, or precisely how many springs were left to Housman's lad in which to go about the woodlands to see the cherry hung with snow.

Verse was one of Miss Groby's delights because there was so much in both its form and content that could be counted. I believe she would have got an enormous thrill out of Wordsworth's famous lines about Lucy if they had been written this way:

> A violet by a mossy stone
> Half hidden from the eye,
> Fair as a star when ninety-eight
> Are shining in the sky.

It is hard for me to believe that Miss Groby ever saw any famous work of literature from far enough away to know what it meant. She was forever climbing up the margins of books and crawling between their lines, hunting for the little gold of phrase, making marks with a pencil. As Palamides hunted the Questing Beast, she hunted the Figure of Speech. She hunted it through the clangorous halls of Shakespeare and through the green forests of Scott.

Night after night, for homework, Miss Groby set us to searching in "Ivanhoe" and "Julius Caesar" for metaphors, similes, metonymies, apostrophes, personifications, and all the rest. It got so that figures of speech jumped out of the pages at you, obscuring the sense and pattern of the novel or play you were trying to read. "Friends, Romans, countrymen, lend me your ears." Take that, for instance. There is an unusual but perfect example of Container for the Thing Contained. If you read the funeral oration unwarily—that is to say, for its meaning— you might easily miss the C.F.T.T.C. Antony is, of course, not asking for their ears in the sense that he wants them cut off and handed over; he is asking for the function of those ears, for their power to hear, for, in a word, the thing they contain.

At first I began to fear that all the characters in Shakespeare and Scott were crazy. They confused cause with effect, the sign for the thing signified, the thing held for the thing holding it. But after a while I began to suspect that it was I myself who was crazy. I would find myself lying awake at night saying over and over, "The thinger for the thing contained." In a great but probably misguided attempt to keep my mind on its hinges, I would stare at the ceiling and try to think of an example of the Thing Contained for the Container. It struck me as odd that Miss Groby had never thought of that inversion. I finally hit on one, which I still remember. If a woman were to grab up a bottle of Grade A and say to her husband, "Get away from me or I'll hit you with the milk," that would be a Thing Contained for the Container. The next day in class I raised my hand and brought my curious discovery straight out before Miss Groby and my astonished schoolmates. I was eager and serious about it and it never occurred to me that the other children would laugh. They laughed loudly and long. When Miss Groby had quieted them she said to me rather coldly, "That was not really amusing, James." That's the mixed-up kind of thing that happened to me in my teens.

In later years I came across another excellent example of this figure of speech in a joke long since familiar to people who know vaudeville or burlesque (or radio, for that matter). It goes something like this:

> A: What's your head all bandaged up for?
> B: I got hit with some tomatoes.
> A: How could that bruise you up so bad?
> B: These tomatoes were in a can.

I wonder what Miss Groby would have thought of that one.

I dream of my old English teacher occasionally. It seems that we are always in Sherwood Forest and that from far away I can hear Robin Hood winding his silver horn.

"Drat that man for making such a racket on his cornet!" cries Miss Groby. "He scared away a perfectly darling Container for the Thing Contained, a great, big, beautiful one. It leaped right back into its context when that man blew that cornet. It was the most wonderful Container for the Thing Contained I ever saw here in the Forest of Arden."

"This is Sherwood Forest," I say to her.

"That doesn't make any difference at all that I can see," she says to me.

Then I wake up, tossing and moaning.

2

Controversy in Teacher Education: The Central Issue

STEPHEN M. COREY

Mr. Corey was formerly dean, Teachers College, Columbia University. From 1959 to 1962 he was a consultant with the Ministry of Education in India.

During the next thirty minutes or so I shall try to do three things: First, comment on the difficulty I am having thinking clearly about teacher education when much of what I stand for is under attack; second, develop what seems to me to be the neglected central issue in the current discussions about teacher education; and, finally, suggest briefly what I think we teacher educators ought to be stressing.

OUR UNDERSTANDABLE DEFENSIVENESS

Like most of you, I have spent my professional life working to improve teacher education. From time to time I have been critical of much that we do, as have many of you. By and large, though, I have believed that we were tackling important problems with determination and as much creativity as anyone could be expected to muster. In light of the complexity of the difficulties we faced, I felt that we were making progress with commendable speed. These convictions, and the inevitable identification a person develops with his professional peers, have

From *The Future Challenges Teacher Education* (Eleventh Yearbook), American Association of Colleges for Teacher Education (Oneonta, N. Y.: AACTE, 1958). Reprinted by permission. (Footnotes that appear in the original source have been omitted.)

resulted in my getting strong feelings of support from association with teacher educators. They constitute my primary professional reference group. I am comfortable with them. Their idiosyncracies are mine. I use and understand their language and enjoy their rituals and ceremonies.

All of this, as I know you realize, may be a blessing, but not an unmixed one. To the degree any one of us identifies closely with others who are doing what they can to improve teacher education we resent criticisms of our efforts and our achievements, especially by persons we consider to be outsiders, that is, without much experience in teacher education. With me this resentment is strong and causes me to react to criticisms with surprising defensiveness. I fail, often, to distinguish between what I say that represents my deepest convictions and what I say because I am angry. Occasionally I am apt to think quite inexcusable things about the personal integrity of men and women whose views about teacher education differ sharply from mine. I inquire into their biographies and feel elated at any discovery that suggests weakness or duplicity. Now and then I find myself rejecting certain ideas about teacher education that I have thought promising for a long time merely because these ideas are championed by people who seem to have little respect or sympathy for what my associates and I have been doing through the years.

Of course, we teacher educators are not unique in our reaction to criticism. Doctors, bankers, lawyers, and foundation officials are like us, in this sense at least, and get hurt and defend and rationalize. Right now, though, the amount of criticism you and I are trying to absorb and cope with is unusual. This makes it hard for us to say, "Let's look at this suggestion as dispassionately as we can, and, if it seems promising, try it out under circumstances that will tell us whether or not the proposal has merit." One reason this is hard to do, of course, is that our critics are often as positive that their proposals are right and good as we seem to them to be impervious to new ideas and to be stubborn in defending the *status quo*. Dogmatism begets dogmatism and precludes objectivity or experimentation or fruitful discussion.

Another reason for the poor communication between us and those with whom we argue is the classic mistake antagonists make in not trying, really, to understand one another. I would travel some distance, at my own expense, to listen to the officers of this organization and of the Fund for the Advancement of Education, for example, discuss teacher education in America on one condition. The condition is that the discussion be preceded by something that Carl Rogers insists is necessary for any meeting of minds: namely, each side must first state what it believes are the assumptions and beliefs and recommendations of the other side and keep on until both groups say, "Yes, that represents our position exactly." I am not sure how long a discussion would last that was preceded by this attempt to understand, but I am sure such discussion would be relatively clear and fruitful.

THE SIDE ISSUES DISTRACT US

The more I have thought and talked and read about the arguments we are having over teacher education, the more convinced I have become that we rarely attend to the real issue. This real issue, which I look at more closely later on, is a basic difference in assumptions and convictions about public education and about the teaching-learning process. Almost all of our attention in the current controversy, however, seems to me to be centered upon peripheral questions that just cannot be settled by polemics. An illustration is our finding ourselves in an argument as to whether or not teachers should have a good liberal or general education. This, I think, is a false issue. The importance of a good general education for teachers can be taken for granted. I do not know anyone who denies that teachers at every level should have a good general education. Many times I have felt, however, that we teacher educators are put in the position of seeming to oppose this basic idea. This we should never allow to happen.

I recognize, as do all of you, that there is much difference of opinion about the nature of general education and the type of college program that gives greatest assurance of achieving it. These are separate problems. Each must eventually be resolved by experimental programs, not by argument. We teacher educators, however, cannot hold everything until we get clear-cut evidence indicating that one approach to general education is far better than another. What do we do in the meantime? In my judgment there is no alternative to basing our practice upon the most careful, even though subjective, analysis of our past experience that we can make and upon whatever implications we can see for general education in what we know about human learning. Conclusions based upon these two ways of reaching judgments about general education programs will differ, of course. They suggest to me, however, several things about general education. First, this kind of education cannot be separated sharply and clearly from professional or vocational or specialized education. Second, the likelihood is remote that a list of discrete courses, developed and fought, bled and died for by discrete departments, will add up to a fine general education for many students; and, third, it is optimistic to hope that a subject matter specialist who does not view his specialty as general education will teach it as general education.

I believe we are on another side issue when we argue whether or not teachers should have special knowledge of whatever it is they are to teach. Of course they should have this special knowledge. To teach history, it is important to know history; to teach science, it is necessary to know science; to teach the English language, one should know the English language. There is an active debate, of course, and some research bearing on the question as to how this special knowledge might best be acquired and what it should consist of. But again these are different questions. They, too, can be answered, if at all, by experimentation, not by heated arguments.

Again, though, we must do our best to prepare the young people we now have as students, and we cannot wait until all the data are in. What about now? My experience with teacher education and what I think I know about transfer of training lead me to the conclusion that a young person who knows he is going to teach physics needs a different kind of physics instruction from the young person who does not intend ever to teach physics. This does not mean, necessarily, that the prospective teacher of physics should learn, in an introductory college course, different subject matter from that taught the prospective atomic scientist or the prospective business man. It does mean, however, that he should be taught physics with continuous attention to the problems a learner faces who is trying to comprehend physics. There is little evidence that the typical college or university teacher of science, or of mathematics, or of history, or of literature teaches his subject so as to provide especial help to someone who, in turn, would like to teach it. I am not implying, necessarily, that students who plan to teach must be segregated in their "major" subject matter courses. I do believe, however, that prospective teachers who are taking a course in American history, for example, would gain a great deal if they were to meet together regularly to do two things, to identify the relationships between what they are learning and what they might be expected to teach and to identify some of the difficulties most young people encounter when they try to learn American history.

We are on another side issue, I believe, when we debate the desirability of having prospective teachers spend a lot of time in public school class rooms. Practice teaching is a valued and integral part of every preservice teacher-education program I know anything about or have heard seriously recommended. The substantial differences of opinion about when practice teaching might best come and about what other kinds of experience it should be associated with had better be dealt with experimentally. But again, what should we do in the meantime? To answer this question, I fall back upon the inferences thoughtful people have made from years of experience with practice teaching as well as upon some of the things I think we know about learning. Both of these approaches lead me to believe that a student ought to be inducted into the realities of teaching-learning situations as soon as he enters a teacher education program. This does not mean, of course, that he starts practice teaching immediately. It does mean, though, that very early in his training he gets back into public school classroom situations where he can practice making observations and assessments and inferences regarding what is going on. Making a sharp separation between teaching theory and teaching practice is an artificial compartmentalization of training experience that reduces the likelihood of transfer. In an ideal teacher education curriculum the student shuttles back and forth between observation and participation and practice teaching, on the one hand, and pedagogical theorizing and conceptualizing on the other. This kind of arrangement is, of course, not at all easy to develop or administer. Until I see evidence, however, that persuades me otherwise, I will look with a great deal of skepticism on any proposal that we separate the acquisition of knowledge about teaching from the acquisition of knowledge of what to teach or from actual field observations and practices that are designed primarily to result in the development of adequate teaching behavior.

Another side issue, it seems to me, is the debate as to whether or not members of a liberal arts faculty or of a department of education should teach the history of education or the philosophy of education or educational psychology or educational sociology to prospective teachers. The extent to which these courses are related to professional problems and to professional motivation is, of course, of great importance. Whether or not, however, *well taught* professional-oriented courses in philosophy or psychology or sociology or history should be offered here or there is another matter that cannot be settled by argument. We should try it both ways under experimental conditions and see what the consequences are.

In the meantime, though, and until these experiments are conducted, my experience leads me to believe that it is unrealistically optimistic to expect that a teacher of philosophy who has no particular interest in education, or in the teaching-learning process, or in the profession of teaching will do a maximally satisfactory job of teaching educational philosophy to prospective teachers. Similarly, I know of no instance where a professor of psychology, not concerned about education, or about the teaching-learning process, or about the profession of teaching, has taught educational psychology to prospective teachers very effectively. Until I see better evidence than I have so far that these foundation courses for teachers can best be taught by faculty members who are not deeply concerned with the professional problems that teachers face, I want them taught by people who have that concern. Heaven knows, even under this circumstance, the teaching is all too often without much meaning.

To conclude my comments on the side issues, I see little point to the argument as to whether or not teachers colleges as separate and single purpose institutions are disappearing. That they are becoming fewer is a fact. What this fact means, of course, is subject to considerable difference of interpretation, but again, these differences cannot be resolved by argument. We need more facts.

BASIC DIFFERENCES IN CONCEPTIONS OF AMERICAN EDUCATION

At the same time that I feel that debating the questions I have just cited, or others like them, misses the real issue, I think I know what this real issue is; and many of you, I suspect, have reached the same conclusion. I believe that the real issue, as I said a moment ago, grows out of basically different conceptions of the purposes of American public education and of the teaching-learning process that gives most promise of fulfilling these purposes. Here is what I mean: If you are disposed to believe that the primary, if not the exclusive, aim of public education is to teach a limited number of important skills or a prede-termined body of important subject matter; that those who are hard to teach this material to should not go to school very long; that the boys and girls who do not learn the skills and the subject matter as fast as adults believe they should are somehow bad and that teachers shouldn't have to contend with them; and that discipline is best engendered in children by imposing on them somewhat fixed and presumably high standards—if you hold these beliefs or others like them, your conclu-sions about teacher education are almost inevitable. You will con-clude that teaching, as such, is not too difficult or too complicated, and that almost anyone can do it commendably *if* he is reasonably bright, is a college graduate, knows enough about what he's trying to teach, and can make children behave.

This conception of education and of teaching is firmly held by large segments of the American public. It is accepted by many college pro-fessors who provide not only the general education for teachers but also the special education in subject matter for high-school and college instructors. This conception gives little support to the idea that protracted preparation for the professional aspects of teaching is necessary. Some teachers are better than others, of course, but this is a consequence of a complex of unpredictable personality and environmental influences and bears little relation to programs of teacher education.

When you believe these things, and, as I have said, many sincere and respectable people do, it is quite reasonable to contend that knowing what is to be taught is by all odds the major responsibility of the teacher and that professors of psychology or history or philosophy or sociology in liberal arts colleges can teach an additional course or can give their current courses a twist that will throw some light on educational questions. Believing these things, it is quite natural to urge that the amount of time being given to professional education might well be reduced so that, as President Griswold recently put it, we can provide for a "massive infusion of the Liberal Arts" into the education of secondary school teachers. Believing these things, it is easy to contend that the tricks of the teacher's trade can best be picked up on the job by the new teacher working hand in hand with the experienced teacher who has himself learned these tricks.

You and I, it seems to me, find it impossible to accept this view of teacher education because we hold different convictions about what American public education should be, about the young people for whom it should be provided, and about the kind of teachers who are needed to facilitate it. Most of us believe that the tremendous variations among boys and girls, variations in their backgrounds, their motivation, and their needs, require that the curriculum be flexible rather than predetermined. Most of us believe that all American boys and girls should have experiences, at least in the elementary and secondary schools, that are maximally meaningful to them at the time and that their judgments are necessary if we are to know what is meaningful. Most of us believe that discipline is a consequence of practice in planning and decision making and of experience with their effects. Most of us believe that good citizenship and health are proper and important educational goals and that these goals are not achieved merely by learning information *about* citizenship or health.

Because of these beliefs most of us take the view that good teaching is exceedingly difficult and complex and dynamic and exacting. Good teaching is of a different order from keeping school. We are certain, too, that the attitudes and feelings and concepts and practices that distinguish the fine teacher have been learned and can, to a substantial degree, be taught. This conviction almost inevitably leads us to the conclusion that the pre-service as well as the in-service education of teachers cannot be casual or incidental and that it cannot be turned over to people with quite different assigned duties. The professional education of teachers must be someone's central concern.

One of the inevitable consequences of our holding these views about American public education and about the kind of preparation that teachers need in order to practice their profession wisely is that they require large amounts of money. Other ways of providing for the education of teachers may be less expensive. This attractive fact, however, should not, it seems to me, be unduly weighed.

I recognize how misleading analogies are, but I want to stress the conviction that the *central* issue which separates those of us who are primarily concerned with teacher education from our critics is a different conception of education and of learning and teaching. For us to agree on teacher education would be about as unlikely as it would be to expect agreement on what should be done for peace in a discussion between Quakers and the West Point faculty. These two groups would go into their discussions with such different assumptions and conceptions of the causes of war as to make it virtually impossible for them to come to common terms on any program for world peace.

WHAT TO DO

Personally, I do not anticipate much reduction of controversy about teacher education until we and our adversaries move a bit closer to one another in our conception of the purpose of public education and what this demands of teachers. I do, however, believe that we teacher educators can do two things that in the long run will benefit everyone. First, we can, in our public discussions, try to see to it that not only those we argue with but we, too, keep our eyes on the central issue. We should miss no chance to point out the implications for the central issue of every teacher education proposal that is made.

I am convinced that our conception of the kind of education that is best for American young people and our conception of the role of the teacher will continue to win adherents. During the past fifty years pressures in the direction of curricular flexibility, of humaneness in relationships between teachers and pupils, of making school work attractive to an ever larger number of boys and girls, and of seeing to it that what is learned is maximally practical in the best sense, as well as pressures to develop teacher education programs that will help achieve these purposes, have been irresistible. As more and more young people continue in school, I do not look for any diminution in the power of these forces. Certainly, temporary setbacks have occurred and will occur again. What worries me most, I guess, is that we may do less than we might to strengthen what appear to me to be forces for good by giving too much attention to the little battles and too little attention to what the war is all about.

A second thing I hope strongly we will work on with increasing dedication is putting our own house in order. I have much more confidence in the correctness of my convictions about American education, about what good teaching requires, and about how teachers ought to be educated than I have in what I as an individual have done here and there to improve the education of teachers. I recognize that new and interesting and promising ideas are being experimented with in teacher education institutions in some places. For the most part, though, I suspect many of us are going on doing much as we have been doing for the past twenty years. I can imagine no more significant single indication of the vitality of teacher education than the existence of a tremendous amount of experimentation and testing of new and promising ideas. This, it seems to me, we ought to be doing much more of. In addition to experimentation related to some of the side issues in teacher education I have commented on, I wish we could move faster than we are, getting evidence in some other critical areas. To what degree are we teacher educators achieving the goals we say we are trying to achieve, for instance? I know of no teacher education institution, although you may, that has good evidence to back up the claims typically made in the front matter of the college bulletin. Another question I would like more evidence on is this: What college experiences, in addition to courses, bring about significant and desirable changes in prospective teachers? There is some reason to believe that the general climate of a teacher education institution has more lasting effects upon the attitudes and dispositions and points of view of its students than do the courses. If this is so we ought to know much more about it than we do.

A third question we know too little about has to do with the kinds of student self-direction that are conducive to effectiveness as a teacher. There is reason to believe that relatively little is done in most teacher education institutions to teach independence. Few people defend this situation, but we need to search much more energetically for ways and means that will increase student independence. . . .

SUMMARY

The argument I have tried to present has not been, I am sure, particularly involved, but I do want to conclude by summarizing my major contentions. First, many of us teacher educators are finding it difficult to be objective and penetrating in our analysis of criticisms of our work because we react to attack, as most people do, by defending what we have done. Second, a great deal of our time and the time of those who differ from us is, in a sense, being wasted through attention to a long list of peripheral issues. Third, the central issue that divides us from those who advocate a different kind of teacher education is centered in a number of fundamentally different conceptions about American education in general and about the role of the teacher. Finally, in light of all of this, the most important things we can do, not only in the near future but in the long run, are to continue to call attention in public debate about teacher education to what the central issue is and, at the same time, to experiment continuously and systematically to put our own house in order.

3

The Two Traditions of Teacher Education in the United States

PAUL WOODRING

Mr. Woodring was formerly a professor at Western Washington College of Education. Now on the staff of the Ford Foundation, he edits "Education in America," the monthly education supplement of the Saturday Review.

Many of the conflicts and confusions found in teacher education today grow out of the fact that we have two distinct traditions of teacher education in the United States. The older tradition, which long controlled the education of secondary teachers, and which still controls the education of college teachers, provides the basis for what may be called the academic or liberal arts view of teacher education. The second tradition—which is newer although it now has a history of well over one hundred years—is that of the professional educator and is most evident in the normal schools and teachers colleges which have long provided a substantial number of elementary teachers and now prepare secondary teachers as well. The teacher education found in the university schools of education is an unsuccessful marriage of the two which has failed so far to synthesize the two philosophies. This failure may be seen in the sharp conflicts of view which may be found between professional educators and academic professors in many an American university.

These two divergent traditions have led to differing conceptions of the proper curriculum for teacher education, and the widespread em-

From *New Directions in Teacher Education* by Paul Woodring (New York: Fund for the Advancement of Education, 1957). Reprinted by permission.

phasis given to these curricular differences has tended to obscure the fact that the underlying conflict is philosophical. The two traditions represent totally different concepts of the nature of man, of the learning process, and of the proper role and limitations of free public schools. Although both traditions stress the importance of the human individual, the older one holds that *formal* education is properly centered in the world of knowledge and is concerned with the development of the mind. The newer tradition prefers to place the stress upon the "whole child." It places great emphasis upon the learning process and interprets this process in a way which extends it far beyond academic or intellectual learning. It is no accident that the newer tradition first gained its foothold in the elementary schools or that higher education has clung more firmly to the older tradition. The secondary schools have been caught between the two.

The early American secondary schools were, in large part, college preparatory institutions and it seemed natural that an academy which prepared students for Yale or Harvard should draw its faculty from among the graduates of those colleges. It was assumed that a sound liberal and academic education was also the best teacher education and that, in selecting teachers, scholarship should be the prime prerequisite. The major responsibility for learning was placed upon the student and, if he failed to learn, the fault was held to be his rather than the teacher's.

The public high schools, which developed during the second half of the nineteenth century, continued this tradition and an A.B. degree was accepted as satisfactory evidence of preparation for high school teaching. The high school teacher was expected to demonstrate competence in his subject, he was not expected to accept any large responsibility for the student's social adjustment or his recreation and rarely did he take an active part in planning the high school curriculum. If he taught his subject well, and lived within community mores, little more was expected of him. Professional training was rarely considered to be a necessary or even a desirable part of the high school teacher's preparation. This concept of the role and the training of the secondary teacher continued well into the present century and even today provides the basis for much of the criticism of the teacher education found in the teachers colleges.

As the academic content of schools and colleges became increasingly departmentalized during the nineteenth century, secondary teachers became more and more specialized. High school teachers, like the college professors who taught them, came to think of themselves less as teachers than as historians, classicists, scientists, or mathematicians. This was something new in the educational world, for the great philosopher-teachers from Socrates to Kant were never specialists in this sense.

Although the new tradition of the teacher as a subject specialist eventually reached down through the secondary school, it never reached into the elementary schools except possibly in the case of music teachers. Teachers for the elementary schools were of a different breed. Rarely, until recent decades, were they college graduates, and rarely were they expected to be scholars. Prior to the development of the normal schools in the second quarter of the nineteenth century, few elementary teachers had any specific instruction for their work and few had themselves progressed beyond the elementary school. Undoubtedly some were kindly and intelligent but others were the Ichabod Cranes—itinerant ne'er-do-wells who taught because they could do nothing else or as a step toward a more remunerative and more respected profession. Far from being a profession, elementary teaching was a temporary job available to almost any literate person who would accept it and who could maintain some degree of order in the classroom.

The normal schools were developed for the specific purpose of improving elementary education by providing a new kind of teacher for the lower schools. Beginning in New England, about 1830, the normal-school movement spread across the country until by 1900 such institutions had come into a dominant position in elementary teacher education. Some were under private auspices while others were state or municipal institutions, and in the rural areas there were many county normal schools offering brief summer courses.

The normal-school movement was sponsored by devoted men and

women and the devotion was to the improvement of elementary education for all. The movement was influenced by the writings of Rousseau, Herbart, Pestalozzi, and Froebel and later James and Dewey.
The early normal schools accepted the prevailing emphasis on the
three R's but added a new emphasis on the nature and needs of the
child as a growing human being. If their view occasionally was senti-
mental, based perhaps upon a too-easy acceptance of Rousseau's doctrine of the inherent goodness of the child in his natural state, it also
was consistent with the growing humanitarianism of the century. It
gave the teacher a new responsibility for understanding the child and
for providing motivation and interest in the learning process. There
seems little doubt that the graduates of the normal schools brought
about great improvement in elementary education.

The early normal schools were in no sense collegiate institutions
and it was not intended that they should be. Students came directly
from the elementary schools and returned as teachers after a period
ranging from a few weeks to two years. Academic instruction was at
best on the level of that provided in the academies with the addition of
instruction in pedagogic skills and a review of the subjects taught in
elementary schools.

It was the rapid development of the free public high school after
1870 that changed all this and resulted in the development of normal
schools into degree granting teachers colleges. By 1900, high school
graduates were available in sufficient numbers so that many normal
schools could require a high school diploma for admission, and by 1920
many normal schools were offering four-year post-high-school courses
terminating in a college degree. By the mid-1930's many normal
schools had changed their names to teachers colleges or colleges of
education and by 1950 many of the state institutions had dropped the
words "teachers" or "of education" from their titles and had become
general or liberal arts colleges, or, in some cases, universities.

The change has been by no means in name only. Liberal arts offerings have been greatly increased and the faculties have been strengthened by the addition of graduates of leading graduate schools. In Ohio,
for example, where teachers colleges went out of existence more than

twenty years ago, the institutions which once were normal schools, and then teachers colleges, at Bowling Green and Kent, are now large state universities with highly diversified offerings. To continue to call such institutions "teachers colleges" because of their historical origin is as meaningless as it would be to refer to the University of Pennsylvania as an academy because it was so designated by its founder.

As a result of these changes the term "teachers college" is fast becoming obsolete. A generation ago there were nearly three hundred such institutions supported by the states in addition to many city and county normal schools of less than collegiate status. Today the normal school has gone the way of the stagecoach and the number of state teachers colleges has dropped to a little over one hundred. The teachers college as an institution separate from universities and liberal arts colleges has disappeared in twenty-one of the forty-eight states although in all these states there are many colleges, both public and private, which prepare teachers along with their other responsibilities.

Most of the teachers colleges which remain are rapidly becoming general colleges in everything but name and many have plans to make requests of state legislatures for changes in their names, scope, and functions. It seems a safe guess that within twenty years, perhaps within ten years, the separate undergraduate teachers colleges will have gone the way of the dodo. The state college which replaces it is a generalized institution in which only a fraction of the students are preparing to become teachers.

One result of this change is that much of the recent criticism of teacher education has missed its proper mark. The critic who attacks teacher education in terms of the teachers college is likely, when he looks around him, to find he is attacking a ghost rather than a reality. The remaining teachers colleges are responsible for the education of only about 20 per cent of all new teachers entering our elementary and secondary schools. In contrast 32 per cent come from private liberal arts colleges and universities and 48 per cent from public liberal arts colleges and universities. It seems clear that if changes are to be made in teacher education we must give our attention to all the colleges that prepare teachers rather than to teachers colleges alone.

Even the remaining teachers colleges have increased their liberal arts offerings until today virtually every subject taught in any liberal arts college is available in some of the better teachers colleges and is taught by men and women with the same academic background as professors in universities and liberal arts colleges—teachers who hold Ph.D. degrees from universities and whose professional commitment is to an academic discipline rather than to education as a profession. The academic world seems to be unaware of the change for the charge is repeatedly made that teachers colleges teach nothing but "methods." It would be more accurate to say that the typical student graduating from a teachers college, if he is preparing for high school teaching, receives about three-fourths of a liberal arts course. If he is preparing for elementary teaching about one-half to two-thirds of his work is in the liberal arts. The *quality* of the liberal education varies from college to college, just as it does in colleges granting the A.B. degree.

It is true, however, that the teachers colleges, as a group, have continued to place a larger emphasis on professional courses than do liberal arts colleges which prepare teachers and this is particularly true of the programs for elementary teachers. The emphasis is not on methods alone, but is on educational psychology, educational principles, and educational philosophy. To refer to these professional courses as "methods" is misleading; the psychology of learning is no more a course in methods than is physiology as taught in a medical school and educational philosophy, if it lives up to its name, is the very antithesis of methodology. Yet the heavy emphasis on professional requirements, and on an extended period of practice teaching, amounting in some colleges to full time for an entire semester, has made it impossible for most teachers colleges to require a full sequence of courses in liberal education and a concentration in a major subject comparable to that usually required for an A.B. degree. One result has been that the graduate of a teachers college, who has greatest need for subject matter concentration on the graduate level, often finds the graduate school reluctant to admit him for a course leading to a master of arts degree in his chosen subject. If he wishes to take graduate work he is forced to take it in education. At the same time the student whose undergraduate work was in the liberal arts frequently is refused admission to a graduate program in education because of his lack of undergraduate professional courses. In each case the student gets more of what he least needs and has no opportunity to fill in the gaps in his preparation.

Many liberal arts colleges have, for many years, offered professional courses for teachers but they have offered them reluctantly and more with an eye to legal requirements for teacher certification than from any real conviction of the value of such courses. Rarely, prior to 1950, did they take the lead in the improvement of the professional part of the teacher's education.

During the first half of the present century, while many liberal arts colleges turned their backs on the problems of teacher education, legal requirements for certification were established in nearly all states. In general the trend was away from certification on the basis of examination and toward certification on the basis of completion of course requirements in colleges and universities. Because the total number of college years required for teaching, particularly for elementary teachers, has steadily increased, there has been increased opportunity for both professional *and* liberal education but the legal requirements have been much more specific about professional courses and have allowed the colleges more discretion in the field of liberal education. Many states specify certain courses which must be taken in professional fields so that the responsibility for curriculum making has, in part, been taken away from the colleges.

When the academic community awoke to what had happened it was loud in its denunciation of the certification laws and the professional educators responsible for them. In the new requirements some thought they saw a conspiracy on the part of professional educators to take the responsibility for teacher education away from the world of scholarship.

There was no conspiracy, of course, but it is quite true that the responsibility for teacher education had been allowed to slip out of the hands of the academic scholars. What happened was that while the liberal arts colleges were preoccupied with other things, while they ignored the problems of teacher education, a like-minded group of school administrators and other professional educators came to agreement among themselves on the necessity for professional preparation for teachers and transmitted their convictions into law. It was during this same period that the educators became imbued with a new philosophy of education, one far removed from the academic traditions of the liberal arts colleges.

Many liberal arts professors remained convinced that professional courses of any kind were inconsistent with the proper aims of the liberal arts college and that the presence of such courses in the curriculum would vitiate the liberal arts program. It was feared that the increasingly heavy load of professional requirements would make it impossible to prepare teachers with a sound liberal arts background and a number of colleges refused to offer any professional courses whatever. Professional educators, however, were adamant in their insistence that professional requirements could not be lowered and ought, indeed, to be raised still higher.

The conflict between the two points of view reached a climax in the early 1950's with the publication of numerous controversial books and magazine articles and a renewed public interest in the schools and their teachers. It was into this atmosphere of confusion, uncertainty, and acrimony that the Fund for the Advancement of Education was born and the work of the Fund in teacher education can be assessed only in terms of these problems, their history, and their consequences.

With encouragement and financial assistance from the Fund a number of liberal arts faculties have, in the past five years, explored the problems of teacher education. The faculties which have given careful attention to the problems have come, often reluctantly, to the conclusion that a certain amount of professional preparation is a necessary background for both elementary and secondary teachers, regardless of legal requirements for certification. Some have sought ways of providing this outside the regular four-year liberal arts curriculum, either through summer school courses or during a fifth year which includes an internship in the public schools with correlated professional seminars or classes. A few, after a thorough investigation of the entire problem of teacher preparation, have introduced reorganized professional courses into the undergraduate curriculum. As the findings from these projects are correlated and disseminated new patterns begin to emerge.

If we assume that teacher preparation must include *both* liberal and professional education and that these two must be brought into harmony with each other in some organized pattern, there would appear to be four ways of approaching the problem:

1. A fifth year of professional training and experience can be provided for liberal arts graduates.
2. Liberal arts colleges can be encouraged to incorporate essential professional training into their programs in ways which will not vitiate the liberal arts program.
3. Universities can be encouraged to devise new programs which represent the best thinking of both academic and professional faculties.
4. Teachers colleges can be assisted in providing better liberal arts programs and in reorganizing their professional courses in such a way as to eliminate proliferation and duplication.

The fourth possibility has so far received little attention from the Fund for the Advancement of Education. Perhaps the reason is that the presidents of teachers colleges have shown too little indication of willingness to attack these problems vigorously and have submitted too few imaginative proposals for Fund assistance.

Much more attention has been given to programs of teacher education within liberal arts colleges and universities but the major emphasis, during the early years of the Fund's existence, has been upon fifth-year programs for liberal arts graduates. This emphasis has opened a new source of teacher supply and has provided for the schools many liberally educated teachers who without the new programs would have been lost to the profession.

The long-range solutions, however, must affect all institutions which educate teachers whether they be universities, teachers colleges, or colleges of liberal arts. We cannot ignore the fact that the greater numbers of our teachers always have come, not from the upper income groups where parents prefer to have their children enter the more remunerative professions, but from among the more intelligent boys and girls of the lower economic classes who look upon the teaching profession as an opportunity to be of service while moving upward from the unskilled and skilled labor groups. Such potential teachers are not found, in large numbers, among the graduates of the more socially selective private colleges. They must be found wherever they are and provided with opportunity for the best kind of teacher education we know how to give them.

Never has there been a greater need for research and experimentation in teacher education and teacher recruitment, but neither has there been a time when experimentation was so certain to lead to controversy. The conflict of views has been brought to the attention of the American people at a time when the teacher shortage is one of alarming magnitude and threatens, at the higher levels particularly, to become increasingly serious.

Programs for the improvement of teacher education must include an effort to synthesize the conflicting views and at the same time must look for new sources in teacher recruitment. Experimental attacks must be bold, imaginative, and philosophically oriented as well as adequately financed. Money alone is useless unless it is coupled with sound ideas. . . .

4

What—and How—to Teach Teachers

JOHN H. FISCHER

Formerly dean of Teachers College, Columbia University, Mr. Fischer has been president of Teachers College since 1962.

Of the 425,000 students who were graduated from American colleges this past June, 142,500 are said to be prepared to teach in the elementary or secondary schools. How well they have been prepared is a matter of opinion, and opinions on this subject vary widely. The recent action of the New York State Board of Regents, raising the requirement for a standard elementary school-teaching certificate from four years of college study to five, is persuasive evidence that present programs of teacher education are not fully satisfactory.

The question of what—or who—makes a good teacher is by no means new. Four hundred years ago in England, Sir Thomas Elyot was complaining, "Lorde God, howe many good and clean wittes of children be nowe a days perished by ignorant school maisters." And across the Channel not many years later, Montaigne, implying that more is involved in good education than substituting information for ignorance, recorded his agreement with the proverb that "the greatest scholars are not the wisest men."

Difficult as it is for even wise men to agree on what a teacher should know or what he should be able to do, almost everybody who has gone to school remembers some instructor who exemplifies, for him, teaching at its best.

This is the way many middle-aged alumni of a boys' high school in one Eastern city remember a Latin teacher. As he taught it, the ancient language came alive and many of his boys became aggressive, serious students. They well recall how the quiet force of his learning stimulated them to learn, but, in retrospect, they value even more his rare combination of fine character and perceptive teaching that gave them a deeper understanding not only of Latin but of themselves.

An eighth-grade mathematics instructor is frequently cited by her former students for her ability to make the intricate patterns of algebra clear and fascinating, and for her unusual patience in working with the slower students while every day in the same class she lifted ceilings for the brighter ones. Another woman has worked for years with children whose intelligence appears so limited that they are legally classified as only "trainable." With ingenuity and understanding matched only by the quality of her solicitude, she has brought child after child to a level of performance far beyond what parents or other teachers ever thought possible.

Successful teachers differ in countless ways, but almost invariably they share an unusual capacity for reaching students as individuals. This is not to say that their own formal learning is unimportant, but that in addition to possessing knowledge they know how to employ it to their pupils' benefit.

I had the good fortune to begin my own career under a teacher who understood these twin aspects of good teaching. Miss Ida V. Flowers was the principal of Baltimore's Montebello School when I came there thirty-two years ago, the ink still wet on my normal-school diploma, to teach a sixth-grade class. Long before the ritual of public obeisance to excellence became fashionable, excellence was pursued in her school as a matter of course. The possibility that either students or faculty members might pitch their efforts at a lower level was simply not considered—by Miss Flowers or anybody else in the school. She took for granted—and let us know it—that every teacher was to be concerned with the intellectual development of his pupils. She excused no weakness in subject matter and she held us responsible for using the best pedagogical practices to teach it.

With her encouragement, and her unfailing help, we steadily improved our competency in planning lessons, in using a variety of teaching materials, and in testing and counseling our pupils. Never since have I seen a school where more constant attention was devoted to refining teaching techniques, or more thought given to building a curriculum based on both high academic standards and sound psychological principles. Much of the difficulty in analyzing teaching and learning to do it well stems from a major difference between teaching and other professions. Whereas the architect, the lawyer or the surgeon usually serves his client or patient by doing something *to* him or *for* him, the teacher, when he performs his work best, does it *with* his student.

To a degree that is true in few, if any, other professions, a teacher must be steadily and closely involved with the learner's activity, sensitive to his reactions, and responsive to his progress and his perplexity. The greater the variety of children with whom the teacher deals, the more puzzling and demanding his task becomes. If he is to work effectively with children, especially those whose cultural backgrounds or intelligence levels differ markedly from his own, the teacher must know something of the ways children mature, how they learn, what motivates them, and the ways physical, emotional and social factors influence learning and teaching.

That the teacher should be a well-educated person is so patently clear as to require no argument. Without a comprehensive view of the humanities, the social sciences, the natural sciences and the arts, no one can responsibly undertake to induct a young person into the culture and problems of the modern world. Unless a teacher understands the major academic disciplines well enough to use them as his own tools for refining experience into usable knowledge, there is small hope that he will be able to help his pupils think effectively or use the ideas they encounter. He should, moreover, have studied at least one subject in enough depth to have a respectable knowledge of it.

But while liberal studies and mastery of "content" are necessary components of every teacher's education, they are by no means sufficient preparation for skillful classroom work. The standard cliché-filled debate on whether the prospective teacher should learn what to teach or how to teach is a pointless waste of time. He obviously needs both, and more: he must also understand whom he teaches and why.

Any appraisal of current programs in teacher education, and any projection of better ones, must start from two inescapable facts. One is that a greater number and variety of people than ever before now require genuine education. Compulsory attendance and universal schooling for basic literacy are obviously no longer an adequate response to a world in which both personal involvement and national survival call for substantial intellectual activity by a large majority of the population.

The second fact is the endless expansion of knowledge. This trend presents the school with two groups of problems: how to select what should be taught, and how to teach it more effectively.

Even in much simpler times, education has never been a matter merely of letting children do what comes naturally. Although specific purposes change from time to time, formal education is always a process of deliberate cultivation. The principal source of energy the teacher uses in the process is the dynamic power of the student's growth and maturation.

Since one who understands this force is certain to teach better than he could without that knowledge, the teacher's professional training should be based on the study of human growth and development. To this general background should be added specific skill in instruction. The teacher must know as much as possible about the nature of learning, the ways of motivating students, and teaching techniques suitable for particular subjects, students or situations.

Another group of ideas important in teacher education is being put forward by Professors Jerome Bruner and Philip Phenix, the first a Harvard psychologist, the other a philosopher in Teachers College at Columbia. They propose that the academic subjects or disciplines be taught, not as groups of facts and principles to be memorized, but rather as "ways of knowing" or "strategies of inquiry."

The principal focus in teacher education, as they see it, should be on the processes by which the student can learn to use his mind to understand not only what he finds in books but what he encounters in the world around him. With more teachers prepared for this sort of instruction, students might learn to use authoritative materials more perceptively and less slavishly, to apply imagination and intuition as well as memory to the unpredictable problems that lie far out beyond the last commencement.

Teacher education will have to respond to the fast-breaking technological developments in communication media and in machines for storing and retrieving information. Modern technology has been producing potential teaching tools faster than teachers have learned to use them. As a consequence, schools are far less efficient than they could be if teachers were properly prepared to use even the simpler devices already available.

Tomorrow's teachers will have to know the appropriate uses of open- and closed-current television, of films, tapes, projectors and recorders. Educational "systems" will include components more complex than blackboards, textbooks and maps. The teacher's task will require him to use these instruments, singly and in combination, with large groups, small groups and individual students. Most important, he will need to understand how such devices can be applied to enhance the student's capacity to employ his own mind to solve the learning problems he discovers for himself.

Future teachers will not work independently, as the teacher of the one-room school did and as many still do today. School people are beginning to accept the fact that just as children differ, so do teachers vary in interests, talents and techniques, and that when they work in groups these differences can usefully complement each other. In more and more schools, assistants are being engaged to relieve teachers of routine functions and free them to concentrate on their more demanding duties. But teaching with a colleague or an assistant may be more difficult than teaching alone unless one is prepared to organize his work in suitable ways. This problem, too, will need to be reflected in teacher education.

It is a rare college that can claim to be preparing new teachers or helping experienced ones to work in the schools these developments portend. The most valid criticism of current programs in teacher education is not that there is too much professional work but that there is too little of the right kind. It is already clear, as the New York State action shows, that if every teacher is to be a liberally educated person and a well-qualified professional, the customary four-year college course simply does not allow enough time. Something like a six-year combination of college, graduate study and supervised internship seems a more realistic estimate of what is necessary.

Nor will even the best teacher be able to keep abreast of new developments without periodic opportunities for advanced study and research. Undoubtedly, school systems will have to adopt some variation of the university sabbatical scheme, or the practice of the military forces which regularly assign officers to graduate institutions for advanced study.

Yet, when all of the improvements that can now be imagined have been made, it will still not be possible to teach the college student or the experienced instructor everything that a teacher should know. For, although teaching can profit enormously, as it has, by drawing on the sciences, the humanities and the other arts, it remains itself one of the most complex of all the arts, and therefore somewhat beyond exact analysis and precise prescription.

A part of every successful teacher's performance is explainable only in terms of his own experience, his own sensitivity, his own imagination. To what extent such artistry is learned—or how, or where—is a mystery as elusive as the origin of any other talent. But because "natural" teachers occur too seldom to furnish a faculty for every school, and because even the best talent can be improved by being informed, disciplined and criticized, high-quality programs of teacher education will continue to be needed and will continue to grow.

The immediate responsibility of leaders in teacher education, especially in the strongest and most influential institutions, is to stimulate fresh approaches and to support imaginative experiments. The teacher's classic and complementary obligation, to foster a proper respect for existing excellence and simultaneously to encourage new promise, is nowhere more relevant, more urgent or more important than in teaching teachers.

5

Teachers Get the Worst Education

JAMES D. KOERNER

Formerly a faculty member at Kansas State and Massachusetts Institute of Technology, Mr. Koerner is now president of the board of the Council for Basic Education. His book, The Miseducation of American Teachers, *was published in 1963.*

The people who train our teachers are incompetent. With rare exceptions they lack the intellect and the educational background to turn out first-rate teachers for the nation's classrooms. Their lack amounts to the single greatest weakness of American education today and a frightening threat to the America of tomorrow. For the quality of teacher training determines the quality of our teachers, which in turn determines the worth of our children's education.

"The blunt fact," says Sterling M. McMurrin, former U. S. Commissioner of Education, "is that many of our teachers are not properly qualified to handle the responsibility we have placed on them. . . . It is a national scandal . . . that large numbers of them are inadequately prepared in the subject matter that they teach." Little wonder that many of the youngsters who stream from the public schools become clerical help who cannot spell or file, workers who cannot read and comprehend directions, citizens ignorant to the point of political and public irresponsibility, and college freshmen who must be put through remedial courses in many subjects before they can proceed with higher education.

Inevitably this catalog of failures leads to one question: How well are teachers prepared for teaching? Having just completed a two-year

---

From *The Saturday Evening Post*, June 1, 1963. Reprinted by permission of the author.

study of the subject for the Relm Foundation of Ann Arbor, Mich., I regret to report that the training of teachers and school administrators is probably the worst in all U.S. higher education. This is true not only at the teachers colleges but also at most universities, including the prestigious ones. Compare the faculty teaching education at a great university like California at Berkeley, or even at a more average institution like Boston University, with the other academic and professional faculties on the same campus. The quality of research done by the non-education faculties, the books they produce, the professional journals they write for, and the reputation they enjoy in their respective academic and student communities (a very accurate yardstick of prestige)—all such comparisons emphasize the inferior status of the education people.

The Commission on Human Resources and Advanced Training reported in 1954 the results of a large-scale survey of students headed for graduate degrees. Those majoring in education were fifth from the bottom in a list of 19 fields, trailed only by those in physical education, home economics, business and commerce, and dentistry. More recently Dr. Lindsey Harmon of the National Academy of Sciences reported on a study which compared intelligence scores and other factors for all people who took doctorate degrees in 1958. On every one of these tests the education graduates finished at the bottom.

Such results are hardly surprising when one considers the makeup of the typical education faculty. It consists of former school administrators and people whose careers and whose own schooling were concentrated in the field of education. The education faculty member is poorly grounded in the liberal arts, often having done very little work in them as an undergraduate and *none* as a graduate student. For example, if he is a professor of mathematics education, he will have spent a great deal of time learning the methods of teaching mathematics and the reasons for teaching or not teaching it, and he will have spent much time in the other trivia of professional education. But he will not have devoted much effort to the study of mathematics itself. The low caliber of the education faculties caused one professor of education at a Wisconsin college to say, "I think we should kick everybody in education out as incompetents and reorganize the field with able people."

The problem of educating teachers thus becomes a circular trap. The admission standards to graduate work in teaching and education are notoriously low, sometimes nonexistent. Inferior people therefore enter and muddle through inferior programs to earn inferior graduate degrees in such subjects as "Secondary School Administration," "Guidance Counseling" or "Teacher Education" itself. Some go on for doctoral degrees in such specialized disciplines as "Intergroup Relations," "Audio-Visual Aids" and "Camping."

These graduates become school administrators who hire teachers and set standards in public schools. Or they staff state departments of education, professional associations and accrediting agencies. Or they become professors of education in other colleges where they proceed to turn out more teachers and more masters and doctors of education. The ramifications run on to infinity.

Improving undergraduate training of classroom teachers clearly depends on some prior reform at the top—the graduate level, the source of the teachers' teachers. For uneducated educators attract the least desirable candidates for teaching, and poor students gravitate naturally to poor departments.

This explains why undergraduates in education generally come from the bottom of the academic barrel, along with students in agriculture and business administration—a fact familiar to most academicians and reinforced by every major study that has been made of the subject. We can look at one of the first such studies, a classic of its kind, titled *The Student and His Knowledge*, done in Pennsylvania and reported in 1938 to the Carnegie Foundation for the Advancement of Teaching. Or we can look at a more recent one like the 1955 report from the Educational Testing Service reviewing the results of tests given to nearly half a million college students during the Korean War. The pattern seems to remain constant: Prospective teachers show up badly in both achievement and native ability when compared with college students in other fields. Thus not only are the education faculties inadequate but their education students show the same intellectual shortcomings.

This unhappy condition prevails for a combination of reasons, not all the fault of educationists. But the educationists' bland acceptance of poor students and their adamant failure to weed out the incompetent has kept a kind of Gresham's law at work these many years in teacher education. In those few programs that have moved in the opposite direction, insisting upon superior ability in candidates for teaching, and creating rigorous academic programs of some prestige for them, the educationist has discovered that education, far from losing candidates, soon begins to attract better people than it ever had, and more of them. The Master of Arts in Teaching program at Yale University, and the undergraduate program for elementary teachers at St. Louis University, and the Bachelor of Arts program for high-school teachers at Grinnell College, are examples of high-quality programs that demonstrate what *can* be done. But the great majority of our teacher-training programs have yet to take to heart one of John Dewey's observations: "All other reforms are conditioned upon reform in the quality and character of those who engage in the teaching profession."

Not only are most prospective teachers inferior in quality to start with; the training they receive, with its heavy emphasis on education courses, only serves to stifle what talents they have. I recently managed to look into a good many of these pedagogical courses, to survey extensively the materials used, and to talk with many hundreds of students involved in them. The students' verdict is overwhelmingly negative—often bitterly so, particularly among the better students, the kind most needed in teaching. They resent the number of courses in teaching methods they are forced to take and the time and money they must thereby waste.

Two factors account for the dullness and intellectual sterility that characterize the education classroom: first, the lack of real depth and scholarship on the instructor's part, and second, the well-known addiction of educationists to the fragmentation, inflation and proliferation of courses and content.

The average high-school teacher of an academic subject has spent nearly one quarter of his college time taking education courses. He has had, therefore, just three quarters of the time available to students in other fields in which to cram both a general liberal education and a major subject of some consequence. (Those who aim to teach non-academic subjects, such as home economics, industrial arts and physical education—and also those who teach art and music—spend even more time in education courses, often so much more that they can be said to have acquired a higher education only by a distortion of the term.)

The elementary teacher is even less educated. She spends over 40 percent of her four undergraduate years taking courses in education. A fed-up elementary teacher remarked, "Every education major wishes she had chosen something else. The courses consist of one dull, repetitious thing after another. Every course starts out with six weeks of 'developmental psychology'—an introductory phase full of such labored truisms as 'The Whole Child comes to school,' 'Children develop at different rates,' and so forth."

Most of these vices persist because the educational establishment combines the worst features of other protectionist, self-serving bureaucracies while exhibiting few of the virtues of real professional leadership or guardianship of the public interest. The politics of education are extremely exclusive, giving very little voice to the academic faculty, the lay public or, indeed, to anyone else outside the educationist fraternity. Enormous power over public education is thus exercised through a maze of interlocking professional education agencies such as the National Education Association and its many divisions, the U. S. Office of Education, the accrediting agencies, and the education units of our colleges and universities. All these bodies are manned by educationists who learned their trade with or from one another and who today complement and reinforce one another's entrenched policies.

Even the language in which members of this establishment communicate, or fail to communicate, tends to exclude anyone but the initiate from their counsels. This weird and pernicious patois, which can most charitably be called Educanto, abounds in twisted syntax, clustered clichés and ugly coinages. It is a world unto itself wherein, for example, superior students must be called "fortunate deviates," and retarded children become "exceptional children"; a world in which one speaks not of encouraging a student's academic interests, but of providing "enriched need arousal," or of "motivating purposeful goal-oriented behavior"; a world in which students "socialize to their peer groups," or if they fail to do so become "isolates" who must be "integrated" into the "appropriate activity constructs."

If the great power of the establishment were used to maintain high standards in the profession and to staff the schools of America with teachers of unquestioned ability, one would no more quarrel with it than with the centralized control of, say, the A.M.A. over medical education. But much too often this power is used solely in the interests of the establishment, for the aggrandizement of special groups, to perpetuate a dogmatic orthodoxy, to protect jobs and status, or to maintain the low intellectual standards of an entrenched system of teacher training.

Reform from the inside is no easier in education than in any other large social organism of vested interests. None of the most promising developments in teacher education today have come from the establishment. All have originated with private foundations, with groups of academic scholars, with such agencies as the National Science Foundation, and with the general public. Pressure for reform must continue to come from "outside." But it must take account of the political realities of the education profession and avoid pushing too fast for sweeping reforms, because the establishment's support is necessary if any reform measure is to succeed. Educationists will not buy any scheme that threatens the *status quo* too sharply. I therefore pass over the more radical reforms that are needed—such as the abolition of the undergraduate school or department of education; the creation of mandatory qualifying examinations for teachers and of full-time teaching apprenticeships requiring no education courses at all; and the granting of greater freedom to school boards, which are now hedged about at every turn by professional controls, in hiring their own teachers. Instead, here are a few of the more modest, more realistic, forward steps that could be taken in the immediate future, with the cooperation of educationists themselves:

1. No undergraduate should be permitted to major in education, and all students, including elementary teachers and special school personnel, should concentrate on some academic subject. 2. The number of education courses required by the colleges should be restricted to state requirements, instead of being arbitrarily set (usually higher) by the colleges. 3. Education courses that are directly related to such aca-

demic disciplines as psychology, history' and philosophy should be taught by trained and bona fide psychologists, historians, and philosophers, not by persons whose graduate work has been in education or simply in methods of teaching these subjects. If these courses are worth having at all, and if they are to remain mandatory in all the training programs, they should at least be put into the hands of competent professors. 4. Standards at the graduate level *must* be improved if anything is to come of the other reforms. Course offerings should be drastically reduced. Candidates for the graduate degrees in education should be screened at least as rigorously as those in academic fields. And course work for all degrees should be concentrated at least 60 or 70 percent in the orthodox academic subjects.

This is little enough. Even so, the effects of only a few such reforms could have a revolutionary effect on teacher training. Whether change can come fast enough in this crucial enterprise to meet the problems of exploding enrollments, the expansion of knowledge itself, and the various other educational exigencies of the nation, I really don't know.

But one thing is sure. Change will not come soon enough if the public remains apathetic, if it continues to tolerate monolithic control of American education by a self-perpetuating establishment founded on mediocrity.

6

Essential Qualifications
of Teachers for the New Era

CLARENCE H. FAUST

Mr. Faust is president of the Fund for the Advancement of Education, and vice president of the Ford Foundation.

. . . [O]ur best hope for realizing the promising possibilities that the new era holds out for mankind lies in attempting to develop the human intelligence to its fullest. To this task the American educational system must be dedicated. And teachers for the new era must be the kinds of persons with the kinds of preparation necessary to carry on this task successfully.

To describe the ideal teacher of the future, then, we need to consider two questions, for one of which I have already, in a general way, suggested an answer. The first question is: What shall be the purpose of our schools or, more specifically, of our high schools? For surely we cannot describe the teacher we need without a clear idea of the functions the teacher is to fulfil. The second question is: What, given a clear view of the purposes of the schools, should be their organization and method of operation? For surely we cannot describe the kinds of teachers we need and desire without knowing how they are to function and just what they are expected to do in order to achieve the results we hope for. Let me try to take up these two questions in at least enough detail to initiate discussion of the problem and perhaps to stimulate my readers to set up a sounder point of view.

"Essential Qualifications of Teachers for the New Era" by Clarence H. Faust is reprinted from *The High School in a New Era* edited by Francis S. Chase and Harold A. Anderson, by permission of The University of Chicago Press. © 1958 by The University of Chicago.

STAFFING SCHOOLS TO DEVELOP CAPACITY
TO ACQUIRE WISDOM

The first question is: What conception of the functions of the schools should determine the kinds of teachers needed for them? The answer I have suggested—that the function of the schools is the fullest possible development of the intelligence—is no doubt too general for our purpose, except in one respect. If correct, it establishes a priority for attention to mental growth as compared with attention to social adjustment, to physical health, to merely vocational skills.

Such establishing of priority may be of no little importance. We have done much, as I see it, to confuse the schools and render them ineffective by loading them with many tasks without establishing any priorities among the assignments. There is current a strange perversion of the doctrine of "the whole child," which, having asserted the wholeness of the student, proceeds to segment him; to divide him into mental, physical, and social compartments; to divide him into citizen, producer, and consumer, and so on, and does this without making any distinctions or setting any priorities among these parts or aspects. As a result, physical education, social adjustment, consumer education, citizenship education, and general education seem all of equal importance. But if we are to consider the whole child, as indeed I believe we should, are we not obliged to consider the relationship of the various aspects of his behavior and responsibilities? And are we not obliged to try to determine what principle makes for wholeness? I suggest that, if we consider these questions, we shall conclude that, though physical health, emotional stability, and social skills are important, the central and governing principle of the wholeness of human beings is, or ought to be, intelligence. Without the development of this quality, physical health is mere animal strength. Without the guidance of intelligence, emotional life is an irresolvable conflict of passionate drives and will inevitably be ordered only by external power and authority. Without intelligence, social adjustment degenerates into mere conformism. Surely education, while recognizing the physical and non-rational aspects of human nature, must proceed on the assumption that these may be, and need to be, intelligently organized and directed.

With respect to the development of intelligence, three points may be worth considering. The first involves a recognition of the differences in capacity for intellectual development. In the past decade we have rightly become increasingly concerned about the problem of the gifted. The new concern about the gifted is a valuable development in American education, both in the interests of society, which needs the fullest possible development of the capacities of our ablest youth, and in the interests of the individual, who is, after all, the ultimate concern of a society which exists not to maintain its own group strength but to provide the fullest development of individual capacities.

Concern about the gifted should lead us to concern about teachers competent to insure the development of talent. This competence does not, fortunately, require teachers who are themselves geniuses. It does require teachers who are prepared to assist students to be better than themselves. Indeed one might lay it down as a fundamental principle that the task for education is constantly to make the next generation better than ourselves, to make students better than their teachers, for only in this way can we have any assurance of future progress.

The idea that teachers should be prepared to assist students to go far beyond themselves implies that the teacher must not be content simply to inform the student of the present state of knowledge or to confirm him in the present view of things but must stimulate him to independent endeavors to go beyond our present knowledge and our present conceptions.

Closely connected, too, with this conception of the teacher's role is the view that the teacher ought to be prepared to encourage uniqueness and difference rather than to require conformity. It is one of the most serious dangers of any highly organized society such as ours that it encourages, especially in times of stress, the development of the organization man, the social and intellectual conformist, the well-balanced and well-adjusted individual, and tends to discourage, if not to suppress, the unique, the different, the independent, the pioneer. We should do well not only to suffer, but to welcome, independence even when it seems troublesome, dissent even when it is annoying, individuality even when it seems to border on oddity. Only so can we hope to provide the climate in which new ideas can flourish and genius can flower.

Finally, free and independent intelligence may not only exhibit itself in unconventional forms but may cover a variety of abilities. It expresses itself in the development of technical know-how, in the development of scientific insight, in discriminating appreciation of the arts, and in the acquisition of philosophic insight and wisdom. I should like to plead that, in high-school and early college education, we put the emphasis upon the development of wisdom, the capacity to make sound and independent judgments about fundamental human problems—about the better and the worse in human associations, about the significance and ends of human life, about the nature of human responsibility.

What I have in mind may be suggested by the almost feverish discussions generated by the Russian production of a satellite. One would suppose from some of the talk about the satellite, even among educators, that America's failure to be first in the field was a result of the failure of our schools to train a sufficient number of able scientists. This seems to me to miss the point entirely. We certainly have as many good scientists as have the Russians, and, if we were not first in launching a satellite, it is not because our high schools and colleges over the past generation have failed to produce the men who could have planned, constructed, and launched a satellite into space. We did not produce the first satellite simply because we had not devoted our energies and resources to this task. Whether we should have done so, whether the decisions which lay behind our not doing so were sound are questions not of scientific, but of political, wisdom. If the political decision is to be challenged and if the decision can be traced to a failure of our schools, we should have to say that the schools had failed, not in teaching science, but in developing in our people and in our leaders the political wisdom required to reach a better conclusion.

In any case, the appearance of the satellite dramatized a fundamental problem—how mankind may achieve peace. This again is not a scientific problem. It cannot be solved by technicians or managed by the highest reaches of material know-how. It calls for wisdom about human beings and human society, their desires, their ways, their true purposes. Because problems of this kind are the most urgent problems of the next generation, our schools need to give highest priority to the development of wisdom about man and about human affairs.

We need, then, in providing the teachers for the new era, to be concerned above all with finding, enlisting, and properly preparing teachers who will be competent to assist students in the development of the capacity of youth to acquire wisdom, which I am democrat enough to believe is far beyond our usual expectations. For developing this capacity we shall need to enlist our best minds in teaching and to make sure that they receive as broad and as deep a liberal or general education as possible.

Now I know the objection which will be immediately raised to the proposal that schools give priority to the development of what I have called wisdom. It will be pointed out that students differ widely in ability and in interests and that it is therefore impossible to aim so high for all students. Let me hasten to reply that I am not talking about college-preparatory work, which may well be inappropriate for a portion of our high-school students who lack the ability or the interest or both to make college work profitable or desirable. And I certainly recognize that, if we attempt at least to lay the foundations for the development of wisdom about man and society in all students, we cannot use the same materials or the same methods, or sustain the same pace of learning for all. What we need to find (and this is one of the great challenges for the teachers of the new era) are appropriate though different means to develop some degree of wisdom about fundamental human concerns in students having different interests and capacities. The so-called slow learner and the inadequately motivated student may not study the same materials, or be guided by the same methods, or manage to maintain the same pace, as those who are gifted and well motivated. But I am convinced that, if we give our minds earnestly enough to the problem and experiment wisely and boldly enough, we shall be able to find the materials, the methods, and the pace that will enable all but the mentally defective to acquire some grasp and some insight into the questions with which as human beings and as citizens in a democratic society they will have to deal.

I do not see how we can otherwise avoid giving up our confidence in democracy, which depends on the assumption that the judgments of the majority will, in the long run, be trustworthy. We give up that confidence, it seems to me, if we assume that only a fraction of our young people are capable of acquiring what I have called wisdom and that others can be given only vocational skills, can become only the equivalent in a technological society of the hewers of wood and the drawers of water.

The finding of appropriate ways to develop the intelligence of young people, with full recognition of the differences in their native ability, so that they can make wise choices concerning the purposes and order-ing of their individual lives and the ends and the ordering of society and government is, I am convinced, the great problem of the modern American high school and will certainly be the great problem of the high school of the new era. Ideally, the high school of the future must be "comprehensive" in a somewhat different sense from that now ordinarily given to the term. It needs to be comprehensive, not by pro-viding in one institutional arrangement for college-preparatory, termi-nal, and vocational education, but comprehensive in providing a range of programs and in employing appropriately different materials, methods, and pace, for developing in all students (up to the limits of their capacity) the knowledge of, the insight into, and the ability to think independently about, mankind's individual and collective con-cerns—thinking that deserves the designation of wisdom.

ORGANIZATION OF SCHOOLS DETERMINES
KINDS OF TEACHERS REQUIRED

A second set of considerations with respect to the teacher of the future arises from the question of how the schools of the future are to be or-ganized and to operate. It is all too easy to suppose that our present modes of deploying teaching resources are not merely contrivances to handle, more or less effectively, the task of educating the young but that they are somehow natural and inevitable. It seems to me that our present utilization of teachers is hopelessly inadequate to the task of education that we as a people have set for ourselves. We have rightly committed ourselves to universal education. This year more than forty million students are enrolled in our schools and colleges. Yet our arrangements for relating teachers to students are, so to speak, in a horse-and-buggy stage.

The sheer pressure of numbers will force us to reconsider them. The biggest school in the biggest city is, in effect, simply a collection of little red schoolhouses. In a kind of egg-crate arrangement, we provide one teacher for every thirty students, requiring that teacher to perform all the chores of the teacher in the little red schoolhouse except attending a potbellied stove. Probably little more than half a teacher's time in our elementary schools is spent in tasks requiring professional competence. The teacher takes off rubbers and puts them on, collects the milk money, polices the play-ground and lunchroom, does a good deal of mere clerical work. The teaching profession is the only profession that has not participated in the revolution of the past fifty years, in which technicians and aides relieve the professionally competent person of non-professional chores so as to enable him to concentrate his time and professional activities and to make his competence available to larger numbers. Surely in the schools of the future, teachers will be provided various aids to enlarge the scope of their professional effectiveness. Otherwise, it would seem impossible to staff our schools with enough able people. Already the shortages at all levels have reached alarming, if not crisis, proportions.

We shall be driven also to draw into service in the schools, on some part-time basis, large numbers of college-bred people in the community who have not prepared to make a career of teaching. Dr. Henry Chauncey, of the Educational Testing Service, pointed out some years ago that, paradoxically, we find ourselves unable to provide enough teachers to read enough English papers to enable students to learn to write well, while at the same time there are in many communities college-bred women who have majored in English and who, with some orientation for the task, could read more papers than the students need to write. Something like the same situation obtains with respect to foreign languages. We are forced to employ for instruction in foreign languages many teachers who are inadequately prepared to teach French or German or Spanish well. And in these same communities, college-bred women who have majored in a foreign language could be recruited for part-time service in the high schools.

We have only begun to realize the possibilities that the powerful new medium of communication in our day, television, has as an educational instrument. Television could be as important in spreading the benefits of education and raising the quality of education as was the first great visual aid, the printed book. It would enable us to make the best teachers in the land available in every far corner. It would enable us to bring events all over the world into every classroom. With it, we could command for the classrooms in every hamlet the resources of our finest museums, orchestras, and dramatic companies.

The co-ordination of these new elements in education would open an enlarged and, I believe, enticing prospect for the career teachers whose task it would be to see that these elements were properly related and directed to achieve the highest quality of education and who might themselves serve that essential and critical function, long ago described by Socrates, of the midwife assisting the birth of knowledge in individual minds.

All this need not necessarily make education more mechanical. It need not give it an assembly-line form. I should hope, indeed, that even the largest schools of the future might follow the lead of some contemporary high schools in organizing themselves in groups of three or four hundred students with a number of faculty members regularly assigned to them—groups small enough so that teachers and students might learn to know each other well individually, groups that could be different enough to take care adequately of students having different abilities and, at the same time, could allow the faculty greater initiative in devising educational programs than a large monolithic school makes possible. Under such an arrangement, teachers might work in teams, each devoting himself to his special interests and competences.

What I am saying would imply that teachers for the high school of the new era would not, in ability, preparation, or function, be cast in one mold. The staff of the high school would include many members of the community not now drawn into its service. It would include aides to take care of much of the clerical work and of the non-professional chores now through necessity performed by full-time, professionally prepared teachers. It would draw upon the part-time services of many specialists in the community, for such things as the reading of English papers and for instruction in foreign languages. It would draw upon the part-time services of men in business and industry—accountants to assist in the teaching of mathematics, for example, and laboratory men in industry for assistance in the teaching of science. It would draw upon businessmen and lawyers for assistance in the social studies. It would depend upon full-time, career teachers for the co-ordination and effective direction of these resources. It would make use of persons having the collection of abilities required for effective teaching over television.

The increasing proportion of college graduates in our population and the prospect of increasing leisure in our society should make these plans feasible and practical. In short, our prospects justify us in assuming that we shall be in a position to command the time, or a significant part of the time, of large numbers of our population for the purposes of education.

A NEW VIEW OF UNIVERSAL EDUCATION

I should like here to repeat a suggestion I have made elsewhere: that we take a new and larger view of our national commitment to universal education. We have come to see, in the last decade, that our commitment to universal education means that education must become everybody's business, in the sense that citizens need to interest themselves in our schools, need to be informed about their problems and requirements, and need to give them their financial and moral support. The work of the National Citizens Council for Better Schools over the past six or seven years has dramatically demonstrated the growing awareness in this country of the need for citizen participation in the solution of school problems.

I am suggesting that there is another sense in which, if we are to have universal education of high quality, virtually everyone must be involved, namely, through widespread participation in the educational work of our schools. Young people as they acquire knowledge should begin to assist in the education of those less mature, and our technological developments will make it possible to enlist an increasingly large number of competent adults for work of various kinds in our educational system. Indeed, as the proportion of adults who have graduated from college increases, these resources should be increasingly valuable.

We should turn to them, not as a move of desperation to man our schools at the expense of educational quality, but as a consequence of a fuller and richer conception of the responsibility of all our people for the education of all our youth and as a means for improving our educational system. We should discover in them, furthermore, a new and potent instrument of adult education, for, as many of us have discovered from experience, one learns most, not as a pupil, but as a teacher.

We should be required, if we took this view of universal education, to think of the school, not as a building within the walls of which a separate professional class of society takes care of the instruction of youth, but as an institution which through its professional staff coordinates the educational efforts of the community, drawing upon all the community's resources to lay the foundations for lifelong learning—and teaching—in the community's young people.

Teacher-training institutions would need to enlarge their ideas and practices so that, instead of providing a single road into teaching marked by required courses in professional education and leading simply to one kind of teaching certificate, they would direct and coordinate a wide range of programs along appropriately different paths for preparing many persons to make a wide range of useful contributions to education. They would need, first, to extend, broaden, and deepen the education of those who propose to enter immediately on a full-time career in teaching so as to prepare them adequately for the larger and more important role they would need to take in co-ordinating and leading the educational work of local communities. They would need also to provide short courses for teachers' aides, develop special programs for preparing older college graduates in the community to do effectively a variety of educational work in the schools, work out programs (perhaps combinations of summer conferences and independent-reading plans) for enlisting and preparing people in industry, business, government, and the professions to do part-time work in our schools, and contrive programs for preparing people as they approach retirement to make substantial contributions to our educational system. It need hardly be said that, since teaching is a demanding art, these programs would need to be carefully developed and tested.

These measures would rest on a conception of universal education as involving not merely an extensive period of schooling for all young people but as coextensive with the life of each individual, so that learning and, as soon as possible, teaching, would begin in youth and proceed throughout life. It would involve the conception of education as not merely a means to an end (that is, to the maintenance and development of our technical know-how, or to the strengthening of our society against the threats of totalitarian states, or as a means for increasing the occupational competence and the career success of individuals) but as itself among the very highest ends of life.

Views of this sort and the practices flowing from them would add a new dimension or, it would be better to say, a new foundation, to the conception we hold of America as a dynamic society. We should think of our society as dynamic, not merely in material productivity, but in intellectual and spiritual power, one in which education—including schooling, self-education, and education through teaching—was a major concern of all its members throughout their lives. Then we might indeed have good reason to hope that the bold experiment in the democratic way of life initiated by our Founding Fathers would long endure, that the society flowing from it would grow in wisdom, strength, and promise, and that increasingly it would realize its fundamental purpose—the fullest and richest possible development of each individual person in it.

7

What Is a Good Teacher?

HARL R. DOUGLASS

Director Emeritus of the College of Education, University of Colorado, Mr. Douglass is also the author of many books and articles on public education.

Many careful investigations have been made in an effort to determine what factors are most closely associated with successful teaching and by what means one's success in teaching might be most accurately predicted. The net result of all of these studies is that no particular factor seems to be closely associated with success in teaching and it is yet impossible to predict success in teaching with any great amount of accuracy. Nevertheless, there seem to be certain characteristics or qualities which characterize a good teacher and successful teaching. Some of these cannot be measured quantitatively. For instance, exact degrees of success in teaching can be measured only roughly. It is impossible to show by statistical means the degree of relationship between these factors and teaching success.

In the first place it seems clear that in the light of modern knowledge of human growth and development and in the light of modern philosophy of education that a good teacher thinks constantly and plans teaching and learning activities in terms of their probable contribution to the direction and acceleration of the all-around growth and the development of the learner. The concept of a good teacher as one who is best able to get learners to master the content of the school's subject is becoming rather generally accepted.

A good teacher is one who thinks properly in terms of the preparation of young people for life—preparation of young people to perform

From *The High School Journal*, January 1958. Reprinted by permission.

well in the situations which they will face as citizens, as workers, as members of homes, in their leisure life, and in their attainment of physical and mental health. Furthermore, a good teacher is one who has established interest in continued learning and prepared youngsters for continued learning in school, in college, and after school days are over.

A good teacher is constantly alert to recognize and exploit opportunities to provide experiences for learners which will contribute to the acquisition of appropriate information, contacts, understandings, physical, social and intellectual skills, physical, social and intellectual habits, ideals, attitudes, interests and tastes—appropriate types of growth of these various types which will contribute to preparation for life's activities.

Throughout childhood and adolescence young people are feeling their way in a world which is still a strange world to them and there is a great need for a feeling of security—the younger the child the greater the need and the more the need is felt. Therefore, a good teacher makes sure he is effective in enabling young people to feel a considerable degree of security. The amount needed is different for each individual but it is common with all and many pupils who seem most secure are in their hearts quite insecure. Young people need to feel that "the teacher likes me and has confidence in me," and that he or she has at least a reasonable degree of acceptance by their fellow learners.

The entire mental, intellectual, and social life of individuals is activated and largely determined by the demand of each individual ego for recognition and expression. A good teacher provides opportunity for each youngster to develop and give expression to his desire for activity and creativity and for the child's initiative. A good teacher sees that each youngster has at least a modest degree of success in obtaining the goals of all learning activity. The goals must be an individual matter and there must be different standards for each individual by which his success is judged. Each individual must find opportunity for recognition of his or her work.

A good teacher is constantly aware of the fact that one cannot teach a class—a class cannot learn as a class. A class has no common learning antenna or equipment; each individual has his own. A good teacher teaches the individual. This means that a good teacher makes at least some adaptation from time to time of the learning activity to the individual's capacity, previously developed abilities, and educational background, to his interests, and to his present and future needs. A good teacher, therefore, spends considerable time and great effort in finding out all that he or she can about each individual child—consulting the accumulated data in the school records, in observing a child carefully at school, in discussing a child with the parents and with the child's previous teacher.

A good teacher makes her work as concrete as possible. A good teacher avoids the acceptance of verbalism and excessive reliance upon words as a means of teaching and as a means of demonstration to the children of the degree to which they have learned.

A good teacher uses audio-visual means to a great extent—film, slides, charts, diagrams, exhibits, and trips into the community.

A good teacher exerts great effort to see that the content of various subjects is related in the learning activities of the pupils to the community, to life activities and life needs. Realizing by that method that better understanding and learning may be assured, that retention of what is learned will be increased, and the ability to use in life situations what is learned will be increased.

A good teacher provides for a great deal of definite learning activity other than reading material from books both in class and out of class. A good teacher interests youngsters in learning activities which will involve thinking, investigation, organization of material and ideas, written and oral expression, and actual construction of things which they can handle. A good teacher will frequently provide for the use and application of what is learned in their life-situations of children. A good teacher also provides for learning activities which includes homework of a type involving the use of the parents as consultants in the gathering of data and this sort of homework is a substitute at least in part for the usual study at home as preparation for recitation and the preparation of paper work at home to be handed in at school.

A good teacher finds time somehow, somewhere, to keep up with the rapidly changing ideas and the more rapidly changing world. A good teacher attempts to become less and less an academic hermit living in times gone by. A good teacher makes an unusual effort to see more adults and not restrict his or her life to life with children and books. A good teacher does provide time for a great amount of reading to enable her to keep up with the world and does not rely too much upon what small amount of knowledge assimilated in high school and college.

A good teacher uses modern methods of evaluation and reacts accordingly. Believing in the all around development and growth of her children she is always looking for ways to observe whether or not young people are growing on all fronts, whether or not they have developed social adjustments, emotional balance, appropriate ideals, intellectual skills, and character growth of that sort as well as the acquisition of schoolbook information. This means observation of youngsters throughout the school day.

A good teacher also develops better methods of reporting to parents. She does not rely entirely upon old fashioned formal report cards. She reports on all aspects of human growth; she does more and more reporting in person and over the telephone and by notes to parents. The good teacher has a great belief in the importance of the work of a teacher and is dedicated to the tasks of the teacher and to assisting young people to grow up and to live lives of happiness to themselves and of usefulness to their fellowman. The good teacher is constantly studying to improve his or her effectiveness. The good teacher belongs to appropriate educational professional organizations and reads a number of professional journals and participates eagerly and actively in in-service teacher growth activities of her school or school system.

A good teacher has developed a very high sense of professional ethics involving professional relationships with her colleagues and professional, academic freedom, and good public relations. A good teacher realizes that the fact of the greatness of American people is traceable in a large part to the effectiveness of public education. For that reason, a good teacher is willing to spend time and energy in developing on the part of the public an understanding and appreciation of the problems and needs of the schools in which the teacher plays a part. The good teacher is therefore constantly an emissary of the schools in the community and regards that as an important part of her work as a good teacher.

To be sure, not every good teacher is or does all the things in the fore-going paragraphs, but the teacher who does none of those things is certainly not a good teacher in any sense of the word. Furthermore, a teacher is good to the extent that she does all of these things and to the extent that she does them well. Some teachers are, as they have always been and as they always will be, better teachers than others. To do all of these things requires an impossible amount of time, time not available to most teachers. A good teacher is a teacher who is able to budget time, reduce the amount of time spent on relatively non-essentials and things of lesser importance, and therefore, find time to be and do most of the things mentioned in this description of the good teacher.

It is rare that a teacher meets all of these standards in the first few years of his or her teaching experience. Most teachers grow toward these ideals and continue to attempt to grow as long as they teach. The good teacher is, therefore, not only a good teacher but is in the process of becoming a better teacher.

8

Teachers Amid Changing Expectations

DAVID RIESMAN

Professor of sociology at Harvard, Mr. Riesman is author of The Lonely Crowd, Faces in the Crowd, Individualism Reconsidered, *and other books. He has also been on the faculty at the University of Chicago and the Johns Hopkins University.*

There are a number of ways to study school teachers and their careers, and my colleagues and I at the University of Chicago have been experimenting with a few of these ways.[1] We can study teachers, so to speak, from outside, in terms of social class and ethnic origin, in terms of the sorts of schools they choose to teach in (where they have a choice), and in terms of the expectations other people—superintendents, parents, other publics—have of them and how they control these expectations, succumb to them, or sabotage them. We can also study them, so to speak, from inside, in terms of their aspirations at various stages of their careers, the often deeply buried expectations they have of themselves, the models they admire and the models they reject. I shall draw in my remarks today on both sorts of investigation, but I should warn you that the studies have all been conducted in the Midwest, mainly in Chicago, Small-Town Illinois, and Kansas City, Missouri; that they have all been of public schools; and therefore what I have to say is limited geographically and in other ways to the very tentative observations and interpretations our work has so far been able to make.

From the *Harvard Educational Review*, Spring 1954. Reprinted by permission.

[1] See Howard S. Becker, "The Career of the Chicago Public School Teacher," *American Journal of Sociology*, 1952, 57, pp. 470–477. John Winget's study of teachers' transfers in Chicago has not been published. For a significant general overview, see W. Lloyd Warner, Robert J. Havighurst, and Martin B. Loeb, *Who Shall be Educated?*, Harper & Bros., 1944.

To take an example, Warren Peterson, who has been in charge of our Kansas City study of middle-aged high school teachers, has discovered that many of them were born in rural areas, taught first in small towns, and moved to Kansas City to escape the instability of small town school board politics, which can oust a principal overnight, as well as for the opportunities to specialize that a big city high school offers. He has also found that the Kansas City pupils of these rural-born teachers do not see the latter as career models for themselves, and thus this metropolitan system does not replenish itself from within but continues to recruit from the Kansas, Nebraska, and Missouri countryside. Here in New York I imagine it is quite different, with teachers growing up in the system who were born here, and thus perhaps more able to recruit in their own image girls who want to be like them. And of course there are a whole series of different private school worlds. . . .

A few years ago my colleague, Everett C. Hughes, inaugurated a series of studies of Chicago public school teachers, and much of what wisdom I have concerning the teacher's career I have gained from him. One study interviewed the graduating class at the Chicago Teachers College in order to determine the social backgrounds and aspirations of these people. It would seem that the majority of them were going into teaching not because of any great missionary zeal either for geometry or for children but in order to raise their social position and economic security. They came, if not from rural areas, then from the upper edge of the working class; their brothers were apt to be storekeepers, policemen, skilled machinists. This and other teachers colleges proved attractive in part because they offered an inexpensive A.B.—inexpensive not only in tuition and accessibility but also in intellectual demands made on the candidates. In other words, to help these prospective teachers raise themselves in the social system through education—and education is now, I would think, the principal avenue of social mobility in this country—the educational system itself had to drop a notch or two. The teachers who teach in such a teachers college as is to be found in Chicago or in Kirksville or Warrensburg, Missouri, Pittsburg, Kansas, or Canton, Illinois, are themselves socially mobile: they are not generally the products of a highly cultivated milieu nor have they sought out cultivation in their studies. Sights are lowered throughout the teacher training system (save in those few which train school superintendents to move from Pasadena to Scarsdale to Kansas City to Harvard or what have you) for aspirants who are satisfied if they can enter the lower-middle class as members in good standing.

Another study, by Howard S. Becker, took up the problem from there and examined the preferences Chicago elementary public school teachers expressed for various schools in the system. This could be readily done because after a year teachers are permitted to apply for transfer, and it could be seen which schools were the favorite ones. We can state the result in terms of three types of schools. Most teachers understandably wished to escape from the slum schools, especially in the Negro areas. Only a few were willing to stay there, in rare cases out of a feeling of mission or devotion to a magnanimous principal and in other cases (as discovered through interviews) because a lazy teacher had resigned herself to the very limited police-woman demands of such schools, had found a way to control her charges, and did not want to risk her sinecure. (Incidentally, the result of this transfer system is that most beginning teachers are compelled to start their teaching in such a school, with such hardboiled colleagues, encountering what Professor Hughes terms "reality shock," such as the need to ward off knifings, for which they have not been prepared in teachers college—the result often being a despairing cynicism.)

A few teachers want to transfer from the slum schools to the very "good" schools in upper-middle-class areas, schools let us say like the High School of Music and Art here (not that we do have anything like this in the Midwest, so far as I know). Most of the parents whose children attend such a school are college graduates; they have an active PTA; they have more education than the teacher and they and their children expect a lot. For this reason, the majority of teachers avoid such schools. Instead, they seek out schools where the parents are no more than high school graduates—educated enough to value the school and assist the teachers in disciplining the child, but not educated enough to make trouble by having exalted hopes for their children, hopes measured against their own remembered schooling or the top school performances in the area or even the country at large. Such parents may also belong to a PTA, which is in such a neighborhood apt to be a transmission belt for teachers who become skilled in handling parents of less education to whom they need not defer. The fact that these parents do look up to the teachers (whereas college-educated parents look down and working-class parents are apt to ignore or resent) helps support the precarious claim the teachers have to middle-class social status. Such status is also supported if the school is located in a pleasant white and preferably Anglo-Saxon district, a "good address" where the teacher is not ashamed to have her friends meet her.

This pattern of choices is very different from those of the occasional teacher who, less frequently I think than a generation ago, enters the public school system from an upper-class family as a genteel way of having an intellectual career. The latter sort of teacher does not depend on her clients, that is on her charges, for her status; she carries her status with her in her family background. And so she will sometimes choose the slum school or the slum child because of the challenge involved, since her own distance from the slum is so great that she is not threatened. Likewise, the older pattern by which many American scholars earned their way through graduate school by bouts of secondary school teaching supplied the system with ambitious men, devoted either to making money or to their subjects or both, but not identified with the secondary school teaching profession as their permanent claim to recognition. Now, of course, the stranglehold of the education industry is such that it is hard for such amateur teachers to enter the public schools at all except during periods of unusual shortages; nor do they, in a full employment society, so often need to take a couple of years out to earn the money for their further studies.

Increasingly, indeed, public school teaching becomes professionalized and therefore attracts people who want the label of certified "teacher" in order to escape their origins and establish new ties. Warren Peterson's Kansas City study shows many such teachers never stirring outside of the world of their school: they are apt to live with another teacher, have only teachers for friends, and spend such little leisure as they have either on school-connected tasks or in accumulating further credits. Because they do not move in the outside world, they manage to escape the usual public attitudes about school teachers as rigid, spinsterly, not quite fully human creatures—attitudes many of us are likely to have about those who "knew us when" and saw us in our formative years. Nevertheless, as already indicated, they tend to judge themselves less by what they teach than by whom they teach it to: again and again in the interviews they will say that their children come from good families or are well brought up, and they esteem themselves in the reflected light of their clients rather than (as sometimes happens in universities) in the reflected light of the subject taught: chemistry or English or ancient history. Their homes, in which we have interviewed them, emphasize "good taste" of what strikes me as a rather pedestrian sort; and this is not because of community pressure from which in a large city they are reasonably free so long as they don't get in the newspapers, but because they themselves (even though as I've said so much of their leisure is spent with other teachers) have not developed a separate set of cultural standards but accept those of the general lower-middle-class white-collar population. Once they have gotten into their favorite school, they are content to stay there, if neither the principal nor the neighborhood changes; but they are not ambitious to rise higher in the system, to become principals themselves—for one thing, the top posts are mostly monopolized by men, and, for another thing, they do not want the responsibility. In other words, like other professional and interest groups, they look to the group itself for advance as a body. Their aspirations are bound up with the school system as a whole.

Yet in spite of the career pattern, teachers are expected not to complain when faced with changing expectations of their relations to parents and children, or with new sorts of children. Listen, for instance, to one of our interviews with a high school teacher, now in her middle sixties:

"When Mr. X was here it was a good school, a school you could be proud of, one of the best in the country. But now! A few days ago one of the boys, one of the leaders in the ROTC set off a stink bomb. That kind of thing just wouldn't have happened when Mr. X was there. . . . [Under the new man] teaching is more difficult than it used to be. . . . The parents out there are the problem, and the [new] principal is always yielding to them. When Mr. X was there, the best thing he ever did for the school was to make it clear to everybody that he would tolerate no interference. And he didn't!"

Now, she continued, parents are allowed to complain that the work is not interesting, or that it takes too much time. This new accessibility is regarded as democratic, and the new principal regards himself as democratic, as against the former autocrat. No wonder that this teacher, when asked what is her biggest trouble, states it is tiring to have to listen to so many talkative people!

Similarly, when Negroes started entering the South Side schools in Chicago, many teachers were marooned among pupils whom they were expected to help but who threatened them, sometimes physically, often emotionally. Just when they had achieved a nice school, this status was swept away in a tidal wave of urban migration. Yet, if they complained, they would be called undemocratic and bigoted, just as the teacher whom I have quoted would be called undemocratic or old-fashioned if she complained. Understandably, many public school teachers become skilled in double-talk, skilled in concealing emotions even from themselves—a theme I shall return to later.

Now, however, I want to point out certain parallels between the attitudes and motivations of these teachers and the attitudes and motivations of the families whose children they are traditionally supposed to be introducing to the world of high culture, the world of scholarship and intellect. Joseph Kahl recently published in the HARVARD EDUCATIONAL REVIEW a study[2] of the aspirations of a group of high school boys, intelligent enough to go to college, some of whom were and some of whom were not going on. All were of lower-middle-class or working-class origin. Those who planned to go to college did so because of family-backed pressure for advancement; they saw a college degree as the passport to a better position, and not as a form of access to ideas. The stimulus to go never came from a teacher or from a book, always

---

[2] Joseph A. Kahl, "Education and Occupational Aspirations of 'Common Man' Boys," *Harvard Educational Review*, 1953, 23, 186–203.

from parents or friends. When the parents were interviewed, they, too, had a narrow perspective: education was something to be got through, as a route to something else. Thus, a bread salesman spoke as follows concerning his hopes for one of his sons:

"I tried to tell him where he isn't going to be a doctor lawyer or anything like that, I told him he should learn English and learn to meet people. Then he could go out and sell something worthwhile where a sale would amount to something for him. . . . I took typing, shorthand, bookkeeping and we had Latin, French, Geometry. We had everything. But anything I would know then I've forgotten now. . . . I suppose there are some kids who set their mind to some goal and plug at it, but the majority of kids I have talked to take what comes. Just get along. . . . I don't think a high school diploma is so important. I mean only in so far as you might apply for a job and if you can say, 'I have a diploma,' it might help get the job, but other than that I don't see that it ever did me any good" (*ibid.*, pp. 194–5).

The cultural and occupational perspectives of this father are not very extensive. And the school is likely to meet his son half-way by giving him the diploma at a small price in intellectual effort and by becoming the arena in which he can learn to sell something, particularly himself. For there seems to me to be an increasing pressure on the school teacher to make her classroom as lifelike as possible—a pressure from the community and from the new-style school superintendents but also from within the teacher herself. Being lifelike, for instance, may mean, as it did for the high school principal in Park Forest, Illinois, that he is proud his audio-visual equipment cost more than the books in his library; it may represent the outlook of the principal of a junior high school in Urbana, expressed at a meeting of the National Association of Secondary-School Principals:[3]

---

[3] This perhaps unrepresentative manifesto is quoted in Arthur E. Bestor, *Educational Wastelands*, University of Illinois Press, 1953, pp. 55–56, and discussed there and in Richard Hofstadter, "Democracy and Anti-Intellectualism in America," *Michigan Alumnus Quarterly Review*, 1953, 59, at p. 294. See also William H. Whyte, Jr., "The Future, c/o Park Forest," *Fortune*, June 1953, 47, at p. 194. Let me emphasize again the limited data from which my own tentative conclusions are drawn; all Midwestern schools are far from being alike; I am speaking of tendencies only; there is an obvious danger that such tendencies—and professors' reactions to them—will be overgeneralized and the immense complexity of trends and countertrends in the schools insufficiently studied and appreciated.

"Through the years we've built a sort of halo around reading, writing, and arithmetic. . . . The Three R's for All Children, and All Children for the Three R's! That was it. We've made some progress in getting rid of that slogan. But every now and then some mother with a Phi Beta Kappa award or some employer who has hired a girl who can't spell stirs up a fuss about the schools . . . and ground is lost. . . . When we come to the realization that not every child has to read, figure, write and spell . . . that many of them either cannot or will not master these chores . . . then we shall be on the road to improving the junior high curriculum. Between this day and that a lot of selling must take place. But it's coming. We shall some day accept the thought that it is just as illogical to assume that every boy must be able to read as it is that each one must be able to perform on a violin, that it is no more reasonable to require that each girl shall spell well than it is that each one shall bake a good cherry pie. . . .

"When adults finally realize that fact, everyone will be happier . . . and schools will be nicer places in which to live. . . . "*

I think you can see that many of these principals and officials who believe themselves to be heretical and ahead of their times have picked up some of the cliches of progressive education in order to lower still further the intellectual tone of the schools to the point where this approximates what the lower-middle-class parent and child expect of the school. The paradox of course is that progressive education in its initial formulation was the product of highly intellectual teachers—individualists who became aware of the constrictions and limitations of traditional schools and wanted to found schools which would not only encourage aesthetic sensitivity and group cohesion but would do an even better intellectual job, because more individualized. These pioneers could take a lot for granted, and they wanted to give the children in their care—as we so often want to give our own children—the things they had missed in their own childhoods. But in the mediocre public school, the dancing class or the gym can take the place of the Latin class or the Library—of all those reminders of cultivation which are meaningless or threatening to the teachers and often to the parents who feel uncomfortable in the teacher's presence, because after all she has been to college and they haven't. Here anti-intellectualism latent in some varieties of progressive education may become institutionalized,

---

* *Editors' Note:* Riesman's quotation is from an article by A. H. Lauchner. For the complete text of Mr. Lauchner's article, see pages 81–91 of this book.

sloganized, and solidified so that these children can in turn grow up to demand no more of themselves and of their schools than the cultivation of those social skills in which American middle-class youngsters are already so proficient. . . .

The teachers who have contributed to this result have done so partly by virtue of their own career problems. In the Warren Peterson interviews with high school teachers, the poignant note comes up again and again that these teachers were shy in their own high school days. They feel this was bad, that they should have been more outgoing. In their relations with other teachers, they have established a coterie which they missed in school, and to the extent that they bring any particular aims to their teaching they are apt to want to appear vivacious, warm, and outgoing in class. (One could make an interesting comparison here with current imagery of ministers and clergymen.) That a great many public school teachers do in fact accept these aims appears when we move from analysis of the choices they make and the outlines of their careers to a more directly psychological level—when we try to see the expectations they have for themselves underneath the protective coating of cynicism and careerism. My colleague, Hedda Bolgar, a clinical psychologist, has been carrying on what amounts to group therapy sessions with public school teachers in Chicago and Milwaukee, and finding, once the initial stiffness is overcome, that they harbor the most idealistic but impossible expectations of omnicompetence in the classroom. They expect themselves to respond sympathetically to individual problem children, even psychotic ones that would baffle an experienced psychiatrist. What with the current emphasis on psychology, they can no longer simply reject a child as a trouble-maker, or if they do they will feel guilty about it. Overtly, they may resist the expectation that there is no child they cannot handle, no child to whose needs they cannot minister while preventing it from dominating the group; they may say to one another: "Who does the school board think we are, parking such little bastards with us?" Overtly, they may think they have done their job if they keep the kids out of a messy home five hours a day, and they may, as our studies show, punish a teacher who does too much for the children, who is too enthusiastic—who is a scab or rate-buster in setting too high standards of performance. But underneath they seem to be demanding of themselves therapeutic or motherly relations with all the children. Just because they think of themselves not only as teachers of a subject but also as teachers of an age-grade (as the nursery school outlook spreads upward through the elementary and even high school grades), they are at once tempted and betrayed by an ideal of omnicompetence. Though they are in fact in the position of the Old Woman Who Lived in a Shoe, they somehow accept the inner responsibility for making up in their own persons for all the deficiencies in the community. They feel badly, not only realistically but also guiltily, if "their" children break windows or go to jail or drop out, no matter what the objective situation—much as mothers often feel. I suggest that the cynicism with which many teachers talk among themselves is thus in part a defense against a still unextinguished if often unconscious ideal image of themselves as unruffled, indefinitely expansible reservoirs of total competence. If it were not for this image, the teachers as a close-knit colleague group could cope well enough with the well-meant interferences by social workers, psychiatrists, superintendents, educators, and others who directly and indirectly are reinforcing this image of what the teacher should be, pushing it always further from the traditional conception of the teacher as a subject-matter specialist.

This pressure has come about in part because of the progressive educators and the private school model, where zealously devoted teachers, working with small groups, could accomplish wonders, and in part because of the nursery school model, where miracles were done by teachers who were unable to fall back on teaching reading or figuring to these preliterate tribes of the 4s, 5s, and 6s! But it has also come about because, as I have indicated, the emphasis on social skills in the schools coincides with the growing emphasis in the community at large. The Urbana school principal, you will recall, thought he had a selling job to do. I wish that were so. Actually, as our society becomes more play oriented and less work oriented, more willing to admit personal sensitivity and warmth to the roster of virtues, more concerned with the group and less with the individual, there is an unfor-

tunate congruence between schools seeking to be life-like and life itself. It is unfortunate for the teachers themselves because, as Dr. Bolgar's material shows, the effort on their part to be relaxed and outgoing imposes impossible strains. When Dr. Bolgar points out to them
that they are not psychiatrists and cannot expect themselves to help
problem children, but only at best not to harm them, they react first
with anger at the threat to their omnicompetence, but eventually with
relief. And there is some evidence that they become better, less har-
rassed teachers when they can fully realize inside as well as in their
tough talk that their function is limited—primarily, to teach a subject—and that they cannot as individuals compensate for all the ways
in which our social organization now puts children in school because it
doesn't want them in the labor force or because it has no other place
for the disturbed child at the moment.

But it is not only the typical teacher who suffers from the new demands for her own "social skills" but also the teacher of an older type
who has been delivering a more traditional product. I recall an interview with a high school drama teacher, the daughter of a highly cultivated newspaper editor, who had come back to the big city of her
birth and started teaching school there in her late thirties, after a divorce. This teacher, a cosmopolitan person, has a remarkable gift for
exciting her pupils' interest in the theatre and in radio; she is proud of
graduates on Broadway and in Hollywood. But her fellow-teachers, to
put it mildly, are not very fond of her. In their view, she cares too
much about the drama and too little about children. They complain
that her productions demand too much time and effort, that the
children who get so enthusiastic about putting on plays have little time
for other subjects and for sociability, and they feel that the plays
should involve more of the children in their production even at the cost
of making the performances less professional. It would be more democratic, they say, to give everybody a chance, and the drama, like other
activities, is seen as one more way to encourage group participation
rather than as a way to encourage vocations in the theatre.

Thus, these teachers are expressing the commonly held view that it
is less important for children to have contact with a teacher who cares

profoundly about a subject-matter or craft, than with one who cares profoundly about children. (To be sure, these concerns are not necessarily incompatible: the teacher who cares about the theatre can be particularly attached to those pupils who also care about it.) I need hardly tell you that the colleagues of this teacher find ways to sabotage her efforts, such as arranging that the auditorium is to be used for band practice when she has planned her dress rehearsal there, and that the principal, a younger man who believes that the duty of the school is to cultivate the total personality of the child, has made life very difficult for her. What he wants is a good working team of teachers, not stars in the Broadway firmament.

Yet it would be going much too far to say that these newer types of teachers and school officials are completely unconcerned about subject-matter or even that in most public schools they form a majority; rather, they mark a trend. In taking on responsibility for the child's social and emotional development, they have not wholly relinquished the older responsibility for intellectual development and discipline. Perhaps it is their very ambivalence about partially contending tasks and ideals that makes them so angry with a teacher like this drama teacher, because she unqualifiedly and unequivocally represents not only high and secure social status and urbanity but also the not entirely demoted status of the traditional culture. However, the over-all result of the combination of internal and external pressures on the public school teacher appears often to be cumulative mediocrity. Teachers who have been shy and want to be "outgoing" are going to care a bit too much whether the children respond pleasantly to her as a person and get along well with each other; teachers who have entered the profession to escape the farm or the working class are going to care a bit too much for the paraphernalia of professionalism, such as teacher talk about classroom skills and audio-visual aids, as against intellectual talk about poetry and the Mendelian laws. And this emphasis will reflect the desires of the families on whose low-level aspirations Dr. Kahl has reported. The schools, as I have said, will be like life, only more so. . . .

To put my view most sharply, I believe that teachers, in selecting among the expectations held out to them, should take account of the potential the schools have for what we might call "counter-cyclical" action. Just as Keynesian economics would have the government and banks save in a time of inflation and spend in a time of depression, so teachers have the opportunity to oppose "life" in its momentary excesses. A generation or so ago it made sense for teachers to be preoccupied with social skills, and there are still many underprivileged children who lack access to those skills. But today, for the most part, many situations and devices outside the school are cultivating those abilities. Children in the home are listened to—they are no longer seen and not heard; they become good little communicators very early. They can and do use the movies, TV, comics, and magazines like *Seventeen*, as well as each other's example, to learn proper social behavior. Nevertheless, as I have pointed out, both parents and teachers, conscious of their own childhood inadequacies and gaucheries, are giving many children what amounts to post graduate education in sociability, when what they need, for the most part, is something very different, namely protection for those long-term intellectual and humanistic interests that are momentarily at a discount. Otherwise, the potentially gifted and creative child will be prevented from rising.

In saying this, I have the ironical misgiving that I may only be adding to expectations for omnicompetence that are already unrealistic. Just as I would not expect a banker who believed a depression was coming to invest his personal fortune as a way of increasing purchasing power, so I do not expect individual teachers to carry the whole system on their backs while beginning a counter-cyclical revolution. Rather, I want them to minimize trying to be psychiatrists, mothers, moralists, to minimize making citizens, democrats, tolerant children, and so on, and to concentrate more than many now are encouraged to do on their roles as teachers of specific subjects—a job no one else now can do and for which they can be trained even if at present they aren't. They must resist requests to do other jobs, such as guidance, no matter how flattering these requests. They must especially resist their own self-demands, which are so much harder to cope with than the demands from outside—no union can be of help in that quarter. They must see that the schools can never reform society, or do all its dirty work, but only put brakes on it and help a few exceptional children to go far beyond their narrow origins. It is up to the school principals and super-intendents to defend the teachers against pressures for lowering of standards and to insist on high competence in subject matter in their appointees. In turn this means that these authorities must support teachers like the drama teacher I have referred to who are eccentric in their devotion to their subject-matter and who consequently may not be the best team-players in the teacher colleague-group.

That a principal who supports and inspires his teachers in this way can make a substantial difference is the one heartening conclusion to be drawn from the Hughes-Becker studies I have mentioned. In these studies, there were a few schools in slum districts from which teachers did not try to flee, even when entitled to do so by length of service. And these turned out to be schools where the principal was of such caliber as to win the devotion of his teachers—as his reputation spread, he could even attract them. The principal therefore can, if he has the quality and character, reverse the usual situation in which the most deprived children are taught either by the most inexperienced or by the most hardened and indifferent teachers. He can, in fact, reverse the vicious cycle of mediocrity.

Where are such leaders to come from? As long as, in a great many states, teachers go through education departments, I have very little hope: these and the teachers colleges are seldom centers of intellectual excitement or cultivation. But the changing values of our society are leading to the decision of many young people that they do not want to make money or a social success but to lead a useful life of service. Many of these, as they are apt to put it, want to work with children, and some of them may develop an interest in a subject-matter which they wish to communicate to children. Perhaps the majority of these will go into private schools, where counter-cyclical tendencies can in all probability be best preserved and experimented with, or into those other model schools, such as New Trier or Scarsdale, where a subur-ban community, prosperous and enlightened, chooses to run its own private school at its own public expense. Just as I want pupils in school to encounter subjects where there is a chance that their sights may be raised, though most will miss or resent the chance, so I want teachers to encounter model schools even though most would prefer not to teach in them. Such models offer the best prospect I see for teachers to get over the fantastic expectation that they should re-enact the current fashion of contemporary life in the school room, an expectation that renders them often miserable and confused, without satisfying the dormant claims of that minority of children, the seed-corn of future creativity and future hopes, who could profit from challenge and from access to those tools and techniques by which the greatest human achievements are made possible.

9

How We Drive Teachers to Quit

RICHARD MERYMAN

Mr. Meryman is an associate editor of Life.

For approximately 125,000 teachers, one in every 12 now working in our public schools, this will be their last year in the profession. Probably a third of them will be the best teachers, the best minds, the ones best able to ignite and fan the enthusiasm of their students.

Many will be retiring or leaving for marriage and a family. But too many will quit permanently because they are fed up. Their ambition and self-respect will take them into business or other professions. They will, of course, leave behind a hard core of excellent, dedicated teachers who remain the heart of U. S. education. But they also leave behind an increasing proportion of tired time-servers.

To replace the 125,000 who left last year, only 106,000 college graduates entered the teaching profession. This year 30,000 additional teachers were needed to relieve teaching loads in overcrowded classrooms.

While the well-publicized low pay in public schools helps drive out top teachers, there is another less known but deeply important factor. Teachers leave the profession because their satisfaction and enthusiasm have been finally suffocated by what can be called The System.

Interviews with ex-teachers across the country, who freely discussed why they quit, brought a startling chorus of blame addressed to The System. By the teachers' definition, The System consists of: (1) know-nothing school boards, (2) insecure, inadequate principals, (3) doting parents, (4) rebellious or apathetic children, and (5) poorly-

From *Life*, November 16, 1962. Courtesy *Life* Magazine; © 1962 Time Inc.

trained teachers drawn from the bottom of the college-educated group. The System produces not explosive, dramatic incidents but a succession of frustrations, of petty worries, an accumulation of angers that go far beyond normal griping. The idealistic young teacher who hopes to be stimulated by his working environment finds instead that his intelligence is repeatedly insulted. The repetition of incidents similar to the following is the cause of the querulous attitude of many teachers and ex-teachers:

In Los Angeles the head of a math department who had spent 300 hours of his own time devising a new curriculum had his pay docked for leaving school during several free final class periods. In Yuma, Ariz., an English teacher was required to stand in supermarkets and hand out bills for a school bond issue. In a Santa Monica, Calif., school the principal waited every morning beside the register where teachers signed in and gave sarcastic greeting to latecomers. An assistant principal in Cleveland, Ohio, said to an elementary teacher who was planning to introduce a little French, "They don't need a language. Everyone speaks English all over the world. I just spent two weeks in Haiti without any French."

"The kind of people you most want to hang on to are often the ones you lose," says Sterling McMurrin, the U. S. Commissioner of Education who recently resigned to return to his position on the University of Utah faculty. "Many first-rate individuals go into teaching, but they aren't treated as people with enormous talent, great skill, training and education."

"The most important problem in education," says John H. Fischer, dean of Teachers College, Columbia University, "is to get everybody to recognize that teaching *really* is one of the most important occupations in the country."

Virtually all teachers basically enjoy teaching and want to excel at their jobs. Many who teach in the nation's thousands of well-run, well-staffed schools really do enjoy it (and excel at it) for years. But the simple truth is that the profession's appeal does not endure long enough for enough teachers.

The average continuous teaching career in U. S. public schools lasts only five years. A survey of a class from the University of Illinois College of Education showed that 30% quit after teaching two years, and that 40% did not go into teaching at all, despite their certification. In Utah two years ago, 1,044 (12% of the total) teachers left their jobs. A survey to determine who quit and why showed that one third of these teachers were rated "very good" and 14% "excellent." The reasons most frequently cited for leaving by "excellent" teachers were working conditions.

"If teaching has the reputation for being a lousy job," says the dean of Harvard University's Graduate School of Education, Frank Keppel,* "it's not because anybody minds working hard—and every job has its harassments. But there's got to be something to keep a good person interested, some hope that the career will bring him considerable amounts of influence and excitement."

Teachers who are openly critical of The System maintain that the local school board does best by its teachers when it has the least to do with them. However, instead of sticking to broad policy and pushing for better education, school boards too often yield to temptation and constantly look over the shoulders of the professional educators.

The problem, many teachers feel, frequently stems from the type of individual who seeks a position on the school board. Most school board members are elected—and campaigns cost money. The financial support sometimes comes from a special interest group; when the position's prestige can be a valuable asset, the candidate himself may foot the bill. The board often ends up with a strong and determined representation of successful businessmen—"the butcher, baker and candlestick maker," as an ex-teacher described them.

It is only natural for such men to apply business standards to running the schools. "Making things go smoothly," and "being a hard man with a dollar" are often the major boasts of school board members. They regard as troublemakers educators and laymen who are movers and shakers, who fight a running battle for higher standards in the schools and the money to pay for them.

Such school boards tend to hire the second element in The System:

---

* *Editors' Note:* Francis Keppel is now U. S. Commissioner of Education.

principals and their assistants whom teachers find more concerned with pleasing the school boards and individual parents than with helping and supporting their staffs.

No one has more control over the school climate than the principal. Yet the principal who lowers teacher morale by relying on petty discipline is not uncommon in the land.

A Long Island, N.Y., principal frequently got on the public address system, piped into every classroom where the children could hear it, and ranted at his teachers for not obeying his rules. A group of teachers there bitterly called themselves "The Incapable Fools Club."

In a Chicago suburb a social studies teacher of eight years' service paused in the hall to talk to another teacher after the bell had rung and his pupils were in the classroom. The assistant principal came by on his regular checkup and reprovingly pointed at him and then at the door of his room. "I was to go into the room like a sheepish child," said the teacher. "When I complained to him, he said, 'You don't believe in discipline.' " . . .

Through lack of imagination—or simply lack of administrative help—the principal passes on to the teacher a series of petty chores that cut deeply into class time. Teachers find themselves serving as penny-ante bankers who collect milk money, cracker money, cafeteria money, savings bank money, contributions to various charities, student organization dues. They are asked to sell tickets for athletic events, yearbooks, school emblems, class pins, even accident insurance. Then of course there are the teachers' traditional "extra" duties: supervising afterschool activities of the pupils, attending faculty meetings and P.T.A. meetings. In all, according to a research report from the National Association of Secondary-School Principals, nearly one-fifth of a teacher's day—and his energy and ingenuity—is spent at jobs which could be performed by nonprofessionals or by automated devices.

But the most demeaning duty which administrators ask of teachers is the role of policeman. A young lady who quit a New York City high school to become a magazine reporter gave this description of the humiliation involved: "Things begin to wear on you, and you take a hard look at where you are and then have to decide whether you want to go through the various garbage disposal assignments for 30 years to make a career out of teaching. Garbage disposal assignments are the hall jobs and cafeteria jobs and watch-dog jobs a teacher has to take.

"Hall patrol duties are usually bad because you have to keep outsiders out of the school and the kids inside. Neither is easy. And you get involved in going into student rest rooms and throwing out the smokers. None of this has much to do with teaching, nor does it leave you the kind of dignity or capacity for friendship with the kids a teacher needs."

Some principals measure classroom success in ways that encourage overextended teachers to shortchange their pupils. The quiet classroom—a principal's delight—can mean that children are doing undemanding make-work at their desks, or it may mean they are ritualistically covering prescribed ground for a weekly test. "Low test grades reflect on the teachers, not the class," said a current Los Angeles teacher. "The [System's] big emphasis, therefore, is on the tests, not on what the teacher could explore beyond the textbooks. Many times the kids ask, 'Are we responsible for this on the test?' I see red every time that happens."

An English teacher in San Francisco who quit to go into textbook publishing said, "The ones who just sit in their jobs rise to positions of eminence. But those teachers most dedicated to the students, the ones with lofty ideals, often wind up in hot water. They're accused of giving too much homework, expecting too much of their students."

Parents who add to the teacher's burden by meddling, complaining and making special requests are a powerful part of The System. Much of the parental interference in the classroom is done with the best intentions but it nevertheless reduces the teacher's chances of personal fulfillment—and sometimes upsets the course of education.

In one Texas school which pursued a program of "homogeneous grouping," children of roughly equal performance were put together in the same class. Though the practice is frequently controversial, the teachers there found that it improved their effectiveness. A minority of the parents, including several with influence whose children were assigned to slow classes, raised a furor. This year the system was abandoned. "You can't blame a guy for not chopping his own head off," said the principal in defense of his surrender. "Besides, any program the parents are not really for just isn't going to work. You'd be surprised. When the parents are dissatisfied, the dissatisfaction goes into the children, who hear the gripes of the parents at home."

Teachers get nasty notes asking that their child's grades be reconsidered. Some parents even appeal to the board of education, claiming that the grades reflect the teaching, not the child.

"Schools are an emotional outlet for parents' anxieties, a natural scapegoat," said a Los Angeles assistant principal. "Parents are *supposed* to be interested, so everybody thinks he has a legitimate right to criticize.

"The unhappy parents keep at you, needling day after day. The administrators have to cater to the public. Their very security depends on a happy community. As a result, schools are being ruined because they're run 90% by public relations."

Almost all teachers work under the shadow of censorship. A teacher in Arizona who later quit to join a college faculty, explained to her class that Communists, however misguided, act from the premise that what they do is right, not evil. One of her pupils went home and gave a garbled report of her statement. The boy's uncle, who was president of the board of education, heard about it.

"It was discussed at the board meeting," the teacher said. "The interpretation was that I was teaching my pupils that Communism is good—me a Roman Catholic educated by Jesuits and a registered Republican! My case was scheduled to come up formally before the Board of Education. While all this was happening, nobody spoke to me. An old friend finally stepped in and settled the situation, but it could have been messy. There was no respect for my integrity. I was successfully challenged in my own classroom by a child who misquoted me."

Ironically, teachers sometimes suffer just as much because of parents who are overdependent on them. "A teacher never has any private life," reported a former Houston, Texas teacher. "I was called at all hours by parents who wanted advice." One parent called her to ask if her child should wear a raincoat. She said, "If you tell them, 'Why don't you look out the window and decide that for yourself?' then you aren't being a kind, patient teacher."

Today the community provides the teacher with very little prestige and sometimes actually goes out of its way to make him feel hapless. Townspeople telephoned one Connecticut man (who finally quit teaching) and offered him baby-sitting jobs. "When I refused," he said, "and maybe my voice showed something, some of the callers actually told me, 'Oh, I thought all teachers did it.' "

In one Detroit school humiliated teachers reported they must go down to the basement boiler room to smoke. They are not permitted to smoke within sight of the pupils, and the boiler room is the only place available to them.

In most U. S. communities today the most popular measure of prestige is income. Only 2% of all teachers make $7,000 and over, and the average income which communities pay beginning teachers is $4,100.

A Harvard University report described one inevitable result of the relatively poor pay levels in the teaching profession with these words: "They (teachers) live on the fringes of the middle class. But they cannot afford to indulge in the tastes of their peers. . . . They—and their wives and children—make admirable sacrifices. But in doing so, they confirm society's impressions of a lowly group, not quite first-class and deserving of no better than the hand-me-downs of our civilization."

However, despite the widespread lack of palpable prestige and their feelings of harassment by school boards, by administrators, and by parents, teachers still reach for the unique professional satisfaction that comes behind the closed classroom door. There, with whatever talent and energy they possess, they harvest the real rewards of teaching.

A former high school teacher, who moved up to a college where she could teach "without restraints on myself as a human being," said: "The most joyous moment is when sparks start flying, and something comes clear, a meaning the students hadn't thought of in terms of their own lives. This is the most exciting thing that can happen in education—to have a child ask a probing or new question about tough material or surprise you with a thoughtful answer. You hear from them years later and learn they have continued their interest, and then you know you led them into something they had to have to live."

But the pupils, who supply the teacher with his greatest rewards, are also the fourth factor in The System—one that is inevitably linked to the factor of parents. Many classrooms are being turned into virtual out-patient clinics, where all adolescent problems are supposed to be handled. . . .

Many children return home after school to an empty house. The mother is gone—holding a job to help boost family income. A high school teacher in Chicago reported that some boys in his classes work as much as six hours a day after school, often to earn the down payment and instalment money for an automobile of their own. Sometimes, when they cannot keep up on the payments, they drop out of school to take a full-time job rather than lose their investment. So the teacher is frequently confronted by children who largely look after themselves.

"Such a child," said this teacher, "may be malnourished, tired, emotionally upset from lack of care—and has small patience for any sustained mental or physical activity—or for even staying in one place."

While established teachers are frequently rewarded with advanced classes, new, potentially top teachers, fresh from college theory courses are often thrust in front of dull, bored, even belligerent students.

One young woman, bitter and disillusioned, quit teaching after one year in a Long Island, N. Y., school. She had five classes of students with median I.Q.s in the 80s. "Some boys would come into the room yelling," she said, "and then the other kids would yell and get up out of the seats and form into groups. I went home sick every night for months. I lost all sympathy for those kids and I really didn't care a thing about them. I wanted them quiet and I got them quiet."

Under such circumstances it is easy for the emphasis on discipline to overwhelm that on instruction. "You're not supposed to teach kids to think, but to be robots," said another ex-teacher. "Teachers become obsessed with details like keeping a line of children straight at all costs. No talking. No running. Nothing positive, all negative. At their desks the children at my school were supposed to sit with their hands folded and their eyes trained on you.

"The answer? Get teachers who are flexible. But where are they, and why would they want to enter such a life?"

Flexibility, patience and dexterity are all required if the teacher hopes to keep up with her daily rounds. In Detroit an experienced guidance counselor said: "When you visit a high school guidance counselor what do you expect to see? Do you expect to see a frenzied person at a desk in front of a study hall trying to deal with a mother mad at her kid for truancy, while the child is coming apart emotionally, while two phones are ringing, while kids are constantly coming and getting passes signed to go to the bathroom? It would give you a lot of confidence in the guidance counselor, wouldn't it? But that's the way it usually is."

Finally, The System itself circles viciously and tends to lower the over-all quality of instruction as the best teachers leave. Faced with the mediocrity of their colleagues, the more scholarly, idealistic teachers feel unhappily isolated.

Dr. Salomon Rettig, a psychologist who conducted a series of interviews with teachers in Ohio, said, "I was very glad to get away." The teachers, he found, were choked, had no freedom of expression. They were not being stimulated nor were they stimulating others. "They are a highly selected kind of person," Dr. Rettig said, "compared to other professional people: a highly intelligent person on one hand, and on the other hand one who doesn't mind being told by rules, parents, supervisors what he or she can and can't do.

"And the teacher thinks he is disliked, that nobody cares about him really. You would expect their sense of restriction to be transmitted to the children. I'll bet 100 to one there is no genuine freedom of expression in their classrooms."

At the University of Chicago three sociologists tested a group of women teachers with an average of 10 years' experience. The group showed no drives at all to accomplish demanding tasks, to do things better than other people, to analyze themselves and others, or to show sympathy toward any person in trouble.

These sociologists arrived at two conclusions in explaining why the traditional public image of the old maidish male or female school-teacher often fits. First, individuals are gradually pressed into the typical teacher mold by the sheer weight of The System. But secondly, and crucially important, colleges of education throughout the U.S. attract a kind of person psychologically precast to fit the mold—undemanding and noncompetitive. Unfortunately, colleges of education tend to become havens for students who are well down in the academic barrel. . . .

Low-level students who attend low-standard colleges usually end up as inferior teachers. By way of illustration, take the subject of English. A recent study showed that half the individuals teaching high school and junior high English in the U. S. today did not major in English at college.

During a special study project, Dr. Paul B. Diederich, senior research associate with the Educational Testing Service, saw many hundreds of student papers which had been corrected by U. S. high school English teachers. He concluded in his report "that the average English teacher . . . is barely literate, capricious in judgment . . . hard to decipher, eager to misinterpret. . . . "

In one northern state, less than half of the 315 teachers who gave courses in world history had studied modern European history, and less than 10% of them had studied Far Eastern history. (Twenty percent of the social science teachers majored in physical education.)

There are, of course, teachers who overcome the handicaps of inadequate training and develop into first-rate educators.

One such teacher was recalled by a former pupil: "I remember," he said, "I once handed her a poem I had written and she said, 'This is beautiful.' It was dirty and smudged and misspelled, too, but to her it was beautiful. I melted. She invited me and two other boys in class to her room to read T. S. Eliot to us.

"I went back to see her a few years ago, to see what her magic was, and there was no magic. She seemed pedestrian and dull, or maybe just old. But she had been magic to us. And on her shelves she has volumes written by her old students."

What can be done to beat The System and keep good teachers at their jobs? "All of us have to get together to find the way," said a Californian. "We have to risk self-examination, risk close scrutiny, risk reprisals against those doing their best to correct the mess. Maybe if we get stronger people, they may be able to defend themselves, be able to speak out, become part of The System and change it."

Around the country the educational machinery *is* in the throes of redesign. States are stiffening teacher certification requirements. Leading colleges of education are improving "how to teach" courses and toughening academic standards. Universities and foundations are rewriting public school curricula to update them according to today's needs in today's world. Part-time lay help to ease the teachers' housekeeping load in the classroom is on the increase. A technological teaching revolution is adding film strips, teaching machines and educational television as invaluable new resources that are easily tapped by hardpressed teachers.

But some theorists, like Harvard's Dean Keppel, believe that such steps are not enough. These educators call for a dramatic reorganization. To this end, Harvard has pioneered a major experiment in "Team Teaching," a technique that is now successfully being used in Pittsburgh and in at least 50 other cities.

The concept involves two innovations. A group as large as 120 students is taught by a single team of a half dozen or more teachers. Depending on the material to be taught, the entire group of pupils may be assembled in one large lecture hall or, on another day, split into dozenpupil seminars. The result is flexibility, in teaching and in programming. Children can be grouped more flexibly by ability and teachers can specialize in the kind of teaching they do best.

But most important, team teaching creates a teacher hierarchy and the prestigious position of the team leader—a goal for aspirations which does not eliminate the teacher from teaching by shunting him into administration. And other teachers have time for special and influential assignments, such as planning the curriculum, appraising textbooks, finding ways to teach low achievement children.

Team teaching also means an increase in the number of positions warranting high salaries. "What you must do," said Keppel, "is invest in a magnet at the top to pull everything up." Thus, even a few salaries at a level competitive with other professions would be an incentive to all teachers.

Keppel believes that these top-salaried, high-responsibility jobs should exist for one out of every five teachers—a total of 300,000—and could lengthen today's five-year career average to 30 years. Then only one new teacher would be needed where six must now be found.

But to be effective, even a sound new technique such as team teaching demands the overturning of all the old, ingrained habits and attitudes and institutions which allow The System to exist. It demands from everybody—principals, teachers, parents, pupils—new imagination and determination. Only in this way will America keep its talented teachers and find its better schools.

10

Why We Teach

LEON DIAMOND

Mr. Diamond is a teacher at Morris High School, New York City.

After a quarter century in the classroom, I asked myself why I had entered teaching. Just why I had not seriously asked the question before is a question in itself. Perhaps it was because I had so often told myself that I taught for altruistic reasons—to serve humanity by strengthening the character and sense of young people. But I also recalled that I had—so long ago—wanted a job with a regular wage. Because time—twenty-five years of it—forced me to ask with urgency, my mind became flooded with memories, vague feelings, contradictory impressions—I wanted very much to straighten them out. It seemed imperative to know what had made me decide upon my life's work.

Very soon I was obliged to admit that not all of my reasons for teaching were praiseworthy. So in telling you something about them, I shall use the expedient of the editorial "We." No doubt I do so to lessen the impact of self-blame. Yet the use of "We" may not be entirely improper because I have, after all, been teaching for twenty-five years. In that time I have known a good many teachers, with the result that I feel my reasons are by no means unique. In talking about myself, I may have something to say about all teachers.

What, then, may have induced us to teach?

From *High Points*, March 1961. Reprinted by permission. *High Points* is published by the Board of Education of the City of New York.

PRESTIGE, OR POSSESSED BY OTHERS

Many of us decide to teach not because we possess interest and ability but because we want prestige. We feel that a teaching license will impress others.

The wish to be thought well of by others is often a valuable incentive. Urged by this motive, we labor at some useful work for a lifetime, whereas without it we would drift. However, such ambition is easily corrupted by opportunism. We then do only the deeds that might bring approbation, regardless of their benefit to ourselves or to our fellows. Any strenuous drive for success can become damaging, particularly for one whose self-respect has been eroded during his childhood. This is the person who must drive himself to please others or, rather, to obtain their praise which he needs to support a tottering ego.

Only momentarily can prestige allay self-condemnation. Yet because prestige assuages somewhat, it is sought in larger and larger doses. Some seek it to the point of frenzy (which can be a coldly logical fury), while their personalities steadily deteriorate. However, we have all heard that self-fulfillment and not prestige should be the first reward of any work. That so many of us fail to act upon this information may be due to the fact that we do not consider the matter with the seriousness it requires. Were we to do so, we might find that the hankering for prestige is but a distortion of the simple human need to be liked. We all want to be liked. But those who really like us, like us for ourselves and not for what we have gained in the way of reputation or position.

MONEY, OR KEEPING UP WITH THE POOR

The "realistic" desire for income and the "good life" made possible by adequate income has brought many of us to the classroom. True, salary scales are often shockingly low. But if material reward is our chief concern, we shall never be satisfied. Nor shall we ever be able to achieve that good life for which the school exists. A truly good life implies both quality and variety of satisfactions and not just the amassing of material goods to impress one's neighbors. If our self-respect depends upon the opinion of a neighbor, and that opinion upon the size of our salary, we are evidently identifying ourselves with that neighbor, not with ourselves and our needs as teachers, that is, persons able to bear the dishonor of being a trifle different in their requirements for satisfactory living.

But if we like, we may choose to live as well as our neighbor, only we must use care in selecting a neighborhood.

Undue desire for possessions is, again, a distortion of our need to be liked. If we do not like ourselves, we are quick to feel that others do not like us. Whereupon we attempt to impress and even to overwhelm them with accessories—not with what we are, but with what we own. However, there is the dilemma: If we do not choose to share our possessions, people will not like us. If we do, we shall soon find ourselves bereft of possessions and, once more, feel that we are disliked.

SECURITY, OR HOW TO EMBALM ONESELF

Desire for security also impels many to teach. We want economic security—a paycheck which, though not quite up to our expectations, is, at least, regularly forthcoming. We also anticipate security in respectable routine. We see it in the continuance of a chosen style of living—for instance, the intellectual or bookish life. We expect to find it in work marked by the absence of competitive stress (though here the fledgling-pedagogue may have some surprises in store for him).

As with possessions, the important thing is to know the adequate. Security is certainly a legitimate aim. But how much security is desirable? And how much obstructs the maturing of our personalities and therefore prevents us from helping young people to grow?

Where anxiety for security dominates, what determines behavior is the fear of change and, therefore, of taking chances. The mind is passive and does not willingly extend itself into action. However, it may use many brave words which are thought a good enough substitute for courage in experiment.

The person who cannot risk action is one who must blindly and compulsively repeat his childhood experiences of rebuff and check. True, he yearns to take chances. But he is doomed to find good reasons for refraining because, in each of his abortive attempts to act, he is bound to experience once more the defeats of early childhood.

LEISURE, OR HOW TO RETIRE ON MAXIMUM SALARY

To many of us, the chief attraction of our work is long vacations and short working days. We justify the need for these advantages with the argument that teaching is by no means easy, that—with the best of conditions—it is a strain.

But often it is because we are bored or have over-conscientiously "worked ourselves to the bone" that a vacation is so eagerly sought. As for boredom, what one usually hears from the bored instructor is that his students are not stimulating. They lack either interest or aptitude. Instead of being challenged, they sit like logs. But this might be a rationalization. The teacher who, whatever his intellectual attainments, finds no challenge in his students, may be indifferent to them. A good teacher is always stimulated to greater efforts by any inadequacy in his students, for his work is to turn the inadequate into the adequate. Boredom may not be quite what the bored instructor supposes it to be—a proof of his intellectual superiority. It may rather be a safety device used to prevent his students from knowing him, which of course they do. To be cured of his boredom, he must try to see it as part of a distance-mechanism induced by fears that his students, despite some inadequacy in spelling or grammar or mathematics and other trivia, are too bright, too knowing, too perceptive of him.

The overly-conscientious teacher is equally bored, equally indifferent to the learning needs and personalities of his students. Such a self-sacrificing person will devote his "all" to teaching. This is to say that the tensions arising from feelings of inadequacy are somewhat discharged by work. Despite some residual strain, some weariness, he feels that he is doing a praiseworthy, even a noble job, one that is turning his students into "scholars" like himself. And what is more gratifying than to force imitation of oneself even though one is forcing only an artificial and therefore ultimately unsatisfactory growth? But it is only the person lacking a self-respecting self who seeks to foist that self upon others.

Scholarship, when a natural attribute of the personality, is indeed precious. But when artificially and strenuously acquired because it is thought socially acceptable, it is far from being admirable. The would-be scholar who turns to books to mask his actual self—thought a shameful thing—from the sight of others, will not go very far. But his problems will—together with those he gives to his students.

INGLORIOUS, BUT NOT MUTE

Then there are many who turn to teaching because they wish to create but find that their productions of word, of brush, of musical theme, and so on, are not wanted, or that they lack the requisite talent. So, often severely frustrated, they teach much less than they criticize. Or else they engage in talent-scouting. By belittling or over-encouraging, they try to relieve the hurt of a disappointed ego.

A frustrated person cannot very well teach because frustration produces an easily triggered resentment. Thus, he often assumes that he is not understood by his students, to which he adds the feeling that they are of inferior intellectual or artistic caliber. In their turn, they resent his attitude and soon he is in serious difficulties. He can, of course, retreat from them. He can develop an indifference to their attitude. By "well-organized" point-by-point instruction from which he does not dare to deviate, he can establish some semblance of control.

With the few that heed him, who possess, perhaps, some talent, he can make only second-rate creators. For he teaches them to use art not as an entrance into life but as a means of escape from its rigorous tests. But, then, he has escaped. He has escaped from an unheated studio but only to suffer a lingering death in the classroom.

PETER PAN, PEDAGOGUE

Another reason that impels us to teach is that we wish to be with young people. We say—and certainly it should be true—that we enjoy their company, their unforced curiosity, their abounding energy. We add that it keeps us young.

—Perhaps too young. It is at least possible that we enjoy the company of youngsters for the reason that we cannot enjoy or even tolerate the company of adults. But then, adults are apt to be knowledgeable. They may find out our inadequacies and prove over-critical. They may even reject us, and this we cannot risk. Therefore teaching, permitting companionship with less critical children, exerts a strong appeal.

What mechanism lies behind this choice? If, during his childhood, a teacher has been rejected by his parents (or feels that he has), he often turns to himself, retreating both from age-mates and adults. Later, when he is himself an adult, he continues to retreat from grown-ups because they represent threatening parental prototypes. But the young no longer threaten him. He has gained, if not insight, at least years, and so he can easily identify them with himself during his formative years. He sees them, not as individuals, not as themselves, but as younger forms of himself. Generally, he is quite sympathetic to them because he is, though without knowing it, overly sympathetic to the slight though painful remembrance—which is all he can permit himself—he has of himself as a child. He easily "understands" the suffering of his students, especially when they seem to be abused by adults—in particular, by "overstrict" teachers. But he does not so readily sympathize with their attempts at self-assertion. These he is apt to identify as rebelliousness. After all, he did not rebel—at least consciously. So why should they be permitted that advantage?

Other teachers, also rejected by their parents, choose a course not of permissiveness and "rapport" but of autocratic control. Because things were not so easy with them as children, they do not propose to make it easier for their students. Taking on the role of a despotic parent, they attempt to dominate their pupils, giving them the same treatment they once received. To be sure, they will be feared by the weaker and hated by the stronger, but what of that? They know they will be obeyed and they even anticipate being respected. But if a teacher is a disagreeable martinet, he receives the reward of the martinet—his name embellished with unflattering comments on the walls. On the other hand, if a teacher's satisfaction is derived from being a good fellow, just one of the class, he will again and again find himself frustrated. For his students will see in him no teacher but one like themselves—and will treat him accordingly.

DR. SPOCK OVER THE CLASSROOM

One may also decide to teach out of frustrated parental urge. But this cannot substitute for teaching which is to free from uncritical dependence upon the old, to develop the confidence needed to build a new and better life. Parenthood has, of course, the very same functions. But we often find fathers and mothers so ignorant that they fondly yet stupidly seek to tie children to themselves. Doing so, they make their child a hostage to the old life, a prisoner of conformity. Or as frequently they reject and leave him unprotected. They rob their child of self-confidence so as to enhance their own—which was, of course, reduced by *their* parents.

The teacher cannot commit these errors. He wants to be needed as a teacher and not as a parent. If parents are inadequate, his concern is to reduce the force of hurtful nurturing upon the child. He teaches: which is to say, he helps the young to discern goals and, in time, to attain those that lie within the range of their interests and capacities. He assists his pupils to obtain an impartial insight into their strengths and weaknesses. By helping them to renew themselves through self-confidence, he builds reason which is also generosity, which is love, our human destiny and not the fate of the fox, the ape, the serpent. Nor is the teacher attached to recognition and return. He does his work for the sake of the work which is the making of man.

CURE-ALL OR CURE?

And while the democratic school is *the* agent for social reform, it is not the tool of the reformer who is eager—and we honor the intention—to remove some ill of society through this or that philanthropic, political, economic or other reform. But while the teacher-reformer may not be a purveyor of some trivial panacea, he is certainly a partisan. He is a partisan of the particular and therefore does not belong in the class-room. Actually, we teach to reform our society. But we do so by in-creasing the sense and strength of the reason so that it eventually does whatever it thinks needful. But if the mind is made to haul the heavy carriage of a cause before one attains independence of judgment, it cannot reach its full power.

Not that the teacher should refrain from dealing with causes. But he must do so fairly. While he may even side enthusiastically (for with-out enthusiasm we must suspect the absence of life), he should keep in mind that even as no man has the entire truth, so no cause except the cause of man's unrestricted growth is without shortcoming and there-fore exempt from criticism. It is the teacher whose ego is weak and who therefore cannot trust his original thinking who must recommend and follow a cause with an unqualified assent. By doing so, he inflates the little self-esteem that he has. He feels his life to be valuable and justified. However, he is resorting to a crutch instead of trying exer-cises on the way to cure—these exercises involving the achievement of objectivity in knowing himself.

But most of us are far from being objective about our reasons. In short, we are still human. We teach with a certain interest in our work but we would not be offended by an offer to raise our salaries. We relish the respect occasionally shown us by a few old-fashioned per-sons who still think highly of the teacher. And Fridays we find more welcome than Mondays. Evidently our motives for teaching are still a bit inadequate. But then they are merely inadequate and—taking into account the sort of education *we* have received—by no means blameworthy. But if they are inadequate, what is a better reason for teaching?

THE TEACHER AS LEARNER

A better reason for teaching is that it helps one to learn. A good teacher is first of all intent upon learning because he has found that learning alone releases from the frustrations that always go with ignorance. He also knows that he never can be done with learning, for however much he discovers, he must always find himself ignorant. When the teacher begins his career, he feels the need to prove and expand his theoretical knowledge of the world of nature; of man, the social being; of the human achievement in the arts and sciences. Later, he feels how little he really knows of his own nature, of his complex motives and their often unpredictable outcomes in behavior. Lastly he feels poignantly his ignorance of the mysterious purposes of life and of the human destiny. He tries to get at the truth of one uncertainty after another, and if there is any serious sense in him, he will continue to ask for a lifetime even though he knows that only tentative answers are possible.

While the motive that goads us to learn is desire to get at "the truth," what is most useful about a truth, a fact, a principle, is not its mere power to explain. Much more important is that it helps us to persevere in learning, to ask new and better questions. We know, then, in order to induce us to ask and to keep on asking. By our learning we fulfill ourselves, proving ourselves men and not unthinking brutes. Indeed, our only distinction lies in learning, and it may well be that learning is our true reason for being. This seems to be made clear in our gross anatomy and in our fine neural structure. All our other functions exist that we may learn. We seek sustenance to live, but we live to learn. We enjoy so as to persuade us to learn. We even procreate our kind to learn. The life of man is therefore a never-ending learning, and the teacher, above all others, teaches us this lesson.

Because the teacher has fulfilled himself through his learning, he is able to give to others the finest gift one human being can give to another—an example of learning. Teaching is no difficult labor for him but a natural expression of his function—learning. Only those who learn eagerly can teach greatly. The one function is to the other as expiration is to inspiration. If one enjoys learning, he cannot restrict that enjoyment to himself. He must share it because it is good, and the good is always the shared.

If, in order to teach, the teacher needs ulterior inducements, it simply proves that the teacher has something more to learn. And which one of us does not?

11

A Teachers Union Leader
Views School Problems

CARL J. MEGEL

Mr. Megel, formerly a teacher in the Chicago public schools, is president, AFL-CIO American Federation of Teachers.

The American public-school system faces no problem that cannot be solved nationally, in the states, or in the community, with public, administration, and *teacher* cooperation. Let *teacher* remain underscored for emphasis and perspective in the reader's thinking. The quality of public education depends on teacher-pupil relationship, assuming that the teacher is well qualified.

There are, of course, conditions under which no teacher, whatever his or her qualifications, can teach efficiently. The fact that some teach as well as they do under adverse conditions and unsound policies, such as overcrowded classes and low salaries, creates public apathy to the problem as a whole.

In this atomic age, when most public needs and problems are solved by billion-dollar appropriations and a majority of our public services are generously financed, we still cling to the idea that school teachers ought to be dedicated persons, working for posterity instead of, among other things, a decent living.

In a situation which urgently needs dedicated teachers who wish to follow teaching as a life-long profession, there is little encouragement. Few tenure laws are worthy of the name. A comparatively minute number of school districts provide their teachers with any kind of paid sick leave, health, and longevity insurance, sabbatical leave, or

Originally published in *Teachers College Record*, Vol. LIX (October 1957), pp. 26–31. Reprinted here, as condensed, from *The Education Digest*, Vol. XXIII (January 1958), with author's 1960 revisions in italics. Reprinted by permission.

severance pay. An even smaller number allow their teachers duty-free lunch periods of as much as 30 minutes, and in a majority of districts in cities of over 10,000, a day off for a funeral or a personal emergency means the loss of that day's pay.

Numerous individuals and organizations have attempted to supply answers. Many if not most of them have come from persons with little firsthand knowledge of the teacher's environment. No other profession is today subjected to more irresponsibly conceived cure-alls than the teaching profession. A lack of sound, tested remedies for the teacher shortage is responsible for the loss to the school system of 10 per cent of its teachers annually. The new teacher, starting with enthusiasm and high ideals, frequently meets head-on, and without warning, situations that cause her to conclude, "It's a rat race. I'll get out."

There is the attempt to reinstate the misnamed and discredited merit-rating system of pay which currently is being used as a club over teachers unions to try to force them to abandon requests for higher single-salary schedules. There are the professional growth requirements known to every teacher as "busy work." There is the lowering of professional standards so that school districts may employ non-qualified persons to teach; or housewives to act as teachers' aides. There are the current attempts to substitute mass instruction by television for classroom teacher-pupil relationship. And there are the loyalty (test) oaths that do not apply to all citizens but single out teachers and other public employes.

NOSTRUM CROP

Teachers themselves need to rid the schools and their profession of the seemingly continuous crop of educational nostrums pressed on them by unprofessional administration. Cannot teachers themselves project and carry through a realistic program to give teachers true professional status and security in our modern economy instead of mere lip service?

The suggestions listed here are not solely the present writer's. They were adopted by the delegate body representing the membership of the

American Federation of Teachers, which is comprised of classroom teachers only. They follow:

1. Starting salaries of $6,000 a year reaching *$14,000* in eight or fewer years at the Bachelor's level, with an additional spread of up to $500 for training beyond the Bachelor's degree so that teachers' income may be competitive with those of other professions requiring comparable education and training.

This presupposes a single salary schedule. *The highest B.A. starting salary in the country in Sept. 1960, was $6,150 in high-cost-of-living Fairbanks, Alaska. Lowest among the 855 cities of over 10,000 population surveyed was $2,794 in Sumter, S.C. Maximums paid teachers holding only a Bachelor's range from $3,586, in Sumter, also the nation's lowest, after 14 years, to $9,900 in Valley Stream, N.Y., after 35 years.*

Sumter, S.C., also pays its teachers with Master's degree the lowest starting salary in the country, $3,011, as compared with an Anchorage, Alaska, beginning salary of $6,300.

It is in Master's maximums that teachers' salaries show greatest variances, The same M.A. teacher who is paid a top of only $3,893 in Sumter after 14 years, can earn $10,500 in Valley Stream, New York. The spread is $6,607.

To the experienced school administrator these salary ranges spell teacher turnover, a shifting of teachers from city to city—and faculty disaster. *Yet the Valley Stream maximums represent no quick road to riches. To reach these maximums, 35 years are required.*

2. State tenure laws to protect teachers from being discharged without proved, justifiable cause, after reasonable probation.

The insecurity of year-to-year contracts containing interim clauses that require or provide no hearings for the accused teacher is an impediment to professional permanency. Teacher shortages are significantly less, all other things being equal, in states with laws that enable the dedicated person to enter teaching with the assurance that she can remain in the system without abnormal effort and establish herself as a permanent citizen in the community. The good tenure law spells out valid reasons for dismissal and provides for public hearing, with the teacher represented by counsel of his or her own choice, and also for court appeal if desired by the teacher.

3. Better teacher retirement pensions, supplemented by social security when desired.

In the vast majority of school districts, adequate teacher-retirement pensions are nonexistent. Who would think that any schoolteacher would stay with teaching long enough to need a pension? This, at least, seems to be the question in the minds of many school boards still living in the horse-and-buggy days. Teachers of some states have adopted optional plans to combine pensions and social security.

4. Adequate cumulative sick leave and hospitalization, as well as medical insurance paid for from school funds. Also severance pay.

FRINGE BENEFITS NEEDED

These fringe benefits have long been provided for other employed professional workers of whom special education and training are required. Teachers are salaried professionals and, unlike self-employed professionals, cannot be classified as entrepreneurs. They are salaried workers who, having invested time and money in preparation, are entitled to protection against personal disaster as well as an assurance of personal security after devoting a lifetime to the public service.

5. In every school district, published personnel policies and procedures for hearing teachers' grievances and for assisting with classroom discipline—"open" personnel records which the teacher concerned may inspect.

The necessity for published procedures is recognized by every teacher and most fair-minded administrators, yet few schools have them. It is worthy of note, however, that in 1957 the Massachusetts legislature passed a law requiring school districts to meet this standard. The teacher subjected to erratic personnel procedures is an unhappy person, and the "secret file" of teacher records and ratings is an evil without justification. Procedures for hearing teachers' grievances are essential to the existence and continuity of a permanent teaching staff, and "buck-passing" from principal to teacher in the matter of student discipline has been one cause for a major number of teachers leaving the profession.

RIGHT TO ORGANIZE

6. The right of teachers everywhere to organize, negotiate, and bargain collectively with employers in the recognized American way.

Since teachers are employed professionals rather than independent contractors, it is inevitable that they should group together to negotiate with their employers for their own well-being and welfare.

To quote from George M. Harrison, "Procedures in Collective Bargaining," which appeared in *American Teacher Magazine*, October 1957:

"Collective bargaining being a group instrument, individuals must come together in groups to use it. That is all that happens when individuals organize to form a union. They come together in groups to assert their democratic right to a voice in establishing the rules which govern their own employer-employe relationship. This is what is meant by the term collective bargaining."

Most school administrators who have tried collective bargaining welcome it as a superior procedure for dealing with scores or even hundreds of individual employes. The collective bargain contract is a master agreement for all teachers, subject to give-and-take conferences in which issues are resolved in truly democratic fashion. This is the basis for understanding and cooperation.

A law making collective bargaining mandatory for public employes, if either employer or employe wants it, has . . . been enacted by the Minnesota legislature. . . . It provides for bargaining agent elections and conciliation. *Bargaining is permissive in other states.*

Obviously, the foregoing objectives and procedures are aimed at creating a good professional climate. They are predicated on the thesis that if teacher recruitment (student recruitment) is to be successful and we are to retain an adequate number of teachers in the classrooms, then we must make the profession and its rewards *attractive.* To be attractive to young people in our democracy, teaching must offer teachers the opportunity for a full life, academic freedom, and the pursuit of happiness in any ethical way.

12

Aids to Teaching

JEROME S. BRUNER

Mr. Bruner is professor of psychology at Harvard. He was chairman of a conference on new educational methods held at Woods Hole, Massachusetts, in 1959, under the auspices of the National Academy of Sciences.

There has been a great deal of discussion in recent years about the devices that can be employed to aid in the teaching process. These devices are of many kinds. Some of them are designed to present material to the student of a kind that would not be available to him in his ordinary school experience. Films, TV, microphotographic film, film strips, sound recordings, and the like are among the devices ordinarily employed in such work. Books also serve in this role. These are the tools by which the student is given vicarious though "direct" experience of events. It does not serve much to dismiss such materials as "merely for enrichment," since it is obvious that such enrichment is one of the principal objectives of education. Let us call these *devices for vicarious experience*.

A second type of teaching aid has the function of helping the student to grasp the underlying structure of a phenomenon—to sense the genotype behind the phenotype, to use terms from genetics. The well wrought laboratory experiment or demonstration is the classic aid in such activity. A closer look at our efforts to get students to grasp structure indicates that there are many other devices and exercises that have the same function. The effort to give visible embodiment to ideas in mathematics is of the same order as the laboratory work. The Stern

Reprinted by permission of the publishers from Jerome S. Bruner, *The Process of Education* (Cambridge, Mass.: Harvard University Press, 1960). Copyright, 1960, by The President and Fellows of Harvard College.

blocks, Cuisenaire rods, and Dienes blocks, as well as the demonstrations of Piaget and Inhelder . . . , have the same function. So too do certain kinds of charts and representations, either in animated or still form. Models, such as a model of the molecule or an idealized model of the respiratory system, serve a comparable function. Needless to say, films and television as well as adroitly illustrated books can be adjuncts to the effort at producing clarity and concrete embodiment.

But there are other, more subtle devices that can be and are being used to lead the student to a sense of the conceptual structure of things he observes. Perhaps the best way to characterize them is to call them "sequential programs." There are certain orders of presentation of materials and ideas in any subject that are more likely than others to lead the student to the main idea. The courses being devised by the University of Illinois Committee on School Mathematics, the School Mathematics Study Group, the Physical Science Study Committee, and others are excellent instances of the well conceived sequence designed to lead the student to an understanding of basic ideas and structures.

The whole range of aids from the laboratory exercise through the mathematical blocks to the programmed sequence we shall, for convenience, speak of as *model devices*.

Closely related to these are what might be called *dramatizing devices*. The historical novel that is true in spirit to its subject, the nature film that dramatizes the struggle of a species in its habitat, the exemplification of an experiment executed by a dramatic personality, exposure to greatness in government by a documentary on the life and service of a Winston Churchill—all these can have the dramatic effect of leading the student to identify more closely with a phenomenon or an idea. Undoubtedly, this "aid" in teaching can best be exemplified by the drama-creating personality of a teacher. But there are many additional dramatic aids upon which teachers can and do call—and one wonders whether they are called upon often enough.

Finally, the past decade has witnessed the emergence of various *automatizing devices*, teaching machines, to aid in teaching. While such devices vary quite widely, they have certain features in common. The machine presents a carefully programmed order of problems or exercises to the student, one step at a time. The student responds selectively in one form or another to the alternatives presented in a problem or exercise. The machine then responds immediately, indicating whether the response was or was not correct. If a correct response is made, the machine moves to the next problem. The progression in difficulty from problem to problem is usually quite gradual in order to keep the student from the discouragement of excessive failure.

What one teaches and how one teaches it with the aid of such devices depends upon the skill and wisdom that goes into the construction of a program of problems. The art of programming a machine is, of course, an extension of the art of teaching. To date, most of the programming has been intuitive and has been entrusted to a teacher of known reputation. It has been remarked by teachers who have written tapes for teaching machines that the exercise has the effect of making one highly conscious of the sequence in which one presents problems and of the aims of the sequence—whether, for example, one is trying to get children to memorize material or use material cumulatively in doing progressively more difficult problems.

Perhaps the technically most interesting features of such automatic devices are that they can take some of the load of teaching off the teacher's shoulders, and, perhaps more important, that the machine can provide immediate correction or feedback to the student while he is in the act of learning. It is still far too early to evaluate the eventual use of such devices, and it is highly unfortunate that there have been such exaggerated claims made by both proponents and opponents. Clearly, the machine is not going to replace the teacher—indeed, it may create a demand for more and better teachers if the more onerous part of teaching can be relegated to automatic devices. Nor does it seem likely that machines will have the effect of dehumanizing learning any more than books dehumanize learning. A program for a teaching machine is as personal as a book: it can be laced with humor or be grimly dull, can either be a playful activity or be tediously like a close-order drill.

In sum, then, there exist devices to aid the teacher in extending the student's range of experience, in helping him to understand the underlying structure of the material he is learning, and in dramatizing the significance of what he is learning. There are also devices now being developed that can take some of the load of teaching from the teacher's shoulders. How these aids and devices should be used in concert as a system of aids is, of course, the interesting problem.

The matter of "integration" is nicely illustrated in a report on the teaching films used by the Physical Science Study Committee. "Until quite recently, most educational films were enrichment films, designed primarily to introduce phenomena or experiences that would otherwise be unavailable inside the classroom. Such films are necessarily self-contained, since the producer is ignorant of what his audience has previously learned or what it will go on to learn; he can neither build upon the student's immediate past nor lay the groundwork for his immediate future. In the last few years, another kind of educational film, stimulated to a large extent by television, has made its appearance. These films present the entire substance of a course, and are designed to minimize the need for a teacher. Clearly, it is possible to make extremely useful films in either of these forms, and such films have indeed been made." Stephen White, who has had a major part in producing the films used in the high school physics course prepared by the PSSC, then goes on to say in his report on the film work of that group, "Every film produced by the PSSC must meet two conditions. It must (1) further the presentation of the PSSC course as a whole, and (2) set the tone and level of the course. For the PSSC film is part of a complex that includes also the text, the laboratory, the classroom, the student, and the teacher."

White describes some of the problems of making the film fit. "The film must fit into this complex and never disrupt it. Obviously, this principle imposes serious restrictions on the producer. The most important of these for the PSSC films lies in the relation between the film and the laboratory. Only at his peril may the producer include in a film experiments which the student should and could do in the laboratory. Occasionally such an experiment will be included because it is essential to the logical development of the film's theme, in which case it is done briefly and allusively. More often, it is considered desirable to repeat on film, with more sophisticated apparatus, an experiment that is suitable for the school laboratory; in such cases the film is made in a manner which indicates clearly that it should be shown *after* the student has done the lab work, and the teacher is strongly urged to defer it until that time."

Other elements in the complex must also be taken into account. "Other restrictions on the film require it to follow the logical development, the spirit, and the vocabulary (where it exists) of the text. Finally, the film must always respect the position of the teacher; it must leave for him those activities which are necessary for him if he is to retain the respect of his class. All these are negative, but the film makes positive contributions to the complex as well. It serves the classroom by directing attention to those aspects of the subject which will best stimulate classroom discussion. Thus, the PSSC film on 'Work and Mechanical Energy' deliberately calls attention to the temperature rise in a nail on which work is being done, and thus opens discussion of thermal energy, which the class will meet next. And the film, wherever possible, serves the individual student directly by suggesting work he himself can carry on outside the school; it is for this reason that many PSSC films contain sophisticated experiments performed with simple apparatus."

The writer discusses a second function performed by the integrated teaching film: "The second condition that every film must meet—that of setting level and tone—may well be the most important contribution that the film medium can make. By directing attention to the important questions and the important problems, the film can help assure that all the great mass of fact and concept and theory and application that constitute any field of knowledge will fall into a coherent pattern in which the more important aspects will be clearly differentiated from the trivial. This is most difficult to achieve with the printed word; on film it can be accomplished at times with a gesture. Beyond meeting these two conditions, PSSC attempts in each film to make other substantial contributions to the learning process. Each film shows a real scientist in action, presenting him not as a disembodied intellect but as a normal, active, occasionally fallible human being, dealing rigorously and respectfully with real problems and deriving not only satisfaction but at times excitement from the intellectual pursuit in which he is engaged. It is in this implicit fashion that the films attempt to elucidate the nature of scientists and of the scientific life. . . . The films are scrupulously honest. Experiments that are seen on the screen were carefully performed and are accurately reported. The temptation to use the legerdemain inherent in film processes has been steadily resisted, and in those rare cases where it is used to produce a desirable effect, the student is told explicitly how it is used and why."

The task of the PSSC—the creation of a single high school course in physics—was a specialized one, and the particular problems of the course may not relate to all forms of curriculum construction. Yet there is always a question as to the purpose of any particular device— be it a film of paramecia or a slide projection of a graph or a television show on the Hoover Dam. *The devices themselves cannot dictate their purpose.* Unbridled enthusiasm for audio-visual aids or for teaching machines as panaceas overlooks the paramount importance of what one is trying to accomplish. A perpetual feast of the best teaching films in the world, unrelated to other techniques of teaching, could produce bench-bound passivity. Limiting instruction to a steady diet of classroom recitation supported only by traditional and middling textbooks can make lively subjects dull for the student. The objectives of a curriculum and the balanced means for attaining it should be the guide.

A discussion of teaching aids may seem like an unusual context in which to consider the teacher's role in teaching. Yet, withal, the teacher constitutes the principal aid in the teaching process as it is practiced in our schools. What can be said of the teacher's role in teaching?

It takes no elaborate research to know that communicating knowledge depends in enormous measure upon one's mastery of the knowledge to be communicated. That much is obvious enough—whether the teacher uses other aids or not. It is also quite plain from recent surveys that many primary and secondary school teachers are not, in the view of various official bodies, sufficiently well trained initially to teach their subject. It is also the case that, with the present high turn-over in the teaching profession, even relatively well prepared teachers do not have sufficient opportunity to learn their subjects in that special way that comes from teaching it. For teaching is a superb way of learning. There is a beautiful story about a distinguished college teacher of physics. He reports introducing an advanced class to the quantum theory: "I went through it once and looked up only to find the class full of blank faces—they had obviously not understood. I went through it a second time and they still did not understand it. And so I went through it a third time, and that time *I* understood it."

There are certain measures that must be taken to improve the quality of teachers, steps that have been proposed many times and that need no elaboration here. Better recruitment and the possibility of better selection, better substantive education in teacher training institutions, on-the-job training of younger teachers by more experienced ones, in-service and summer institutes, closed-circuit television to continue the education of teachers, improvement in teachers' salaries—all of these must obviously be pursued as objectives. But equally important is the upgrading of the prestige of the teaching profession. This upgrading will depend upon the degree to which we in America are serious about educational reform and the degree to which efforts are made to improve not only the facilities and salaries available to teachers but the support they can count on from the community and from our universities.

One special matter concerning the teacher as communicator of knowledge must be mentioned: the training and qualifications of the elementary-school teachers. Several references have already been made to the training of children concretely and intuitively in logical operations that will later be taught more formally in upper primary and secondary school. Such teaching requires special training, and it is not clear what the most effective form of training is. Special emphasis should very likely be given to such work—research on how to train teachers for such teaching along with research on the actual teaching of younger pupils.

The teacher is not only a communicator but a model. Somebody who does not see anything beautiful or powerful about mathematics is not likely to ignite others with a sense of the intrinsic excitement of the subject. A teacher who will not or cannot give play to his own intuitiveness is not likely to be effective in encouraging intuition in his students. To be so insecure that he dares not be caught in a mistake does not make a teacher a likely model of daring. If the teacher will not risk a shaky hypothesis, why should the student?

To communicate knowledge and to provide a model of competence, the teacher must be free to teach and to learn. We have not been sufficiently mindful of the ways in which such freedom can be achieved. Notably, we have been neglectful of the uses to which educated parents can be put. Various schools have experimented successfully with plans that use parents for the semiprofessional tasks that keep teachers pinned down. Parents can certainly help in supervising study halls, in grading routine quizzes, in preparing laboratory materials, and in the dozens of routine operations necessary in a school. The effect would be to free the teacher for teaching and study. If the teacher is also learning, teaching takes on a new quality.

The teacher is also an immediately personal symbol of the educational process, a figure with whom students can identify and compare themselves. Who is not able to recall the impact of some particular teacher—an enthusiast, a devotee of a point of view, a disciplinarian whose ardor came from love of a subject, a playful but serious mind? There are many images, and they are precious. Alas, there are also destructive images: the teachers who sapped confidence, the dream killers, and the rest of the cabinet of horrors.

Whitehead once remarked that education should involve an exposure to greatness. Many of us have been fortunate. But there is no simple plan for attracting greatness to the teaching profession. Emphasis on excellence is still the slow but likely way. Might it not be the case, however, that television and film might expand the range of identification figures—models of greatness—within the special limits imposed by one-way communication? We know relatively little about effective identification figures for children at different ages and in different circumstances. Are Olympian models the only ones or the best ones for engaging a child's sense of competence or greatness? Perhaps promising high school students as guest teachers from time to time would do better? They might also lure more talent into teaching.

In sum, then, the teacher's task as comunicator, model, and identification figure can be supported by a wise use of a variety of devices that expand experience, clarify it, and give it personal significance. There need be no conflict between the teacher and the aids to teaching. There will be no conflict if the development of aids takes into account the aims and the requirements of teaching. The film or television show as gimmick, the television system without substance or style in its programs, the pictographically vivid portrayal of the trivial—these will help neither the teacher nor the student. Problems of quality in a curriculum cannot be dodged by the purchase of sixteen-millimeter projection equipment. The National Defense Education Act provides considerable sums of money for the development of audio-visual aids. The intelligent use of that money and of other resources now available will depend upon how well we are able to integrate the technique of the film maker or the program producer with the technique and wisdom of the skillful teacher.

WHO RUNS THE SCHOOLS? | IV

1

The Problem of Control

BURTON R. CLARK

Mr. Clark is a member of the staff at the Center for the Study of Higher Education, University of California, Berkeley.

Whoever controls education is in a position to mold if not control the minds of the next generation. In totalitarian societies, the issue of educational control is decided by centralized state power, behind which lies the power of the ruling party. Education in the Third Reich was controlled by the Nazis through the state apparatus. Education in the U.S.S.R. is explicitly controlled and directed by the Communist Party through the machinery of the central government. No other groups— unions, business associations, churches, other political parties—seriously contend with the state and the ruling party. In short, centralization is combined with a one-party system, and the issue of educational control is fairly well settled. If struggles do take place, they are within the political-educational system itself, and most likely take the form of educational expert versus the noneducational official. Most conflict is therefore thrown into the shadowland of bureaucratic maneuver, since effective power lies almost entirely within the network of bureaucracies.

Democratic societies, in comparison, depend upon a certain amount of free play of group interests, permitting diverse groups to organize and campaign for their own point of view. This characteristic of democratic societies holds whether the educational system is centralized, a national system such as found in France, or decentralized, a mélange

Reprinted by permission from *Educating the Expert Society* by Burton R. Clark © 1962 by Chandler Publishing Company, San Francisco. (Footnotes that appear in the original source have been omitted.)

of discrete state and local systems as in the United States. The degree of centralization does not change the fact of a plurality of interests; what it changes is the level at which factional contention has its greatest play and the kinds of groups who must be heard. In democracies with unified educational systems, interest groups contend at the level of national politics; for example, attempting to influence the policies of the national ministry of education, or the platform of national parties as they struggle for office. In democracies with decentralized educational systems, the battle of interest groups goes on at middle and lower levels of government—the province, the state, the city or town—where, to influence school policy, groups must seek to influence the local board of control or the state legislature. Such is the situation in the United States. The historic and extreme decentralization of education in this country has made control a problem of state and local government, and until recently these have been the locales of nearly all the conflict of interest.

Elementary and secondary education in the United States have been very much *local* matters. Much authority to run the schools has been scattered, placed in the hands of separate districts that numbered over 100,000 in 1945, about 40,000 in 1960, and that will probably still number 10,000 in 1970 after great progress in consolidation. This decentralization has placed the formation of educational policy down at the level of town politics. Such state-level authorities as the state legislature and the state department of education play a role, but in most states this has historically been secondary to local influence. The state authorities generally declare minimum educational standards for the school program, disburse state funds to the local districts, set minimum requirements for the certification of teachers, and sometimes buy and prescribe textbooks for certain grades. But it is the local officials who hire and fire the school personnel, from the superintendent to the "custodial engineer"; they build the buildings; they determine the curriculum for the most part. In short, most key areas of policy formation are in the hands of the local authorities.

School politics in American communities are ostensibly nonpartisan, separate from city hall and the county courthouse, from Republicans and Democrats. Thus the election of board members commonly proceeds without party labels or party slates of candidates. But what is not explicit is often implicit, and the conservative-liberal opposition in a town that may explicitly take the form of Republicans versus Democrats for the city council will find a similar, only unannounced, alignment for the school board. The taxpayers association offers its support (conservative) for certain candidates; the local chapter of the Americans for Democratic Action backs the liberal opponents. Conservative and liberal groups seek candidates for the school board whose opinions are congenial to their own; the candidate may be already within the ranks or at least a frequent lunch partner. Election to the school board is often a first step in the political career of a local man; after board membership has brought some public attention, the man sheds his nonpartisan clothes and runs redressed as a Republican or Democrat for the city council or the office of mayor.

One important division of interest swirling around American public schools in the last quarter of a century has been the proponents of the "three R's"—reading, writing, and arithmetic—versus the believers in progressive education. The most vigorous proponents of the three R's have been traditionalists outraged by changes in the curriculum that tore it from its rigorous academic pattern and annoyed generally by the many social changes that have been tearing apart the fabric of the old. The parents most interested in the progressive school have generally been of liberal persuasion, sympathetic to experimentation and interested in changes that promised to free their children from the traditional lockstep. School personnel during this period have, in most cases, been largely in the progressive camp. Controversy between advocates of the three R's and proponents of progressive education has commonly taken the form of an attack by the "outs" on the "ins"; an attack on current school policy—at board of education meetings and elsewhere—by small, vocal conservative groups from the churches, women's clubs, and business associations.

The battle of traditionalists versus progressives takes many specific forms, and each camp is quite diverse within. One extreme case in the early 1950's centered on classroom discussion of world government.

Certain conservative groups took the position that the schools should not teach anything about the United Nations, especially about UNESCO (the United Nations Educational, Scientific, and Cultural Organization). In Los Angeles, a militant campaign against the schools on this issue was sustained by some church groups and patriotic organizations, who were against imparting information to school children that would in any possible way promote world government. The controversy caused several articulate spokesmen for the anti-UNESCO forces to be elected to the school board, and hastened the departure of the then superintendent of schools. It reverberated throughout the system for some time, leading to adjustments in the curriculum and to apprehension on the part of teachers over the kind of protection they would receive in discussing controversial issues. The neighboring city of Pasadena also experienced an attack by extreme traditionalists on liberal school policies, in even more traumatic form.

Such attacks subsided considerably in the late 1950's. After sputnik the foreground of the traditionalist attack on doctrines and practices of progressive education in the schools has been occupied increasingly by well-educated professionals, notably college professors, who would not be seen dead with the far-right groups. The weapons used by these traditionalists are the critical book, the study report, and the mimeograph machine, rather than the packed audience and the violent denunciation at board meetings. The sense of national concern about the schools, which has become part of the temper of the times, has swung the attention of many educated men of both conservative and liberal persuasion to the schools and motivated them to try to save the schools from what appear to be their progressive faults. Thus driver education became more controversial than world government. The professor-critic is concerned about the interruption of learning by athletic and social activities, rather than about communism in the schools.

University professors, little active over the last half-century in shaping school policy, are becoming again an active force, one similar to community groups in being external to the public schools but unlike them in being within education and there occupying some of the commanding heights. This traditionalist force is manned in part by liberal intellectuals, and has a general esteem among the educated who over the last three or four decades have provided a public base for the innovations of progressive education. New national concerns are producing new national moods and reshaping the adherence of groups to doctrines. The neighborhoods of the well-educated business and professional families are especially in flux; their demands add resonance to the professors' criticism of the schools, though they attempt at the same time to hold to many of the patterns of progressive education. . . .

The clash of interests in the local community over educational policy, interestingly, often takes a form in which organized blocs play only a minor role. The Old-Timer versus the Newcomer is a common schism of this kind, one that has developed in small communities from Maine to California as population movement has taken millions of city folk into the suburbs. These two types are easy to describe. The Old-Timer's family has *been* the community since way back when, and he works in the town or runs a farm; he owns property, often the farmland on which the new suburbs are spreading, or has the little home with land where he hopes to live out a peaceful retirement; his children are grown and out of the schools; he is not too well educated, perhaps completed high school; he likes Main Street quiet and the tax rate low; he sees most of his local taxes going for new sewers and new schools for the Newcomers and he does not like it.

The Newcomer has been on the scene ten years or less; he may be renting but he too is likely to own a house—generally one of the new ones in the tracts out from town; he is a young professional or corporation man and commutes to the nearby city; he is raising a family and his first concern at home—other than the blasted crab grass—is good schools. He sees education as a Good Thing, since he went to college and as a result now has a good job and feels culturally sophisticated. He finds Main Street quaint and the town dead, but still a good place to raise one's children away from the dangers of the city's streets. He wants better schools and playgrounds; he is willing to pay higher taxes and does not see why the Old-Timer is so penny-pinching and reluctant to accept change.

These two sectors of the community find expression in some organizations—the Property Owners Association, the PTA, and Dad's Club—but often fight their main battles as numerical aggregates in which most members are publicly silent. The silent members turn out on election day and vote for or against the school bond issue and then return home to glow or grumble about the results. The schools can be much influenced by these periodic expressions of sentiment. A system that repeatedly passes its bond issues and wins tax-limit increases gains the financial resources for new buildings, more teachers, and varied courses; it also develops a feeling that the town supports the system and its policies. But a series of defeats at the polls, often due to a silent "taxpayers revolt" or a hard-to-explain general distrust of current policy and personnel, pulls the financial rug out from under the "extra" features of a modern system and encourages a mood of staying with the fundamentals.

The cultural and political climate of a community inevitably gets through to the local school system, whether the climate is expressed openly by interest-group spokesmen or is something to be sensed by prolonged, informal contact. Climates may vary from one region of the country to another. Many California towns and cities, expanding rapidly in population and wealth, have a vigorously optimistic climate of opinion on community matters. This climate supports the growth of "progressive" school systems. Experimentation is in the air in many of these communities, with new buildings and new teachers—indeed whole new systems springing up over night—offering the chance to introduce new arrangements in the curriculum and in the treatment of students. Unhampered by tradition, progressive education has been extensively developed in the newly settled areas and suburbs.

A notable contrast to the boom psychology of California is found in the many industrial towns and cities of New England that have continued to experience economic depression and decline even in good times for the nation at large. Here the local citizenry has faced for 20, 30, or 40 years the vicious cycle of industry lost, property values down, taxes up. This state of affairs, unless changed by vigorous effort, promotes a town psychology ranging from "stiff upper lip" to sheer despair. The young and the adventurous leave, throwing the city more than ever into the hands of an aging leadership. The general mood of pessimism, underpinned by the hard fact of scarce money, sharply constrains school development. Educators are typically forced to adopt a traditional, conservative style whether they like it or not.

Lastly, while change and conflict in the local community are characteristic of a society that over all is changing rapidly, there are also many relatively stable communities. Often a small conservative group of city fathers quietly exercises control over town government and school affairs. Power in the hands of a few is coupled with apathy on the part of the vast majority, and the apathy is reinforced by lack of interest and lack of influence. In towns with an oligarchy of city fathers, successful school superintendents are those who learn to consult informally with the few who count, securing their nod before making an important move. Such towns are located from coast to coast but are more heavily concentrated in the long-settled states of the eastern seaboard. Many such towns have been broken out of this pattern by industrial and population movement, such as the flight to the suburbs, which brings new blood willing and able to challenge the old leadership. . . .

A modest upward drift in educational authority is taking place *within* the states, as the school-consolidation movement replaces small districts with larger ones, and as state departments of education and state associations of school personnel grow in size, strength, and number of state-wide rules and requirements.

Yet, in the face of the obstacles to more centralized control, the future clearly will bring more national legislation on public education and enlarged activity in such federal establishments as the United States Office of Education and the National Science Foundation. Many educators and citizens have long been interested in obtaining federal money for the schools, feeling that the local property tax was fast exhausting itself as a financial source and that state treasuries were also showing signs of being unable to finance necessary expansion and improvement. The large increase in the number to be educated, brought on by the high post-1945 birthrate, has called for rapid expansion in school funds—and a greater inclination to look toward Washington. International tension has encouraged a *national* approach to the problems of quantity and quality of American education.

With such forces at work and public interest aroused, we find emerging a comparatively new phenomenon for this country—education in national politics. Leaving aside the matter of school desegregation, interest groups are increasingly submitting, or opposing, various bills on education in the United States Congress. School personnel have their own lobbies; the National Education Association through its Washington headquarters works for "strong" bills on education, for large sums of money for school construction, teachers' salaries, and scholarships. In this they are generally supported by labor unions and liberal organizations, such as the AFL-CIO and Americans for Democratic Action. On the other side, such conservative groups as the United States Chamber of Commerce are chary about federal aid to education and work for weaker legislation. Some groups wish no federal legislation in education at all. Here is a new battleground whose existence is due to education's increasingly important role in our society and to its growth into a big enterprise.

The growing contention over education in national politics is reflected in the attitudes of the two major political parties. Both the Democrats and the Republicans now see education as a national issue, one in which there is political capital and on which positions must be taken. . . .

With the very sharp expansion of interest of the two parties in 1960 also went a new-found interest in science and technology. Republican platforms had said nothing about these matters until 1960, except for a few words about an Atoms for Peace proposal in 1956. The Democratic platforms have had items about atomic energy since 1948, with a major plank on this subject in 1956, but had not expanded into a broader consideration of science and technology. In 1960, both parties had major planks, one on "Science" and the other on "Science and Technology," with the Democrats underscoring "the special role of our Federal Government in support of basic and applied research," and the Republicans maintaining that "Government must continue to take a responsible role in science to assure that worthwhile endeavors of national significance are not retarded by practical limitations of private and local support."

Federal aid to education is controversial precisely because it is thought to bear heavily on control. The common understanding is that he who gives the money calls the tune, thus that federal financing means federal control and the undercutting of local and state authority. Those experienced in finance and organization can usually testify that this belief has some basis in fact. Earlier we indicated that public colleges were generally subject more to state than to local community pressures, and this is in part because of funds coming from state rather than local government. Yet it is clear that the degree of control exercised through the allotment of money can vary within wide limits, from virtually no impact to dominance. Federal funds can be allotted and directly supervised by an arm of the national government, that is, a ministry or department of education. Or they can be disbursed to an existing decentralized and varied structure of state offices, separate schools, and independent colleges in ways that change relatively little the distribution of authority.

The federal government has been in the business of subsidizing the colleges of agriculture of state universities since 1887. Have these colleges come under governmental control or supervision because of the federal grants? Apparently the grants have not been the means of federal political control. The pressures on these agricultural colleges have continued to come from the state and local areas in which they are located; and the federal money has strengthened the colleges so that they are better able to resist these state and local political pressures as well as others. Agricultural education and research remains decentralized and has been made into a more independent force, while continually dependent on the federal funds. The ways in which funds are allotted are thus more important in determining control than is the amount of the financial support or the sheer fact that money is given at all. The national government will play a greater role in American education in the future—dispensing scholarships, supporting research, paying for new buildings, and even contributing to teachers' salaries. Yet, it is also likely that compared with other countries the educational structure will remain decentralized.

One of the basic problems of this decentralized structure in an age of rapid technological and social change is its consequences for institutional adaptation. Decentralized systems possess certain flexibilities that systems under central control do not have. The "lower" units can innovate or experiment or change as they see fit, and new patterns can thus arise. But highly decentralized systems are also difficult to influence quickly and decisively with new ideas and often have the inflexibility of institutional drift. When each autonomous subsystem decides for itself what is best, the composite institutional trend "just happens." Thousands of school boards separately make policies on the basis of what is best for the local town or area—and what the decisions add up to is the national product.

In earlier eras, it mattered relatively little, perhaps, whether the national outcome was appropriate to the national need. Now it matters greatly. We have shown earlier that education is adaptive to changing occupational requirements and social conditions. Yet it is an open question whether a decentralized institution operating under local impulse can adapt rapidly and appropriately to the needs of a society in which other institutions are more centralized and changing at a very high rate, primarily under the impulse of a technological revolution. . . .

2

False Claims in School Control Drive*

ROGER A. FREEMAN

Mr. Freeman is Senior Staff Member, The Hoover Institution on War, Revolution, and Peace, Stanford University. He served on the White House staff during the Eisenhower Administration.

A powerful movement is underway to shift control over your local school policies to a nationally organized bureaucracy.

The Eighty-seventh Congress is being told that federal funds will quickly solve the public schools' financial problems and raise the quality of education to higher levels.

In reality, enactment of a federal aid program would be detrimental because:

1. It would hinder progress toward urgently needed improvements in local school systems, such as fuller and more effective use of available manpower and facilities.

2. It would shift control over school policies from parents, lay boards, and communities to a remote group of bureaucrats.

3. It would be a fateful step toward the absolute concentration of governmental powers in Washington to transfer responsibility for the largest domestic service—education—to the national level.

4. It would damage civic morale and set a bad example for youth by demonstrating that the way to get the things we want is not to work

From *Nation's Business*, March 1961. Copyright 1961 by *Nation's Business*, published by the Chamber of Commerce of the United States, Washington 6, D.C. Reprinted by permission.

* *Editors' Note:* In a letter to the editors of this book, Mr. Freeman made the following statement concerning this article: " . . . the editor [of *Nation's Business*] changed it materially without my knowledge, put another title on it, altered some figures incorrectly, etc. . . . "

and pay for them but to seek a way to shift the cost to somebody else.

At the heart of the education controversy is not the question of how much money the public schools need and how it can be provided, or how many classrooms or teachers they should have, or how much the teacher should be paid. The fundamental issue is big government versus home rule.

The drive for federal control, although a century old, will be pushed with special vigor this year because federal aid proponents know that unless a bill is passed soon the arguments for it will disappear.

The growth of school finances, the building of classrooms, the addition of new teachers have far surpassed what friends and foes of federal school aid dreamed of only a few years ago. The White House Conference on Education in 1955 proposed that school funds be doubled within ten years. In the six years since then, school support rose at a decennial rate of 152 per cent. States and communities have been increasing their school appropriations by about $1 billion each year for almost a decade.

It is not likely that state and local officials would keep doing so if Congress showed a willingness to raise the needed funds either through boosting taxes or by deficit financing. Federal aid might have the effect of pushing the need for higher taxes, or greater deficits, to the federal level. In the end, then, the schools' total resources would not be larger but the policy direction would be transferred to Washington.

To be sure, most federal aid bills include a clause prohibiting federal control of school programs. This declaration is necessary because the overwhelming majority of the American people want to keep control at the local level.

But when the professors of education and the school administrators talk, not to Congress, but to each other, they speak a different language. Let's listen to some of them.

An editorial in *The Nation's Schools* (September 1960) said:

"There is something quite naïve in the way we school people talk about federal control of education. Some of us seem to think that federal influence on education can be prevented simply by stating that it shall not exist. . . . Federal direction is inherent in any federal law or any federal court decision pertaining to education."

An editorial in *Overview* (formerly the *School Executive*), monthly magazine of the school administrators, said in November 1960:

"The United States is inexorably moving toward a national system of education. . . . The long-held views that education is largely a personal concern and that educational policy should be made by local units of government will have to go. . . . The national welfare demands a national system of education. . . . "

"GRASS-ROOTS-ISM" ATTACKED

Other educators demand "a gradual weakening of local autonomy over the school and a gradual emergence of control mechanisms that are not so socially and politically proximate to the educational worker." Some deride "our historical love affair with what might be called 'grass-roots-ism' in American education."

One federal aid advocate—Myron Lieberman of the Educational Research Council of Greater Cleveland—declares that "local control of education has clearly outlived its usefulness on the American scene," that "local control cannot in practice be reconciled with the ideals of a democratic society," and that "our present system of local control is far more conducive to totalitarianism than a national system of schools would be." In his book, *The Future of Public Education*, Mr. Lieberman proposes that "local control of education by laymen should be limited to peripheral and ceremonial functions of education." He states that "the crux of the matter is that centralization itself will hasten the establishment of professional autonomy." Mr. Lieberman concludes: "I am convinced that we are about to move rapidly toward a national system of education."

If education becomes federalized it will not be because the people want this to happen. The National Education Association and the American Association of School Administrators have stated: "At no one time will they [the people] clearly and decisively take action to make the national government the predominant agent of educational control. Rather, national control of schools will come by a process of accretion and infiltration. This is how it has happened thus far."

It is significant that the demand for federal aid does not come from those who are legally responsible for the schools and their support—the boards of education and state governments. No witness representing a state or local board of education has appeared before a congressional committee to testify in favor of federal aid for some years. Several have testified against it.

The success of the overwhelming majority of school bond and tax issues and the steeply rising size of school income demonstrate that the American people are interested in and willing to support their schools in the traditional manner without compulsion by the national government. But they do need more factual information. It is essential to give adequate publicity to the facts. . . .

The promise that federal aid will give taxpayers and schools something for nothing—money that won't cost anybody anything—has made an undeniable impact. Those in favor if it are confident. The staff of the Office of Education was doubled within the past three years and its expenditures more than quadrupled in the past six years. But this is barely a beginning. A memorandum circulated within the Office last fall predicted that "the role of the Office of Education is going to explode in the decade ahead."

The authors of the memorandum pointed to the success of the Life Adjustment Education Movement which the Office of Education sponsored 14 years ago and outlined a plan to "develop a national policy in education," to reshape curricula and organization and remodel the public schools. This should be brought about by the enactment of general federal aid, by "a federal contribution far beyond anything seen in the past."

Whether these hopes—which clearly are against the wishes and the best interests of the American people—materialize will depend on the attitude of Congress.

3

Higher Education Is a National Problem*

JOSEPH S. CLARK

Mr. Clark (Dem., Pa.) is a United States Senator.

Surely democratic government is a tool to be used by the people to solve their collective problems and to improve their collective lot. Yet a multitude of influential Americans regard their national government with suspicion and hostility. One would think, to hear the talk, that to turn to Washington in a time of need would be more like surrendering to a foreign power than utilizing one's own resources. The "conventional wisdom" in America still agrees with Jefferson that "that government is best which governs least." If chaos results and problems are swept under the rug, never mind; we are the same free people who drove the minions of George III into the Atlantic.

This inbred and deep-seated distrust of government may have had sound historical roots in the eighteenth century, but it is dangerous indeed in the twentieth. For it is only our national government that can mobilize and direct the resources of our society when they must be mobilized. And we should all ponder whether the United States as an unmobilized society can long compete with the determined, mobilized, aggressive society that confronts us today from the other side of the iron curtain.

This distrust of government, which has always been present in American thought, goes back to our unfortunate experiences with

From *Saturday Review Education Supplement* ("Education in America") February 18, 1961. Reprinted by permission. *Saturday Review Education Supplement* is sponsored by the Fund for the Advancement of Education.

* *Editors' Note:* Although Senator Clark is talking specifically about higher education, his point about the Federal Government applies equally well to the controversy over control of the secondary schools.

King George III. It was strengthened by the physical distance between the frontier and Washington, D. C. But the distrust did not break out into open warfare until the days of Franklin Roosevelt. Being unable to prevent the enactment, or later to repeal, many of the specific provisions of the New Deal, its powerful opponents set out to discredit government itself. In the publications they controlled, the fine old term "public servant" disappeared from the lexicon and the derogatory word "bureaucrat" took its place. "Citizens" became "taxpayers"— usually depicted by cartoonists as clad only in a barrel. The word "taxes" was rarely seen without the prefixed adjective "confiscatory" or "crippling" or the synonym "burden." Public spending was referred to always as a "cost," never as a benefit, and normally with the prefix "wasteful."

We have recovered a bit from the worst of the anti-government crusade. Today thoughtful and sensitive men, such as Walter Lippmann and Adlai Stevenson and Senator Fulbright, suggest that the fiscal starvation of public services such as education is a matter for national shame rather than national pride. Yet the conventional wisdom has not been greatly modified. I speak with assurance because the propaganda output flows across a Senator's desk by the ream.

To support the thesis that the Federal Government is essentially evil and should be dismantled, a whole school of economics has grown up. We are told that the oppressive weight of federal taxation is destroying enterprise and stifling investment, that the federal debt is climbing out of control, and that the soundness of the dollar is threatened. We are told that the Federal Government is costly and inefficient and therefore the states should do the job—when every objective test shows that federal employees are better selected, better trained, and better supervised on the average than state employees, and that the federal tax system is more equitable and more efficient than state tax systems.

Since the facts lead us toward the Federal Government, let us be calm. Let us keep our heads and repeat together: "The Federal Government is not our enemy, it is our friend. It is not an alien power, it is the creature of the American people. It will do what they want it to. It is not a monster that can ignore their will."

I will not dwell at length on the objection that federal aid will lead to federal control of the colleges and universities. I will say only that, in my opinion, it is a myth. Surely we are wise enough to legislate and to administer so as to prevent a result we don't desire. To those who oppose federal assistance I ask: What is your alternative? Is it not clear that the only real alternative is a second-class system of higher education? . . .

There are other urgent questions ahead. They are the questions of how much, how, to whom, and what for. I am confident that they too can be answered. In fact, we must answer them, for the purpose of higher education in America is the staffing of freedom. If we cannot staff freedom adequately, history will again take note before the end of this century, as it has before, that an unmobilized society cannot compete successfully with one that is fully mobilized. This is a conclusion which no free American, living in the richest country the world has ever known, in a society founded on Magna Charta, the Declaration of Independence, and the Constitution of the United States, can willingly accept.

4

We Reject Federal Aid

ANTHONY MARINACCIO

Mr. Marinaccio is superintendent of schools, Davenport, Iowa.

In most public school systems, there is no need for asking or expecting federal help. The job can be done at the local level—where it should and must be done if we are to preserve our freedom. America has been built out of this thing we call freedom. People can learn how to handle freedom—to be free—only if they have such powers as free education. Essential to free education is the power of the community to decide for itself what its schools should teach, and how to finance the teaching.

If we allow federal aid to education to come on a big scale, we will be moving—perhaps slowly at first, but more rapidly later on—to centrally directed education that could take us down the same road traveled by Mussolini and Hitler and Stalin and all the totalitarian societies of the past. I don't want this to happen. But it could happen. It's precisely the danger which Washington and Jefferson and Benjamin Franklin were concerned about when they met at the inn in Williamsburg after the Revolutionary War.

"Now that we have won this thing," they said in effect, "are we able to educate the masses of Americans to be free and to have responsibility for control of their freedom—or will chaos result?"

Proponents of federal aid to education continually assure us there will be no control. In Davenport, in Peoria, Ill., in Missouri and in other places where I have had contact with public schools, I found the opposite to be true. Control does follow aid.

From *Nation's Business*, September 1961. Copyright 1961 by *Nation's Business*, published by the Chamber of Commerce of the United States, Washington 6, D.C. Reprinted by permission.

Those who administer aid want to check the programs and courses of study. They suggest programs. They suggest the type of personnel you should hire and what you should pay them. They suggest what you should teach and, through these suggestions, they are actually controlling the situation.

Uncle Sam cannot hand out large sums of money without checking to make sure this money is properly spent. When you get to checking the spending you have to have a standard against which to check it. This becomes control. It is really as it should be. Billions of dollars should not be loosely distributed and their use left unmonitored. So, you're in a vicious circle. If you're running a public school system which receives federal tax dollars, you have to pay attention to what the federal government or its agents say, or you just won't qualify for the funds.

Look at the National Defense Education Act of 1958 which sets up grants for science and mathematics.

The preamble to this Act disclaims any intention to control local schools, yet you should have seen the thick report which we had to prepare in Davenport if we wanted to qualify for NDEA funds. We had to spell out in detail our program, our organization, and so forth. If that isn't control, what is it?

I know of communities which are spending thousands of dollars on science equipment, language laboratories, additional guidance personnel and tests financed from NDEA funds before they are ready for these things and before they know what to do with the new facilities.

This is an outrageous drain on American taxpayers. Many such communities spend the money from NDEA simply because it is there and its availability invites someone to spend it.

One of the things which we should all recognize, realistically, is that if federal aid is ever voted on a massive scale, many communities—including my own—will tend to think that they should apply for it, just to get their share. This is another reason why it is so important that the federal programs be stopped before they get started.

I have studied history, and I am disturbed by the lessons it teaches.

I see some ominous things in our society which emerged in past societies prior to their collapse. One of the most menacing signs is a drift
into centralization, abandonment of individual responsibility.

What is happening in America today is comparable to what happened to Rome and Greece and Egypt. After the individual citizens of
those states rose to great heights and everything became abundant,
they forgot how they got the abundance. We are living better than we
have ever lived, yet I wonder if we are not forgetting how we got
there.

We got there through individual initiative, not by turning to someone else to solve our problems. If we let the centralization trend continue, we will wind up in the predicament described to me by a Russian teacher to whom I talked recently. I asked this teacher why
Khrushchev and the other Soviet leaders are pushing so hard to surpass America.

"We won't have to fight you," this teacher replied with cold im-
personality. "You will fall from within."

The reason why we are drifting toward the superstate and consequent loss of local initiative, stems, I feel, from widespread ignorance
of our economic and political system. Our youngsters—for the most
part—simply do not know what got us where we are today, and what
makes our system tick. The same must be said about our teachers.

In our public schools you see very little in our curricula that even
refers to our system of free enterprise. The student has to elect one
economic course our of 12 years of work, one semester. We teach our
economic system in only an incidental way.

Let me illustrate this: Say a youngster makes a pair of bookends in
shop. He gets the mistaken notion that, since he paid 15 cents for the
two pieces of scrap wood he used, and perhaps 15 cents for his shellac
and what not, the bookends are worth less than a dollar. Then, when
he sees a pair of bookends in a store window for $19.95, he assumes
that somebody is making $19.

If our teachers understood our economic set-up better they would
say:

"Now look, boys, you are going to make a pair of bookends," and then they would study together how bookends are produced by industry; what the overhead cost is; how much goes for taxes; what it costs to supply the tools and to pay the workers. When you put it all together you might find a two per cent margin of profit, or three or four, and that would give the youngsters a more accurate grasp of competitive enterprise.

Why are our teachers so poorly equipped in economics? Many of today's teachers weren't taught economics when they were in school— or, at least weren't motivated to study it. You must add to this the fact that some teachers feel they do not receive an adequate financial return from the society they serve.

RETURN TO OUR EARLIER VALUES

The challenge we face nationally has subtle aspects. When I was a boy young people were quickly acquainted with the fact that they had responsibilities. We carried groceries, or sold door to door. The importance of hard work, initiative and self-reliance was made plain to us not only in our own families, but in our schools and in our communities.

We have slipped away from those principles, and we must get back to them. Our emphasis should not be on having big government do more and more for the individual, but on the individual doing more and more for himself.

If federal aid to education becomes a reality, I am afraid it will mark the first step toward complete control of the education process by government. Dictation would move slowly, but surely, just as it did in Mussolini's Italy, where even the textbooks were changed and Il Duce's picture finally showed up on about every fifth page. The schools would eventually become an agency of government, and many people would take their children out of them, leaving the public institutions to accommodate only the paupers and unfortunates whom no one else would take into their private schools. Even private schools would be drawn to the magnet of federal aid.

We must not let these things happen. The public school is the basis of our strength. It's the bulwark of our society.

In the future we must teach our children to be able to make comparisons between our way of life and communism, but the only way we can teach these things is, first of all, to make sure that they understand what America stands for. Then we should try and teach the truth about communism as nearly as we can see it, and as nearly as we can tell the story. This becomes a difficult thing because our teachers, while they are well meaning and patriotic, generally don't have a foundation which would enable them to compare the American way of life with communism.

I would want to have an intense in-service education program so that our teachers would know. Out of this would come a strong desire to promote the American way.

For a long time I have felt rather comfortable about our relationships with Russia, thinking that someday the people would overthrow their government, but after talking with some Russians, I don't believe they are about to overthrow the government. They have a strong desire, almost a religious feeling, that their country is going to rise to tremendous heights.

They have been imbued with the idea that they are going to surpass America. They have been given a little more than they had—and they had nothing before—and this to them proves that they are making progress.

We must give our youngsters the same faith and strong desire to fight for and to promote American values, and I am afraid that is an area where we are falling down.

We face a difficult job, but we must get this job done, or we truly will fall from within.

5

The Folklore of Local Control

THOMAS D. BAILEY

Mr. Bailey is State Superintendent of Public Instruction, Florida.

Local control of schools as we know it today has certain important values we must not lose in American education. It allows maximum flexibility to meet the local educational needs and desires that differ from those in other communities. Because it involves direct investment of money and effort, it also stimulates community interest in the schools and a desire to make the most effective use of school facilities. Local control exercised through nonpaid—or low-paid—school boards is less expensive and probably more efficient over-all than highly centralized control would be.

But what is local control today? Those who think that such control involves the absolute right of local persons to make decisions without reference to higher authority have accepted folklore as fact, for local control of this type is nonexistent today.

Folklore is appealing. Customs, beliefs, and tales traditionally preserved among people become a part of the common culture. And folklore has a charm of childhood fantasy about it; its convictions linger despite common sense and scientific reasoning.

For example, many Americans still believe that whiskey is good for snake bite. We knock on wood for good luck. We think it is unlucky for three people to get a light from one match. These are examples of inherited folklore—convictions that persist even though they have no basis in reality. As I suggested above, the conviction that absolute local control is still essential or even possible falls in the same category.

From *National Education Association Journal*, December 1961. Reprinted by permission.

The concept of local control in education is a time-honored one, but state and federal influences on education began early in our nation's history. Two good examples are the Northwest Ordinance of 1787 and the Supreme Court decision in the Dartmouth College case in 1819. Local school boards for the past several decades have looked to state governments for financial support to provide adequate educational opportunities for all the people in their districts. Furthermore, such control as local boards exercise over education is done within a framework of state and federal laws, regulations, and directives.

In addition, some influence on the school curriculum has been exercised through the National Defense Education Act with its emphasis on science, mathematics, languages, and guidance. Federal vocational-education programs for many years have generally been influenced by laws and administrative directives. Even subsidies by private agencies, such as Ford Foundation subsidies for educational television, have to a degree "controlled" local school districts that have accepted them.

Accreditation standards by regional agencies control to a considerable degree the practices in local school systems. For years, college entrance requirements have determined to an extent what is taught in secondary schools. State athletic activities associations often rigidly control local schools with respect to certain athletic activities. The fact that such controls are not official does not make them any less real. The point is that such controls limit or remove from the local community the power to make *absolute* decisions.

For some time, local control in education as our forefathers knew it has been obsolescent in certain respects. The first school in which I taught more than forty years ago in South Carolina was a two-teacher school in a rural flagstop community with one general store and about 500 inhabitants. We were three miles from a town of about 2000 population with a good school by the standards of that day. No one gave a thought to school consolidation, because the three miles of sand ruts between the communities were almost impassable for the automobiles in the area.

Several years ago, I drove through this community on a beautiful paved highway. I found that the former little school building had long since become a residence. The children now boarded buses each morning to attend well-equipped consolidated schools. Good roads, transportation, and the demand of our times for improved education have made the concept of local control of education obsolescent.

Today, the need for many small independent school districts is being debated far and wide in our country. These small administrative units—relatively expensive and uneconomical—contribute to mediocrity in education by today's standards. When will we banish the folklore of absolute local control and forget the obsolescence of the past? How soon will we decide on local control of education supported by a more balanced financial effort that provides honest control of excellent education for all?

I like to think of myself as a middle-of-the-roader in a discussion of education, but I have rather frequent experiences with extremists. There are those who are recommending a national curriculum and a national testing program. I have heard it said a few times that the state and federal government should take over the responsibilities of operating public education in order to assure quality education for all. I do not agree with these people. Nor do I agree with those people at the other extreme who declare that localized foolishness would be preferable to centralized wisdom.

It is interesting to note that even citizens most in favor of traditional local controls seldom resist decisions made by a central authority if they agree with those decisions. To my knowledge, few citizens have raised objections to the state requirements for a minimum school term of at least 180 days; minimum qualifications for all teachers; mandated financial accounting for the handling of public funds; earmarking funds for certain purposes such as teachers' salaries, buildings, and transportation; or for prescribed procedures in appointing teachers.

Furthermore, even though absolute local control is a thing of the past, people in communities today can exercise very effective control over the decisions of state and federal agencies and even those of private organizations. Today, more than ever before, modern communications media, well-organized citizen groups, and increased leisure time make it possible for citizens to participate in local, state, and national meetings and to assist in formulating policies that deal with education.

Groups of citizens at the local level can wield such influence through legislators and administrators, not only in state government but also in federal legislation relating to education.

In my opinion, this extension of the influence on education by the citizens in each community is the new and modern approach to local control. Even financial assistance from state or federal agencies may be refused if the terms are contrary to the desires of local school officials.

What then are trends as we move into the "searching sixties"?

The mobility of our population has increased. In one year—1958–59—one million children moved from one geographic area of our country to another, one million moved from one state to another, and two million from one county to another. With this increased mobility, education is a matter of national concern.

The variations which exist with regard to the ability of states to finance good education may be illustrated by these facts: The personal income per child of school age (5–17) in 1959 reached a national average of $8780. The average for Mississippi was $4045; at the top was Connecticut with $12,762. To cite another comparison, during 1958 the number of school-age children (5–17) per 1000 adults (ages 21–64) averaged nationally 470. In Mississippi, there were 612; in Connecticut, 413.

Other comparisons would reveal similar variations. These facts compound the problem facing our nation today.

The demands caused by national defense and international rivalry are now accentuating the obsolescence of old patterns and practices in education. Ex-Senator William Benton of Connecticut, upon his return from Moscow six years ago, warned, "Russian education is a bigger threat than the hydrogen bomb." President Kennedy recently declared, "The human mind is our fundamental resource."

Under today's conditions, can this nation afford to allow any geographical area to continue to take a pauper's oath as the excuse for providing only mediocrity in education? Should there be any geographical area in America where it is an educational liability for a child to be born and thereby be sentenced to poor or mediocre educational opportunities? Can this nation afford to allow large segments of its potential citizens to grow up within a society that is indifferent to the values of excellent education and the very survival of America?

It seems to me that the trends point to a realistic cooperative partnership of local, state, and federal governments in making possible quality education for all who can profit from such opportunities. This effort must of necessity provide for some desirable controls by all three divisions of government in the form of fiscal accounting and reporting.

The initiative of local citizens to improve education at the grassroots level must not be thwarted by any effort to provide financial assistance to local schools from state and federal sources. To those of us who have administrative responsibilities in education, the concept of local control believed by segments of our senior citizens is folklore and for some years has been outmoded.

6

Federal Aid to Education:
A Legal Opinion*

ALANSON W. WILLCOX

Mr. Willcox is the General Counsel of the U. S. Department of Health, Education, and Welfare.

SUMMARY OF CONCLUSIONS WITH RESPECT TO ELEMENTARY AND SECONDARY SCHOOLS

This summary sets out briefly the conclusions reached in the attached memorandum with respect to the application of the first amendment to Federal aid to elementary and secondary schools with religious affiliations. The field of higher education, which presents different factual, historical, and constitutional considerations, is discussed in the body of the memorandum. The memorandum also discusses the problem of obtaining judicial review.

I

The Supreme Court has ruled that the first amendment to the Constitution forbids the use of public funds to "support religious institutions" or "finance religious groups." Legislation which renders support to

From Senate Document No. 29, 87th Congress, 1st Session, May 1, 1961, "Memorandum to the United States Senate Education Subcommittee on the Impact of the First Amendment of the Constitution Upon Federal Aid to Education." (The title of this excerpt was supplied by the editors of the present volume.)

* *Editors' Note:* This excerpt contains only the "conclusions section" of a longer document. For the complete text including the detailed legal arguments, the reader is referred to the document cited.

church schools is unconstitutional in some circumstances. But laws designed to further the education and welfare of youth may not be unconstitutional if they afford only incidental benefits to church schools. For example, public funds may unquestionably be used to provide fire and police protection to church schools.

The line between direct support and incidental benefits is not always easy to determine. Decisions of the Supreme Court and relevant State cases cited and discussed in the accompanying memorandum make it clear that it is easier to determine what the first amendment forbids than what it allows.

II

A. Several unconstitutional proposals can be readily identified

1. Across-the-board grants to church schools may not be made. The Supreme Court has declared:

> No tax in any amount, large or small, can be levied to support religious activities or institutions, whatever they may be called, or whatever form they may adopt to teach or practice religion. (*Everson* v. *Board of Education*, 330 U. S. 1).

Plainly an across-the-board grant is the type of support which the Court has ruled is prohibited. Since no effort is made to earmark the funds for specific purposes, such a broad grant would inevitably facilitate the performance of the religious function of the school. This the first amendment forbids.

2. Across-the-board loans to church schools are equally invalid. A loan represents a grant of credit. When made at a rate of interest below what is normally available to the borrower, it also constitutes a grant of the interest payments which are saved. These benefits plainly have the purpose of providing financial advantage or convenience to the recipient. And like the broad grant, the across-the-board loan would inevitably facilitate religious instruction.

The Supreme Court has ruled that the first amendment forbids the lending of a public classroom for religious instruction during released time (*McCollum* v. *Board of Education*, 333 U. S. 203). The lending of public property and the lending of public credit are constitutionally equivalent forms of Government assistance. In *Zorach* v. *Clauson* (343 U. S. 306), the Supreme Court stated, "Government may not finance religious groups."

3. Tuition payments for all church school pupils are invalid since they accomplish by indirection what grants do directly. The form of governmental assistance is not controlling. Since tuition payments, whether made to the school or to the parent or student, would constitute support of church schools, they are prohibited by the first amendment. State courts have followed the statements of the *Everson* case to invalidate tuition proposals, since such a practice "compels taxpayers to contribute money for the propagation of religious opinions which they may not believe" (*Almond* v. *Day*, 197 Va. 419, 89 S.E. 2d 851; *Swart* v. *South Burlington Town School Districts*, 167 A. 2d 514).

B. *Areas of uncertain constitutionality*

The permissible area of legislation which renders incidental benefits to church schools is not clear. The *Everson* case illustrates the closeness of the question. In upholding bus transportation, a form of assistance in no way connected with the religious function of a church school, the Court divided by 5 to 4. The majority opinion suggested that the statute in question "approaches the verge" of impermissible action under the first amendment (330 U. S., at 16). Nonetheless, bus transportation has been ruled valid, and other collateral benefits like provision of milk and lunches appear equally constitutional, since the benefit is plainly to the health of the child and not to the school itself.

It is also likely that where funds are made available to a church school on a loan basis for special purposes not closely related to religious instruction, constitutional objections may be avoided. An example is title III of the National Defense Education Act which enables church schools to borrow funds for equipment to assist in teaching science, mathematics, and languages. Such programs advance specific national purposes, and their relationship to the religious function of a church school is remote. Moreover, the requirement that such funds be repaid makes it unlikely that a church school will be enabled to free its own funds for religious purposes.

In what other directions this principle of special purpose loans may be extended is difficult to ascertain. Typically secular and sectarian education is so interwoven in church schools as to thwart most possibilities. . . .

7

Federal Aid to Education:
The Catholic Viewpoint*

NATIONAL CATHOLIC
WELFARE CONFERENCE

. . . From the foregoing certain conclusions may be clearly drawn:

1. Education in church-related schools is a public function which, by its nature, is deserving of governmental support.

2. There exists no constitutional bar to aid to education in church-related schools in a degree proportionate to the value of the public function it performs. Such aid to the secular function may take the form of matching grants or long-term loans to institutions, or of scholarships, tuition payments or tax benefits.

3. The parent and child have a constitutional right to choose a church-related educational institution meeting reasonable state requirements as the institution in which the child's education shall be acquired.

4. Government in the United States is without power to impose upon the people a single educational system in which all must participate.

The foregoing conclusions, drawn from the relevant Supreme Court

From "The Constitutionality of the Inclusion of Church-Related Schools in Federal Aid to Education" (prepared by the Legal Department, National Catholic Welfare Conference), *The Georgetown Law Journal*, Winter 1961. Reprinted by permission. (The title of this excerpt was supplied by the editors of the present volume.)

* *Editors' Note:* This excerpt contains only the "conclusions section" of the longer document. For the complete text including the detailed legal arguments the reader is referred to the document cited.

decisions, represent only a part of the justification for aid to education in church-related schools. What must further be considered are results which would flow from a denial of such aid in the face of long-term programs of massive support exclusively to the public schools.

Some of these results would raise serious constitutional problems, while others would render meaningless certain constitutional protections presently enjoyed. These results should be carefully pondered when any program of major federal aid to education is being considered, because they would plainly entail a transformation of a free and pluralist American society into a society in which uniformitarianism would be certain and freedom therefore doubtful. It is indeed true that governmental spending may effect transformations of society; and in no instance is this potential in government spending programs to be more carefully examined than where such programs are directed—as in the case of subsidies for education—toward the formation of the minds of citizens.

Massive spending solely for public schools would in time result in a critical weakening of church-related schools, presaging the ultimate closing of many of them. This, taken in conjunction with the compulsory attendance laws, would mean that most children would be forced to acquire their education in the public schools. *De facto*, parents would no longer enjoy the freedom to send their children to church-related schools. Practically speaking, therefore, the freedom of parent and child protected by the *Pierce* decision would have been rendered meaningless.[113]

Further difficulties appear. The Supreme Court observed in *West*

---

[113] Although economic coercion through governmental action is not to be classified, constitutionally speaking, with statutory coercion such as was considered in the *Pierce* case, the observation made in 1955 by Alanson W. Willcox, presently General Counsel of the Department of Health, Education, and Welfare, should be borne carefully in mind: "Whenever a state imposes a choice between . . . receiving a public benefit, on the one hand, and exercising one's constitutional freedoms, on the other, the state burdens each course to the extent that abandonment of the other is unpalatable. The deterrent to exercise of first amendment freedoms when public benefits are at stake is a real one. . . . Infringement of constitutional rights is nonetheless infringement because accomplished through a conditioning of a privilege." 41 Cornell L.Q. 12, 43-44 (1955).

Virginia State Bd. of Educ. v. Barnette: "If there is any fixed star in our constitutional constellation, it is that no official, high or petty, can prescribe what shall be orthodox in politics, nationalism, religion or other matters of opinion. . . . "[114] Yet an "orthodoxy" is expressed— inescapably so—even in a curriculum from which religious "ortho- doxies" are absent. Removal, through government spending programs, of practical alternatives[115] to public school education would mean that those who, in conscience, desired education in a church-related school would be forced to participate in an education in unacceptable ortho- doxies. Here, as a matter of practicality, would be the social result discountenanced by the Court in *McCollum:* coercion upon the child to participate in schooling, the orientation of which was counter to his beliefs—a *de facto* denial of free exercise of religion.[116]

Not only "free exercise" problems would be encountered by such spending programs; "no establishment" problems would become manifest. This is because there is little guarantee that the public schools can, in actuality, maintain a completely non-"value"-inculcat- ing program. Since life itself, humanity, history, and the social sciences are all involved in the daily life of any educational institution, "values" of one sort or another inevitably creep in. In this connection, it must be asked: If the No Establishment Clause operates to exclude the inculca- tion of religion in the public schools, what, by constitutional defini- tion, is "religion"?

---

[114] 319 U.S. 624, 642 (1943).

[115] The Supreme Court has made note of the absence of alternatives as a standard for judging the coercive effect of given governmental action. The Court pointed out that in the *McCollum* case "the only alternative available to the nonattending students was to remain in their classrooms"; while with respect to the Maryland Sunday laws (which the Court upheld) "the alternatives open to nonlaboring persons . . . are far more diverse." McGowan v. Maryland, 366 U. S. 420, 452 (1961). The absence (in the case of closing of church-related schools, caused by a program of massive governmental support of public schools) of any alternative opportunity to receive a form of education to which millions of citizens would consider themselves conscientiously entitled, would highlight the coercive effect of such a program.

[116] The Court continues to underscore its warnings against such uses of govern- mental power as will tend to coerce beliefs. Torcaso V. Watkins, 367 U. S. 488 (1961).

Leo Pfeffer, of the American Jewish Congress, considers nontheistic beliefs to be "religious":

In this study I shall regard humanism as a religion along with the three major faiths: Protestantism, Catholicism, and Judaism. This, I submit, is not an unreasonable inclusion. Ethical Culture is exclusively humanist but is generally considered a religion.[117]

Lanier Hunt, of the National Council of Churches, is somewhat uncertain of the definition of religion, but is willing to accord it a very broad definition:

By another definition, religion is simply loyalty to ultimate values. . . . In schools, youths look for answers to questions about the origin, destiny, and meaning of life. These are religious questions. In the United States we say that every individual has a right to an education. And this is an expression of a religious conviction about the nature of the universe and man's place in it. Within the wider definition of religion, public education is perhaps the greatest religious force in American life today.[118]

Justice Black's notation in *Torcaso v. Watkins* is to the same effect:

Among religions in this country which do not teach what would generally be considered a belief in the existence of God are Buddhism, Taoism, Ethical Culture, Secular Humanism, and others.[119]

That public schools inculcate values is undeniable. Indeed, it has been said, respecting public school education:

The development of moral and spiritual values is basic to all other educational objectives. Education uninspired by moral and spiritual values is directionless . . . .
    That educational purposes rest on moral and spiritual values has been generally recognized in the public school system. The Educational Policies Commission has previously declared: "Every statement of educational purposes, including this one, depends upon the judgment of some person or group as to what is good and what is bad, what is true and what is false, what is ugly and what is beautiful, what is valuable and what is worthless, in the conduct of human affairs."[120]

---

[117] Pfeffer, Creeds in Competition 5 (1958).
[118] Hunt, Religion and Education, 332 Annals of the Am. Academy of Political Science 99 (1960).
[119] 367 U. S. 488, 495 n.11 (1961).
[120] NEA & AASA, Moral and Spiritual Values in the Public Schools 7 (1951).

The foregoing statement by the Educational Policies Commission of the National Education Association of the United States and the American Association of School Administrators is qualified, it is true, by the statement contained in the same report that public schools must be nondenominational: "As public institutions, the public schools of this nation must be non-denominational. They can have no part in securing acceptance of any one of the numerous systems of belief regarding a supernatural power and the relation of mankind thereto."[121] However, several of the denominations to which Justice Black made reference do not acknowledge a supernatural power. The value-objectives of one of these, the Ethical Culture Movement, are described in the following statement:

A national movement of Ethical (Culture) Societies—religious and educational fellowships based on ethics, believing in the worth, dignity and fine potentialities of the individual, encouraging freedom of thought, committed to the democratic ideal and method, issuing in social action.[122]

Certainly the Court, through Justice Black, cannot have meant to say that the teaching of certain religious value-systems to child citizens is publicly supportable, whereas the teaching of certain others is not. To make a distinction based upon whether the religious value-system embraced the supernatural would be meaningless and invidious. The Court, in *Torcaso*, held the provision of the Maryland Constitution there involved unconstitutional because it favored "one particular sort of believers" ("believers," as the Court had noted, including also those who profess nontheistic religions).[123]

Obviously, under an absolutist interpretation of the first amendment, such value-inculcation must pose serious problems. Again, however, rationality should point to the solution. Value-teaching should not, in principle, be regarded as an evil, to be shouldered out of community life by some deemed necessities of the first amendment. But if such teaching may, *without* first amendment objection, be offered in the public schools which are supported completely by government, then it

---

[121] Id. at 4.
[122] 1961 Yearbook of American Churches 47 (1961).
[123] 367 U. S. at 490.

cannot be said that some compulsive mandate of the first amendment decrees that no government aid whatever can be granted to education in church-related schools because the church-related schools, too, offer a program which inculcates values.

Again, it should be apparent that there is no need for a dilemma seemingly caused by opposed claims of the free exercise clause, on the one hand, and the No Establishment Clause on the other. *It is apparent that the free exercise clause as well as the No Establishment Clause must be recognized as creating limitations upon the spending power of the federal government.* If all governmental spending for education in church-related schools is to be considered ruled out on account of requirements of the No Establishment Clause, governmental spending for education in public schools must also be considered ruled out due to requirements of the free exercise clause. Ours, however, is a Constitution of rationality, not one of absolutes which paralyze social action. And plainly the solution becomes one in which government should be free to make such rational adjustment as best comports with the very real social needs involved.

Apart from the question of precise holdings in cases, constitutional precedent of another sort is available in aid of a solution to the problem here presented: the view often expressed in the more recent Supreme Court decisions respecting freedom of contract, the commerce clause, due process in criminal proceedings, and equal protection, that the Constitution is not static but must be from time to time reinterpreted in view of changed social conditions.[124] These decisions show a hospitality to change, an awareness of widely felt social needs, an admirable balancing of competing interests, and a recognition that the demands of justice are not necessarily met by such slogans as "freedom of contract," or "separate but equal"—or "separation of church and state" (where that phrase is meant to denominate *absolute* separation). Such pat phrases may command constitutional results while ousting rational discussion of the real and complex social problems involved.

---

[124] Emspak v. United States, 349 U. S. 190 (1955); Brown v. Board of Educ., 347 U. S. 483 (1954); Wickard v. Filburn, 317 U. S. 111 (1942); Home Bldg. & Loan Ass'n v. Blaisdell, 290 U. S. 398 (1934).

In the present situation, where it is said that an educational crisis is upon us and that government aid to education is an imperative, it is apparent that the constitutional wisdom of the past is the necessity of the present. There is need to recognize the public contribution of education in church-related schools and to continue to utilize its beneficent contribution to the national weal. The problems involved are predominantly practical: no constitutional bar exists to the aid herein described to education in church-related schools. Practicalities, not slogans, should govern the determinations to be made—determinations which give clear recognition to the rights of parents, the rights of children, the enlargement of freedom, and the preservation of the nation.

8

Public Funds for Public Schools Only

PHILIP BURTON

Dr. Burton is minister of the Community Church of Watertown, Massachusetts. He has been a member of the executive body of the Council of Community Churches.

Many Roman Catholic proponents of tax-subsidized religion are engaging in intricate verbal exercises to invert the meaning of the Constitution's First and Fourteenth amendments and use them against their opponents. Faced with dilemmas posed by expanding population, galloping inflation and canon law imperatives, they are claiming—with amnesiac blandness toward clear dicta of Supreme Court decisions blocking tax-supported religion—that refusal of such support is an unconstitutional limitation of parental rights and religious liberties.

No advocate of tax support for parochial schools denies that such schools are a religious enterprise. *Extra ecclesium nulla salus* is the rationale that accounts for their establishment and compels Catholic parents to use them. Beyond ensuring their right to exist (upheld by the Supreme Court in 1925), the government's obligation toward them is identical with its obligation to the churches themselves. As the Supreme Court has made clear, parochial schools are legally precluded from any tax support whatsoever. If they were to receive such support, the government would thereby acquire the right to regulate them in the same way it regulates public schools, and under such circumstances no religion could be taught in them.

From *The Christian Century*, April 5, 1961. Copyright 1961 Christian Century Foundation. Reprinted by permission from *The Christian Century*.

I

Traditional Roman Catholic opposition to public aid to education in general has been modified in recent years by growing anticipation of sharing in larger benefits for public education at public expense. In 1930 the U. S. Supreme Court drew a distinction between child benefits and aid to religion, and rendered a decision permitting parochial school pupils to share in free textbook distribution. Religious school pupils were in some places being transported at public expense even before any legal clarification by the Supreme Court. The Everson case, which came before the court in 1947, culminated in one of the court's most notable verdicts. By a slim majority of one the court adhered to a precedent, drawn first in the 1930 textbook case, distinguishing between child benefits and aid to religion. On this basis it made public transportation of children attending parochial schools permissible. Four members of the court rejected the distinction and declared such use of tax funds violative of the Constitution. And the whole court concurred in the judgment that the First amendment erects an impregnable wall of separation between church and state and absolutely precludes publicly supported religion. The reasoning of the dissenters was adopted in the McCollum case the following year in an 8-1 decision outlawing the teaching of religion in public classrooms. Taken together, these two Supreme Court decisions settle by a clear negative any real questions as to whether government can subsidize religion.

Comprehensive as this answer seems, those who seek public support for religious enterprises remain undaunted. The extent of their anticipations can be surmised from the nature of the denunciations that have been hurled at the Supreme Court following the Everson and McCollum decisions. The court is charged with departing from tradition and misinterpreting the Constitution. The Constitution, say the accusers, does not prohibit nonpreferential tax support of religion; the court ignores history, logic and law by imposing a novel interpretation upon the First amendment. They further argue that there is no wall of separation between church and state except an imaginary one in the minds of smokers of secular opiums. The misinterpretations the court imposes reject the honored tradition of liberty, deny parental rights and violate freedom of religion. So goes the argument of the proponents of tax-supported religion.

The substance of this argument was articulated last summer by Bishop Lawrence J. Shehan, chairman of the department of education of the National Catholic Welfare Conference. Preaching on August 28 at a Red Mass held at the National Shrine of the Immaculate Conception, Washington, D.C., and attended by three Supreme Court justices (including Chief Justice Earl Warren) and many members of the American Bar Association, Bishop Shehan bluntly posed the question whether the financial burdens of those who send their children to religious schools is an unconstitutional limitation of parental rights and violation of freedom of the practice of religion. While Bishop Shehan put the matter in question form, his own answer was obvious— and clearly contrary to that already established in law by the Supreme Court decisions. Beneath his arcane language is to be found a different concept of the proper relationship between church and state than that which informs the Constitution and guides Supreme Court decisions.

The bishop's logic obviously identifies the Constitution's concern to protect parental and religious rights with a nonexistent governmental duty to incur parents' expenses deriving from exercise of such rights. This kind of logic betrays confusion in the minds of those who invoke its aid. The Constitution upholds the right of parents to send their children to the church of their choice, but maintenance of these legal rights carries no concomitant obligation for the government to, say, pay pew rent in the church chosen. If such a principle were constitutionally valid, legal consistency could claim that the government incurs the obligation to pay any and all expenses involved in a citizen's exercising any one of his constitutional privileges. No claim could be more patently absurd. The financial burden of parochial schools is a private religious problem; nothing relevant to constitutional questions of rights is involved. A clear violation of the Constitution would be perpetrated if the government were to honor the plea for tax support implicit in the presuppositions behind the bishop's question.

Bishop Shehan's approach was not born full grown of his homiletic travail last August 28. Inherent in it is Cardinal McIntyre's notion of circumventing the wall that separates parochial schools from the federal treasury by a ruse to gain funds for such schools through scholarship awards to parents of children attending them. Included also is a conception of child welfare benefits that would include everything from erecting religious school plants to stopping leaky toilets in them. Obviously such grab-bag expenditures could be made to cover the major costs of parochial religious education. This method of breaching the wall of separation between church and state is assumed by its proponents to have no constitutional complications and to nullify the Supreme Court's clearest interpretations of the First amendment. They imply that the government's refusal to adopt some such way of nullifying Supreme Court decisions blocking direct or indirect tax support of these schools is equivalent to violation of Catholics' constitutional rights. The assumption ignores the fact that *no person has constitutional rights to religious education at public expense.* Any citizen possesses the legal right to acquire religious education for himself and his children; these rights have been as fully upheld for Roman Catholic citizens as for others. Obviously it is fallacious to confuse legal rights with private economic problems.

Roman Catholic citizens have the legal right to make use of public schools but are prevented by dicta of their church from doing so. The government does not infringe upon their right to act on the insistence of their church's authorities that they send their children to religious schools not entitled to tax support. The germane core of the point at issue here lies in the fact that Roman Catholics accept for themselves an extralegal position that constrains them to go beyond what the government requires and assume for themselves extra educational costs. This is the crux of the dilemma of dual loyalties upon which the government approach to educational responsibility has in many countries foundered.

Contrary to the view of the Roman Catholic hierarchy, the economic disabilities of those required by their churches to assume the burdens incident to religious education are not in any way the result of government discrimination. They are instead incidental costs of the actualization of rights ensured under the First and Fourteenth amendments. The same amendments which set forth these legal rights prohibit the government from collecting taxes to subsidize the individual's exercise of such rights. The government is not a church and cannot act as one in order to collect church school fees. By due process of law the government collects taxes from all its citizens; it treats Roman Catholic citizens on equal terms with all others. If they complain that they are victims of double taxation without representation, they cannot in good conscience lay blame upon the government. If they refuse to accept their share of what the government provides for all on equal terms, the refusal is not one for which the government is responsible.

Advocates of tax-supported religion increasingly recognize the futility of securing direct tax support and tend to cloak their claim for public support under the guise of proposals that speak of child welfare benefits. Their hopes lie in the dubious distinctions discussed herein and appealed to by the slim majority of one which in the Everson case ruled in favor of free transportation of parochial pupils. The dissenting minority of four in that case saw no such distinctions, and in the 1948 McCollum case their reasoning was adopted as the basis for an 8-1 decision outlawing the teaching of religion in public classrooms.

III

When proponents of tax support for religious schools accuse the court of rejecting the tradition of religious liberty, they have in mind the precedents based on dubious distinctions. Carried to logical conclusions, this recent tradition might open the way for vast public expenditures for religion. Such was not the tradition from which James Madison reasoned when he protested federal compensations for chaplains in the House and Senate on the ground that they are unconstitutional.

Madison knew more intimately the intent of the tradition that informs the First amendment than do some of those who now appeal to tradition against that amendment! Madison knew of no tradition of non-preferential aid to religions; he did know that the authors of the Constitution countenanced neither preferential nor nonpreferential aid to religions at public expense. And he knew of no tradition using "benefits to children" as a subterfuge for extending tax support to religious institutions. In the McCollum case the court was wisely sensitive to the tradition known to Madison and others of his day.

Bishop Shehan cites the government's providing chapels and chaplains for the armed forces and special veterans' programs as the kinds of measures needed to facilitate religious freedom. As a matter of fact, the constitutionality of tax-supported chaplaincies and chapels is highly debatable. Madison opposed them as unconstitutional. One can only wait until the Supreme Court takes on and decides a case involving the issue to be certain of its opinion. It is not inconceivable that the practice might be found illegal. As for special programs for veterans, their purpose was not motivated by any concern either to facilitate or hinder practice of religious freedoms. Much less was their purpose to solve the financial dilemmas of administrators of religious schools! That such was the incidental effect in some instances is hardly to be questioned; it is not certain, however, that all aspects of the administration of the programs could pass a constitutional test.

Such problematic cases may yet provide the occasion for future litigations and decisions; nevertheless the fact remains that the kinds of expenditures uppermost in the minds of advocates of tax support for religion are clearly precluded by law. The law which prohibits teaching of religion in a public classroom cannot be bent to accommodate ruses encompassing scholarship awards, child welfare benefits and loans which would in fact constitute financial aid to religion. The answer to questions presupposing that denial of such requests is an unconstitutional violation of parental rights and freedom of religion is contained in these words by Justice Hugo Black (in the Everson decision): "No tax in any amount . . . can be levied to support any religious activities or institutions." Words could not be clearer!

9

A Liberal Calls for Aid to Church Schools

ROBERT M. HUTCHINS

Formerly Chancellor of the University of Chicago, Mr. Hutchins is now President, Center for the Study of Democratic Institutions, Santa Barbara, California.

Federal aid to education is an absolute necessity. But a political argument over funds for parochial schools, masquerading as a constitutional issue, bars the way. Unfortunately President Kennedy, while calling for $5.3 billion in aid to education over a period of years, is himself guilty of jeopardizing aid to all schools by perpetuating the masquerade.

The President and many others, especially liberals, tell us aid to church-school pupils is a constitutional question. They say there is a wall of separation between church and state forbidding any kind of assistance, direct or indirect, to an educational institution operated under the auspices of a church.

In fact, the Constitution says nothing of separation and makes no mention of a wall. The words of the First Amendment are: "Congress shall make no law respecting an establishment of religion, or prohibiting the free exercise thereof. . . . " The Supreme Court has held that the Fourteenth Amendment makes these words applicable to state legislatures as well as to Congress. Nothing in the words necessarily leads to the conclusion that every form of aid, direct or indirect, to educational institutions under religious auspices is unconstitutional.

We owe the wall not to the Constitution but to a letter from Thomas Jefferson to the Baptist Association of Danbury, Connecticut, in 1802, replying to a complimentary address. Jefferson wrote, "Be-

From the *Saturday Evening Post*, June 8, 1963. Reprinted by permission of Robert M. Hutchins.

lieving with you that religion is a matter which lies solely between man and his God, that he owes account to none other for his faith or his worship, that the legislative powers of Government reach actions only, and not opinions, I contemplate with sovereign reverence that act of the whole American people which declared that their legislature should 'make no law respecting an establishment of religion, or prohibiting the free exercise thereof,' thus building a wall of separation between church and state."

The letter shows that what Jefferson was interested in was freedom of religion. He did not want the Government telling people how or whom or whether they should worship—first, because of the nature of religion, and second, because of the nature of government. Religion was a matter between a man and his God; government should not, if only because it could not, attempt to control the thoughts of men.

The wall Jefferson erected in the name of the First Amendment rose no higher than was necessary to wall off the religious opinions and practices of citizens from interference by government. His letter does *not* suggest that he would have opposed public expenditures that might benefit schools under religious management. And the record shows that he recommended procedures by which students at the University of Virginia, supported by the state and founded by Jefferson, might receive religious instruction.

Jefferson's wall disappeared into the mists of history for 77 years. Then it came back into view when the Supreme Court held that the First Amendment did not protect polygamy among the Mormons. It came back, that is, with a hole in it, through which the Government marched against a practice defended in religion's name. In justifying legislative condemnation of a church's action, Chief Justice Morrison Waite, who wrote the opinion of the court, used the Jefferson doctrine that legislative powers should be limited specifically to regulation of actions.

All was quiet along the wall for 62 years. Then, in 1941 it reappeared, but with another large hole in it, through which a school board in New Jersey drove buses carrying some children to parochial schools. The action was authorized by state law. In 1947 its constitutionality was *upheld*. The majority opinion said, "The First Amendment has erected a wall between church and state. That wall must be kept high and impregnable. We could not approve the slightest breach. New Jersey has not breached it here."

For the last 15 years, whenever there has been a case involving church and state, almost every Supreme Court justice has felt constrained to bow before the wall. The psalms sung in its behalf have grown more eloquent and more moving. It has become one of our more popular figures of speech. But the only effect of the wall on the decisions of the court has been to confuse the opinions of the justices.

The wall is used indiscriminately as a jumping-off point in all cases in which the religion clauses of the First Amendment are invoked. These cases are in general of three quite different kinds: those in which a public agency has used public money in a way benefiting private schools indirectly; those in which a public agency has authorized a program of "released time" for religious instruction in public schools or in connection with public schools; and those in which a public agency has instituted religious exercises in public schools.

Released time and religious exercises put the power of the state behind religion and raise the question of public pressure, direct or indirect, on the consciences of individuals and the consequent limitation of the exercise of their religious freedom. Indirect financial aid to schools under religious auspices does not raise this question. Such aid may actually help the aided pupils to exercise their religious freedom; it cannot be seriously argued that it restricts the religious freedom of those who are not assisted.

For all its talk of the wall, the fact is that the Supreme Court has never held aid to pupils in religious schools unconstitutional. As the court sustained New Jersey in providing transportation for pupils in Catholic schools, so it sustained Louisiana in providing textbooks for children in all schools. The theory in both cases was the same: an overriding public purpose was to be served—the education of the children in the state. The fact that some benefit might incidentally accrue to a private school or to the religious organization that managed it was not significant.

The tax exemption of church schools has never been challenged. Neither have the numerous Government programs of grants, loans, scholarships and tax benefits under such laws as the GI Bill of Rights, the College Housing Act, the School Lunch Act, and the Surplus Property Act, all of which have been available to church-supported institutions. The Kennedy Administration has sonorously opposed Federal aid to church schools. Yet it finds no logical difficulty in recommending in its present bill appropriations to facilitate the recruitment of teachers by parochial as well as by public schools.

My conclusion is that Federal aid to pupils in parochial schools is not a constitutional issue. It is a political issue, a real and important one. It may be stated this way: Will the general welfare be promoted by including parochial-school pupils in a national program of education, or will it be promoted by leaving them out?

In 1961 five and a half million children received education in Catholic elementary and secondary schools. That is a little more than an eighth of all schoolchildren in these categories. If the Constitution does not require us to leave one eighth of our children out of a national program of education, why should we do so?

In the New Jersey bus case, the court said, "It [the state of New Jersey] cannot exclude individual Catholics, Lutherans, Mohammedans, Baptists, Jews, Methodists, Nonbelievers, Presbyterians or the members of any other faith, *because of their faith, or lack of it,* from receiving the benefits of public welfare legislation."

The children in schools supported by religious denominations should not be excluded because of their faith from the benefits of a national program of education. And we can hardly have a national program unless these children are involved in it.

Rep. James J. Delaney of New York has reintroduced a bill to authorize a two-year program of Federal aid to all elementary and secondary schoolchildren in all the states. The bill provides that $20 shall be allotted annually to each pupil to defray part of the cost of his education. Pupils who did not record their intention or desire to attend a private school would be presumed to be destined for a public school, in which case the allotment would be paid to the public educational authority in their community.

This is a GI Bill of Rights for Children in elementary and secondary schools. Over a two-year period it would add $1.7 billion to the resources of these schools. Something more than $100 million a year would go to church-related schools.

Legislation of this sort would quiet the fears of those who are alarmed at the prospect of Federal control. It should calm those who believe that aid to church-related schools means the destruction of the public schools. It should satisfy everybody, except those who hold that a church-related school is the same thing as a church. They might say that legislation authorizing payment of $20 of taxes to a church school was the same as giving a citizen $20 of taxes to put in the plate on Sunday. They might argue that such payments were neither constitutionally possible nor politically wise.

But a school is not an assembly for worship. It does not perform ecclesiastical functions. Payments to a pupil for his education are not payments for the support of worship, of ecclesiastical functions or of the propagation of the faith. The object of education is the development of the mind. This may be conducted under religious auspices, but it is not the same as the development of religion or of the spiritual life. The Supreme Court would not have allowed New Jersey to pay for buses to carry worshipers to church.

A sensational shift in public opinion has been going on over the past two years on the subject of Federal aid to all schools. In March, 1961, the Gallup Poll showed that 57 percent of those interviewed thought Federal aid should go only to public schools; in February, 1963, only 44 per cent of those polled were of this opinion. Apparently the common sense of the American people is winning over the pedantry of their leaders.

10

Local Control of Education

MYRON LIEBERMAN

Mr. Lieberman is a member of the Educational Research Council of Greater Cleveland.

One of the most important educational trends in the next few decades is likely to be the decline of local control of education. Such a development is long overdue. Local control of education has clearly outlived its usefulness on the American scene. Practically, it must give way to a system of educational controls in which local communities play ceremonial rather than policy-making roles. *Intellectually*, it is already a corpse. At least, I propose to treat it as such. . . . The proper way to treat a corpse is to conduct an autopsy upon it and then bury it promptly. Having done this, we can better understand the rationale for the school system which will emerge from the present chaos in education.

An autopsy of local control reveals several reasons for its demise. In the first place, mobility and interdependence have completely undermined the notion that local communities ought to have a free hand in educating their children. Second, national survival now requires educational policies and programs which are not subject to local veto. Third, it is becoming increasingly clear that local control cannot in practice be reconciled with the ideals of a democratic society. Finally, local control is a major cause of the dull parochialism and attenuated totalitarianism that characterizes public education in operation.

Let us analyze these reasons briefly. In order to do so, consider carefully the following question: *Who* should decide whether the children

Reprinted from *The Future of Public Education* by Myron Lieberman by permission of The University of Chicago Press. © 1960 by The University of Chicago. (Footnotes, with one exception, that appear in the original source have been omitted.)

in a given community should be required to learn to read and write?

Some persons would undoubtedly argue that parents should have the right to raise their children as illiterates if they wish to do so. Most people would probably feel that the public ought to have the right of final decision in this matter. Still, there are many publics: local, state, regional, national, international, and even publics which are not defined geographically. Which of these publics should be authorized to have the last word in the matter?

Until a short time ago, every state had a compulsory education law. These laws took the power to decide our hypothetical question out of the hands of parents and local communities. Recently, however, some states have passed standby legislation which would enable them to abolish compulsory education in order to avoid racial integration in their public schools. States cannot be prevented by the federal government from abolishing public education. There is no way that the federal government can force a state legislature or local community to appropriate money to operate public schools. But what about our basic question—should the decision as to whether children shall learn to read and write be properly regarded as one for local communities or even state governments to make?

The reasons why the power to make this decision was taken away from parents and later from local communities will help us to answer this question. One reason was based upon the concept of fair play for the individual child. There was growing acceptance of the belief that a child's chances in life should not depend upon whether his parents or his local community were willing and able to educate him.

Should a child's chances depend upon whether he lives in a state which is willing to educate him? Certainly not as long as we adhere to the concept of an open society, one in which the individual's chances are not determined by fortuitous factors. As far as the individual child is concerned, the extent to which his state government is willing to provide him with an education is as much a fortuitous matter as the socioeconomic status of his parents or the educational values of his local community.

Consider the problem from a social standpoint instead of an individual one. We are an extremely mobile people. Most of us eventually move away from the community in which we received our education. In the year ending in April, 1958, 30,800,000 Americans changed their residence. Over 11,000,000 moved from one county to another; about half this number moved to a different state. Thus, on the average, every American moves to a different state two times during his life. Under these circumstances, does it make sense to insist that the citizens of one state have no right to insist upon literacy for the children of other states? Today, we plead for federal aid to education in order to equalize opportunities between states. Tomorrow, we could hardly contend that the federal government must stand by idly while a state legislature compounded the inequity by depriving children of an education altogether.[1]

As an abstract proposition, it has always been clear that it is undemocratic to permit educational opportunity to be determined by circumstances of race, geographical location, or economic status. It has also been clear that our national welfare was dependent upon the extent to which individual talents were able to flourish, regardless of their social, economic, racial, or geographical origins. Neither the ideal of equality of opportunity nor the fact of our interdependence is new. What is new is the urgency of these things. Proposals for federal aid to education in order to equalize educational opportunities between states have been ignored by Congress for generations. The same proposals, advanced as a counterpoise to Russian scientific progress, are now regarded as insufficient by panic-stricken congressmen who never supported them on equalitarian grounds.

Some idea of the bankruptcy of local control of education may be seen in the statistics concerning selective service registrants disquali-

---

[1] My argument treats control of education by the states as local control of education. Fundamentally, this identification is sound although people do not now think of control at the state level as local control. It is only a matter of time before they do so, and then the control of education at the state level will go the way of control at the parental and community levels. In point of time, the decline of community control over broad educational policy will precede the decline of state control over it, but the same forces that undermine the one will eventually undermine the other.

fied for failure to pass mental tests. In 1956 the lowest rate of rejection for failure was in Montana, where 2.5 per cent of the registrants failed these tests. The highest rate was in Mississippi, where 44.9 per cent of the registrants failed the tests. In ten states, fewer than one out of every twenty registrants failed to pass; in eleven other states, one or more out of every four registrants failed to pass.

The vast differences among the states in the rate of disqualification are not due solely to the differences in the quality of their school systems. A registrant educated in Montana might take his selective service tests in Mississippi or vice versa. The statistics on rejection include the failures to pass because of inherited mental deficiency, and there are other causes for such failure over which the schools have no control. Nevertheless, the differences between the states cannot be explained solely by noneducational causes. Because some states and communities provide a decent minimum education for only a small minority of their children, we must, in all states, draft persons who, for family or occupational reasons, ought not to be in the armed services at all. This is only a small part of the exorbitant price we are paying for local control of education. The intellectual smog that has obscured our grasp of this fact is being cleared away once and for all by such dramatic events as the riots in Little Rock and the Russian conquests of space.

LOCAL CONTROL AND TOTALITARIAN CONTROL

The prevailing point of view is that anything but local control of education, with perhaps a few concessions made to control at the state level, would be a step toward totalitarianism. This view is profoundly mistaken. Our present system of local control is far more conducive to totalitarianism than a national system of schools would be. I know that this statement is not acceptable to the overwhelming majority of the American people, including the teachers, but I am willing to stand on it.

The assertion that our educational system tends toward totalitarian-

ism seems absurd on its face. A totalitarian system is one which de-
delops a massive uniformity of outlook. It is based upon a policy of intellectual protection for a point of view that cannot stand the test of
free discussion. We have a multitude of schools of all denominations
or no denomination at all. Among the teachers and students in our
public schools, there are adherents to every major political, economic,
and religious point of view. What could be further from totalitarianism
than this?

In most states the purposes and the content of education are left to
local school boards to determine. Undoubtedly, there are some constitutional limits to the purposes for which communities may operate
public schools. However, these limits have never been spelled out,
and there is great latitude in what a community might require of its
schools. Since the purposes of education are set forth locally, the predominant groups in the community tend to establish purposes which
accord with their particular religious, political, economic, or social
points of view. As a practical matter, therefore, local control results in
the same kind of intellectual protectionism that characterizes schools
in totalitarian countries.

The basic problem is not that communities define the purpose of
education to be the acceptance of the Protestant faith or unswerving
devotion to the single tax or the inculcation of the tenets of the Democratic party. Some communities have not blinked at adopting purposes
as sectarian as these, but this is not where the problem lies. Even where
a community accepts the most liberal educational purposes for its
public schools, its interpretation of what intermediate objectives and
what educational programs fulfil these purposes may have the same
stultifying effect as outright adherence to a sectarian purpose. Every
pressure group is for the general welfare, but each has its own version
of what measures do in fact promote the general welfare. Similarly,
every pressure group is for a liberal or a democratic education, but has
a special version of what intermediate objectives and what educational
programs lead to this result.

What is crucial is that, at the local level, it is relatively easy for a
preponderant group to enforce a policy of intellectual protectionism for

its sacred cows. Thus the white majorities in Southern communities exclude instruction that is critical of racial segregation. Communities in which fundamentalist sects predominate exclude instruction [favorable to] evolution. Some communities have prohibited the study of the United Nations or of UNESCO. Ours is a heterogeneous country, but in most communities the predominant racial, religious, economic, or political groups are able to veto whatever in the school program displeases them.

Looking at our system as a whole and seeing the existence of public schools teaching diverse doctrines, one might infer that our schools are free. We do not readily recognize the totalitarianism implicit in our situation because not all schools protect the same dogmas. Nonetheless, a diversity of schools based upon intellectual protectionism for different dogmas does not constitute a "democratic school system." At least, it does not do so if "democratic" refers to the education actually provided in these schools instead of to the legal structure which encourages a variety of one-sided programs.

The diversity of our undemocratic schools is not the only factor which maintains the fiction that we have a democratic school system. No matter how successful a group may be in excluding certain facts and ideas from the public schools, television, radio, and other mass media are almost certain to expose students to these facts and ideas. The power structure of American society is such that no single group is able to enforce or to indoctrinate its dogmas on the population as a whole. People look at this situation and say "Our schools have kept us free." They should say "Our freedoms have survived our schools."

THE MYTHOLOGY OF LOCAL CONTROL

Many persons believe that public education was not made a federal responsibility in the Constitution because the founding fathers feared the potentialities for dictatorship in a federal school system. Actually, education was not included as a federal function in the Constitution because the idea of free public education had not even occurred to the founding fathers. At the time of the American Revolution, the concept of universal public education was receiving attention for the first time and then only from a few frontier thinkers. Our decentralized school system was not an inspired stroke of genius but a historical accident, resulting from the fact that the ideal of free public education for all became widely accepted only long after the American Revolution.

Our schools have never been an important foundation of our free society. Our freedom is partly due to a separation of powers which enables us to transact public business reasonably well while avoiding excessive subjection to government officials. Perhaps for this reason we tend to regard the diffusion of power over our schools as an essential element of our free society. But adherence to the general principle that we must avoid excessive concentration of power does not automatically justify every separation or diffusion of it. Everything depends upon the circumstances—what powers are involved, who is to wield them, and so on. It is preposterous to think that merely because their political genius was expressed through a constitution embodying a remarkably successful separation of powers, the founding fathers would align themselves today with the supporters of local control of education.

People are seldom aware of the non-public character of public education. They tend to regard it as a legal concept and to neglect it as an educational concept. However, the ideal of public education means more than having some governmental unit—local, state, or federal—provide the funds to operate schools. Public education has a referent in the quality of education as well as in its financial basis. The qualitative referent is an education in which the search for truth is carried on regardless of what empires topple, interests collapse, or heads roll. Without this, public education is a delusion, as dangerous as the notion that mere government ownership of the means of production will automatically result in their operation for the public welfare instead of for private interests. The socialization of a service at any level of government is no automatic guarantee that the service will be performed in the public interest. The "new class" should have ended all of our illusions on this score.

Public schools, then, are not necessarily infused with a public spirit. Likewise, the fact that a school is privately controlled does not mean that its program is necessarily sectarian in character. The program of some privately controlled institutions such as Harvard is more free of parochial limitations than the programs in most publicly controlled institutions. In short, we cannot assume anything about the educational program of a school merely from a knowledge of whether the school is publicly or privately controlled. Nor can we infer that the educational program of a school is undemocratic merely because the school is locally controlled or that it is democratic merely because the schools are part of a national system. The relationship between the legal status of a school and the quality of its educational program is never one of strict logical implication.

The system of legal controls under which schools operate is only one factor which serves to shape their educational programs. However, it is an extremely important factor. Because a national system of controls is more likely to broaden the purposes of education and to preserve the professional autonomy of teachers, it is much more likely to provide a truly liberal education than a multitude of totalitarian systems under local control. It is a striking fact that in England, which has a national system of education, the teachers are on record as being opposed to local control of education precisely because they fear that it would undermine their professional autonomy. Meanwhile, teachers in the United States, who lack any substantial measure of professional autonomy, continue to act as if local control must be maintained inviolate lest academic freedom (which they do not possess) be imperiled.

The decentralization of our schools is often justified by an appeal to the experimental nature of this situation. We supposedly have fifty state school systems, each of which is free to try something different from the others. Each state has delegated considerable power to local school boards, which supposedly multiplies the experimental possibilities. This is thought to make for progress, since each state and each system is not only free to try something new but is free to benefit from the experience of other systems.

There is no doubt that some change for the better occurs in this way. Nevertheless, such enormous decentralization cannot be justified on the grounds that the different school systems constitute a vast pool of educational experimentation. The different schools do not constitute experiments except in the loosest sense of the word. They do not operate under conditions carefully controlled for purposes of analysis and comparison. They just operate.

Much of the experience of different systems is valuable only on the premise that education should be a state or local responsibility. A school board may indeed be interested in how another community put over a school bond campaign. But if funds came from the federal government, the experience of this or that school system in raising money would be academic.

The truth is that local control of education has obstructed rather than facilitated educational research. By and large, only large urban systems allocate funds to research. Even in these cases, the research is generally limited to problems that are of local concern. Very few school systems support any research that is even theoretically of more than local interest. . . .

In this connection, it is interesting to note that one of the most persistent and most pathetic arguments against a national school system is that such a system would not permit experimentation in the schools. The assumption seems to be that centralized administration is necessarily non-experimental or that it necessarily insists upon uniformity down to every detail. Actually, several federal departments which have centralized administration also subsidize programs of research which dwarf anything we have ever seen in education. The departments of Defense and Agriculture illustrate the possibilities.

If the present structure of American education is not conducive to the support of research, it is well designed to obstruct the utilization of it. On this subject, we need only to compare the lag between the discovery and the application of knowledge in education and the lag in other professions.

In the legal profession, important developments such as Supreme Court decisions are taken into account by all lawyers within a very short period of time. When the Bureau of Internal Revenue makes a ruling which affects a substantial number of tax returns, the accountants generally absorb it within a matter of months. Everyone is familiar with the short period of time between the discovery of an effective polio vaccine and its use by doctors everywhere. In education, however, the lags between discovery and practice are scandalous. These lags are reflected in what is taught as well as in how teachers teach their subjects.

The average person is little aware how long it takes for important new knowledge to be reflected in the public school curriculum. The diffusion of teacher education and of the curriculum is so great that it often takes decades before teachers realize the need to add or delete a subject or to make radical changes in the content of an accepted subject. Even after this hurdle has been passed, tens of thousands of school boards must be persuaded that these changes are desirable. "Go ye therefore and persuade all those who are affected by the decision"— thus reads the Word in textbooks on school administration. The Curriculum Committee of the PTA, the school board, the parents, the students—all must have a voice in a decision which affects them. An infinite number of banana peels lie between the professional decision to modify the curriculum and actual practice in the school.

THE BREAKDOWN OF LOCAL SUPPORT
FOR PUBLIC EDUCATION

The case against local control of education becomes more compelling when we consider the practical problems involved in introducing basic changes that require heavy expenditures. In recent years, our high schools have been severely criticized for their real or alleged neglect of science. For the sake of argument, suppose that we required every high-school student who has the ability to do college work to take three years of physics during his high-school career. At this point, consider only the practical problems involved in implementing this recommendation. How would we get from the status quo to a situation in which all these high-school students take three years of physics? Regardless of whether this particular change is desirable, consider its implementation solely from the standpoint of the difficulties of making any basic curriculum reforms under the present system.

There are over 21,000 high schools across the country. In 1956, only 12,000 of these schools offered one full year's work in physics. As late as 1954, 50 per cent of all schools having tenth-grade pupils did not offer physics at all. These were usually the smaller schools, but it is interesting to note that only one-fourth of all high-school students in 1954 took as much as one full year of physics before graduation. We are thus confronted by thousands of school boards which have seen fit to offer one year's work or none at all in physics. Each board must now be persuaded, one by one, to make drastic changes in its curriculum. Since it is unlikely that the additional work in physics will simply be added to the present curriculum, each board must make its own decision about what subjects shall be reduced or eliminated. Each board must decide what to do with the teachers in subjects to be eliminated.

Even assuming that most school boards could be convinced that more work in physics is desirable, can they be persuaded to implement such a change? If a school is to offer three years of physics instead of one or none, extensive remodeling would almost invariably be required. There would have to be substantial expenditures for new laboratory equipment and supplies. Just how substantial these would have to be is evident from a survey made in March, 1957, by the NEA's Research Division, which covered the needs for instructional equipment in high-school science and mathematics classes. More than half the schools responding to the inquiry from the Research Division reported that they did not even have direct electric current in their physics laboratory. Less than 15 per cent of the schools reporting had a calculator available for mathematics courses. Only one school in five had a graph board in every mathematics classroom; about two out of every five did not have a graph board in any mathematics classroom. The report indicated that 57 cents was the average per pupil expenditure for supplies and consumable equipment in science classrooms.

Before most high schools could offer three years of physics, local school boards would have to adopt salary schedules much more attractive than the prevailing ones. Even though physics is now offered for only one year in the majority of schools which offer it at all, there is already a large and growing shortage of physics teachers. It would be pleasant to think that school boards which have heretofore balked at making minimal expenditures for physics instruction will suddenly be inspired to vote the necessary taxes for an adequate program. Unfortunately, the odds are overwhelmingly against such a development. . . .

It is unlikely that in the next few decades we shall have a federal school system covering the entire country. Such a development would occur only if the failures of states and communities to carry out their educational responsibilities were to be brought home dramatically to the American people by some such event as the abolition of public education in the South. I am convinced, however, that we are about to move rapidly toward a national system of education. What is certain is not the form but the fact that we shall have a much more centralized system of education in the future than we have had in the past. The idea that the present chaos in education is the price one has to pay for living in a democracy, or the even more nonsensical notion that the prevailing educational chaos is one of the foundations of democracy, will linger on but without any real force in our society.

Unquestionably, the most important barrier to a centralized system of public education is the notion that any such system would be "totalitarian" or "undemocratic." We are warned that a centralized system would provide an opportunity for one particular group, say a political party, to seize control of the schools, and by indoctrinating its point of view, maintain itself in power. Since this line of reasoning is undoubtedly the basis of our fear of a centralized school system, I wish to consider it at some length . . .

Those who think along these lines usually point to Soviet Russia to illustrate the dangers of a centralized system of education. But it should be obvious that one cannot assume that a centralized system per se is more likely to be totalitarian than our own. England, France, and the Scandinavian countries all have national systems. In all of these, there is less political interference with teachers than there is in the United States. Put positively, there is more freedom to teach and to learn in all of these national school systems than there is in the over-whelming majority of schools in the United States.

In the United States, how would any particular group, be it political, religious, or economic, achieve such complete control of all schools that it could produce a generation of unthinking disciples? To develop such a generation would require complete control of our mass media. This in turn would presuppose fairly complete control of the govern-ment. Any pressure group which could achieve such controls would have no need to control the schools. Indeed, it could safely permit schools to operate as they do now, preparing generations of civic illiterates who firmly believe they have fulfilled the highest obligations of citizenship when they have flipped a lever in a voting booth.

We already have many schools supported by the federal govern-ment. What evidence is available indicates that the teachers in these federal schools have more, not less, freedom than teachers elsewhere. For example, there is as much or more academic freedom at Howard University, which is supported by federal funds, than there is at the overwhelming majority of institutions of higher education.

People are opposed to a centralized system of schools for many rea-sons, not all of them noble ones. Some of the opposition comes from private school interests which would not share in the federal funds which will undergird such a system. We need private schools, but the arguments which some private school spokesmen make against federal aid or a federal school system are unrealistic. Private educational insti-tutions whose *raison d'être* is to keep the faithful from being exposed to heretical points of view oppose federal aid to education on the grounds that such aid would mean mass conformity and indoctrination. The free and independent mind which these institutions claim to nurture is what some of them fear above everything else.

Nonetheless, it must be conceded that many people have a gnawing fear of a centralized school system which is quite unrelated to any thought that their particular points of view might not survive in such a system. These people do not fear for their points of view in an atmosphere of intellectual freedom. They would not exclude a fair presentation of other points of view in the schools even if they had the power to do so. Their fear is for the integrity of the system, not for the fate of their particular views on political, economic, religious, racial, or other controversial issues.

Ironically, these fears often are based upon experiences with local control. Every inadequacy of a local board reinforces rather than weakens the fear of a federal system. Under the present system, the worst blunders are confined to a limited area. What would happen, people ask, if a national school board or federal school administrator were to engage in the educational follies which characterize some local school boards?

The answer is that it would be a calamity, but the more we centralize our school system (up to a point, of course), the less likely it is that such a calamity will occur. The crucial point is that at the national level, no one group has the kind of power to interfere with the educational program that one sees every day under a system of local control. The rabble rousers who can successfully frighten a large city school system like that of Los Angeles into dropping an essay contest on the United Nations would not have a chance in a federal school system. Nor would the more powerful pressure groups be able to shape the educational program to their own ends. None has sufficient power by itself to do this. Each would be watched and checked if necessary by all the others if it attempted any massive interference with the educational program or with educational personnel. Since no non-professional group would have the power to dictate the educational program or personnel policies, and since teachers would not be subject to local censorship, the teachers would be free to discuss points of view which are now proscribed by local boards of education.

The fact, if it be a fact, that no pressure group would be able to dominate a centralized system might not sound very appealing. Would the integrity of such a system rest upon a balance of power among large national pressure groups, all of whom would subvert the school program to their own ends if they could? If so, what assurance is there that tomorrow, or the day after, the balance of power will not change so as to provide one of these groups, or a combination of them, with the opportunity they seek?

If by "assurance" is meant an ironclad guarantee, of course there is none. We are choosing between practical alternatives, not between mathematical solutions, one of which is the perfect answer. It is local control of education which provides a greater opportunity for national pressure groups to dominate the educational programs of the public schools, on a *national* basis. The reason is that local school boards are unable to withstand the pressures which can be generated by powerful national organizations which know what they want from our schools. However, there is another factor which seems to me to clinch the case for a centralized school system, at least insofar as the criterion of academic freedom is concerned. This factor is the impact which centralization is likely to have upon teachers' organizations and the role which they would play in protecting the integrity of a centralized public school system.

11

Statement on Control

MAX RAFFERTY

Mr. Rafferty is California's State Superintendent of Public Instruction. He was superintendent of the La Cañada, California, School District at the time this statement was made.

High schools have always had a lot more local autonomy than elementary schools in California.

I would like to see the high schools retain their autonomy, and the elementary schools increase theirs.

California education is and should continue to be a Federal concern, a State function, and a local enterprise. In the past, the national government has provided certain types of aids and inducements to local education in the form of *specific* grants for *specialized* purposes relating to the general welfare. These have been largely unaccompanied by controls, and the results have been generally good. No one seriously opposes this sort of Federal interest and aid.

But the rub comes in connection with *generalized* aid to education, and this is the type embodied in the legislation presented to the last two sessions of Congress. Generalized financing of this sort in areas other than education has invariably brought with it some form of Federal control, and for obvious reasons. The national government cannot and will not appropriate and distribute huge sums of money for nonspecific purposes without retaining a large say in how it is to be spent. For this reason, I am opposed to the type of Federal aid to education exemplified in the bills most recently to appear before Congress.

The State has an historic and legal interest in education which is in-

From "Symposium on the Control of the Schools" in the *Journal of Secondary Education*, May 1962. Reprinted by permission.

disputable. It must make reasonably sure that each generation is brought up under such minimum standards of instruction as will insure the continuance and the improvement of the State itself. In California, this interest has been traditionally manifested in the person of the Superintendent of Public Instruction and through the office of the State Department of Education. The proper functions of that Department are and always have been the threefold ones of Leadership, Research, and Service. Nowhere in that triad is to be found the word "control." To the extent that the Department *controls* our textbooks, *controls* our curriculum, and *controls* our personnel, it is behaving wrongly and dangerously.

The greatest peril to local district autonomy, however, lies in the growing tendency on the part of the California legislature to confuse *interest* with *interference*—to pass laws which interfere seriously with matters which have since the founding of our State been considered the proper concern of the local school district.

There is the new law compelling districts to devote a certain percentage of their budgets to salaries for certain kinds of teachers. I happen to have been superintendent during the past seven years of two school districts which paid among the highest teacher salaries in the State, but this enviable goal was not reached as a result of legislative mandate. As a consequence of this new and hasty legislation, many school boards now paying above-average salaries but not exactly fulfilling the percentage requirement are instructing their administrators not to put more money into salaries, but to put less money into other budget categories. They are telling them not to hire guidance people and counselors, and psychometrists because these salaries don't count in the specified percentage category.

Then there is the new polio law. If it really required children to get their shots, it would probably justify having to add all the clerical help which the requirement makes inevitable. But if you have read the law, you know it does nothing of the sort. All it really makes necessary is the spending of a lot more time by local school administrators who already are spending too little time on educational matters.

These are but two examples of a trend which, if allowed to go unchecked, will eventually bring to California the essential features of a European-style, centralized state educational system. It has become the clear and positive duty of the State Superintendent and his Department to oppose this trend, not to encourage it. In the years to come, he must tell the legislature and the people, over and over again if need be, how education in this State has prospered under the stimulus of local interest and willingness to experiment, and how it has lost its impetus whenever it has been forced to chafe under the dead hand of bureaucratic centralization.

For local autonomy cannot feed and grow on mere lip-service. It must be nurtured by citizens who value it, by school people who who respect it, and by a State Superintendent who measures a school district's right to exist not by its size alone, however small, but by the kind of education it sees fit to provide its children, and by the kind of young people it graduates. Unless such leadership is provided—vigorously and soon—the trend now far advanced will achieve its ultimate objective of complete control. If leadership of this sort can be exerted, we may yet succeed in arresting a tendency not yet arrived at the point of no return, and we may emerge upon the sunny uplands of a future of free children and free teachers, working and living together in free schools.

12

The Rights of Teachers

THE NEW REPUBLIC

Although college professors, regional accreditation agencies, state departments of education and even state legislatures have for years made sporadic protests about the way local school boards choose to run "their" school systems, these boards remain a popular, almost sacrosanct, symbol of democracy. Teachers and others who have thought that these boards were behind the times have turned to state legislatures for relief, either in the form of coercive legislation or in the form of seductive subsidies. In most states the legislature has been willing to grant some of these appeals, laying down the law about who can and cannot be hired, what can and cannot be taught, and what minimal standards will be exacted in return for state aid. But because most legislatures, like school boards, are composed of civic leaders familiar with local rather than wider needs—observers with a broader perspective have remained dissatisfied. Some have turned hopefully to Congress; others have argued that the teachers themselves would have to take matters in hand. But because the giant National Education Association was dominated by administrators and was convinced for this and other reasons that local boards of education were the incarnation of Jeffersonian wisdom, teachers have rarely been willing to use coercion when persuasion failed.

Last year, however, the NEA finally began to perk up. Its tiny rival, the American Federation of Teachers (an AFL-CIO affiliate

From *The New Republic*, June 1, 1963. Copyright © 1963 by Harrison-Blaine, Inc. Reprinted by permission.

distinguished from the NEA mainly by its willingness to strike when employers proved obstinate), had used a series of strikes to win recognition as the bargaining agent for New York City's 40,000 teachers, and the NEA feared inroads in other communities where teachers are sufficiently sophisticated to realize that respectability is no substitute for power. So the NEA approved a program of "professional sanctions" to be used when necessary.

The first test came last year at Little Lake, California, a district which the militant California Teachers Association had already sought to blacklist because the local board tried to run it like a piece of corporate property. Resignations and blacklisting hurt Little Lake badly at first, but then the district got national publicity and many teachers eager to move to California wrote Little Lake seeking jobs. All vacancies were filled when school opened in September. The teachers then took a new tack, asking Little Lake voters to eject two of the most offensive board members. The voters obliged last April.

The next test for sanctions will come in Utah, where the Republican Governor has refused to accept the $24 million spending proposals for education of an official commission. The Governor asked for and got only $12 million from the legislature (*NR*, April 13). Utah teachers have voted overwhelmingly not to renew their contracts for next year unless the Governor recants, which he shows no signs of doing.

If the teachers close the schools and win the right to negotiate with the state on the terms under which they will be reopened, the school boards' freedom of decision would be reduced in much the same way as corporate power has been limited by the unions' right to strike. Nor was this fact lost on the National Association of School Boards when it met last month in Denver. After hearing half a dozen speeches on the Utah situation and discussing the matter interminably, the NASB asserted once again that local authority over schools and teachers was "established by law" and "may not be delegated to others." Endorsing the position of the Governor and the Utah School Boards Association, the NASB resolved that, "The Governor and the people of Utah should continue to resist those actions and pressures which would deprive school boards of the legal responsibilities that have proven basic to the educational welfare of children."

However, one incidental fact seems to have been ignored: the Utah School Boards Association itself confessed the inability of the local boards to run their schools when it joined last year in the report urging that the state legislature spend $24 million to solve Utah's school problems. Local authorities, it was evidently felt, could not or would not provide the money.

Local control over education, then, is not even at issue in Utah. The only issue is whether state control should be tempered by the needs and desires of teachers as well as the opinion of local school boards.

13

First Steps in Educational Reform

ARTHUR E. BESTOR

Mr. Bestor, a professor of history at the University of Washington, formerly taught at the University of Illinois. He has been president of the Council for Basic Education and his two books, Educational Wastelands *(1953) and* The Restoration of Learning *(1955), are frequently referred to in debates on education.*

. . . The aims of secondary education can be properly and safely defined only if all aspects of the life of the nation are taken into account. The yawning gap that exists today between those who are actually using intellectual training—in the sciences and professions, in business and public life—and those who are supposed to be laying its foundations in the public schools is, in my judgment, the fundamental cause of the unsatisfactory state of American public education today.

Scholars and scientists must bear much of the blame for permitting this situation to develop. They should have exercised constant vigilance over developments in secondary education. They should have brought their views on public school policy forcefully to the attention of the public and the legislatures. They should have resisted the debasement of college entrance requirements and the seizure by departments of education of control over the training of teachers. They should have provided, through their learned societies, continuous, organized leadership in the process of developing and strengthening the secondary school curriculum. The people expect intellectual guidance from the scientific and scholarly world in matters pertaining to education at every level. It has not been furnished in the recent past. It must be furnished in the future.

From *Educational Wastelands* by Arthur E. Bestor (Urbana, Illinois: University of Illinois Press, 1953). Reprinted by permission.

The first step, as I see it, must be for the learned world to create an agency entirely its own, through which it can state its views on public school policy independently and unitedly. It must be ready at all times to express a considered judgment concerning the intellectual soundness of the programs that are offered in the elementary and secondary schools. It must address the public directly, for they make the final decisions on educational policy. And it must speak with a voice unmistakably its own, not allowing its words to be smothered or twisted or censored by others. If scholars will create for themselves an organ through which they can expound their educational principles with clarity and force, I am confident that they will be listened to with respect.

The basis for such unity indubitably exists. Within the learned world there are differences of opinion, of course, but they are minor differences. Mathematicians and anthropologists may approach their problems in quite different ways; biologists and linguists may not completely understand each other's objectives; historians and sociologists may quarrel over questions of methodology. There will always be—there *must* always be—such differences, for they are the signs of intellectual vigor and of freedom. But scholars and scientists must never lose sight of the overarching fact that they are partners in a single great enterprise—the greatest that engages the attention of mankind. They share a common purpose: the advancement of understanding and the augmentation of that intellectual power upon which mankind depends for its very existence. They share a common respect for knowledge, for the disciplined mind, for independent, objective, disinterested inquiry. Each of them, whatever his specialized interest, must recognize at all times that these common aims and values are far more significant than any points of difference. Each must remember that it is these common aims and values which anti-intellectualism is seeking to undermine. Should it triumph, no field of science or learning will be exempt from disaster.

This sense of common purpose must be embodied in an organization capable of effective action. It is idle to think that scholars and scientists, divided a hundred ways by professional ties within their specialized fields, can exert a real influence upon public educational policy until they present a united front on the matter. They have learned to do so in meeting other problems that confront them. They look to a single great organization, the American Association of University Professors, to safeguard the standards of the profession. They bring the collective wisdom of the learned world to bear upon the broad problems of research through the great federations of learned societies: the National Research Council, the American Council of Learned Societies, and the Social Science Research Council. Such agencies take account of the fact that scholars and scientists can spare little time from their own exacting tasks to undertake responsibilities of a general nature. These societies and councils are organized to function continuously with a permanent staff, and they require of each individual professional man only a limited amount and period of service on working committees. An organization of this kind, I believe, should be created to represent scholarly opinion on public school questions. In the appendix [to *Educational Wastelands*] I reprint the text of a proposal which I have made for a Permanent Scientific and Scholarly Commission on Secondary Education to perform this function.

The commission should be established by the learned societies of the nation, and by them alone. The reason for keeping the commission independent of all political and economic pressure groups, and hence of all nonprofessional associations, is obvious. The exclusion of educational associations is more controversial. This exclusion, while deliberate, is not intended as a gesture of hostility. It is merely a recognition of two facts: that the professional educationists are already thoroughly organized and vocal, and that scholars clearly differ with them on many vital issues of public educational policy. I propose a separate organization of scholars and scientists, not as a repudiation of the ultimate ideal of co-operation between educationists and the learned world in public school matters, but as a means to that end. No true co-operation is likely to take place between two groups, one of which is well organized and the other not. If there is to be genuine agreement, each side must feel that its point of view has been clearly stated and consistently maintained throughout all discussions and negotiations. The professional educationists already have associations to present and defend their position. If scholars are to exert influence in favor of the things they believe in, they must be responsibly represented by men in whose judgment they have full confidence and they must back these men up in an organized way. Then a real meeting of minds with respect to public education can take place, with assurance that the decisions will be concurred in and supported on all sides. Collaboration, to be effective, must rest upon some such firm foundation as this.

An agency of the kind proposed must make clear to the public the reasons why scholarly and scientific opinion ought to be taken into account in the making of public school policy. Educationists have so persistently emphasized the problems of childhood when defining the function of education that they have caused the public almost to forget that the schools have an obligation not merely to the children actually enrolled in them, but to the nation as a whole and to all its mature citizens. Scholars must emphasize the latter obligation, and must point out the unsoundness of public school policies that jeopardize the rest of the nation's educational, intellectual, and scientific activities. . . .

Once the point of view of the learned world on public educational policy is made clear to citizens at large, I am confident that they will give it general and effective support. The time will then have to come to effect a general revision of state legislation and state administrative procedures with respect to public school matters.

14

Pro and Con: Should There Be a National Board of Education?

EDGAR FULLER AND
STERLING M. McMURRIN

Mr. Fuller is Executive Secretary of the Council of Chief State School Officers, an independent corporation. Mr. McMurrin, former U. S. Commissioner of Education, is a professor of philosophy at the University of Utah.

YES!

BY EDGAR FULLER

Much progress has been made in the government of American education in establishing teaching on a professional basis free from partisan interference. In local public schools, considerable freedom from partisan politics has been widely achieved, but at the same time the schools have been kept close to the people. Here nonpartisan boards of laymen determine general educational policies and employ professional educators to administer the programs of instruction. The school board is legally a state agency, locally selected but operating under delegated authority from the state, and as such usually enjoys necessary protection against partisan municipal politics.

A trend toward the nonpartisan board of laymen with the appointed professional officer is also clear at the state level. In recent years states having this system have increased from eight to 23. Many others have developed strong traditions of political nonpartisanship in education. Public and private institutions of higher education also exercise much institutional autonomy on a professional basis. The federal government is increasingly alone in treating education as merely another unit of general government under a political chain of command.

An independent Federal Education Agency would remove influences that now handicap fulfillment of an appropriate role in education by the federal government. It could attract better professional personnel, develop nonpolitical policies and traditions for the agency, and bring the educational role of the federal government into harmony with more acceptable patterns of educational policies and practices.

These patterns call for increased federal nonpartisanship in the spirit that prevails in the state and local control of our best schools and colleges. They require more adequate federal understanding of the nature of state and local autonomy in education, consistently reinforced by improved federal cooperation to maintain it. Within these patterns the people would gain confidence in the Federal Education Agency and in the federal programs it administers. Its leadership would become more respected and trusted, because undesirable political entanglements that are inevitable in the current organization would be avoided.

Creation of such an agency would transfer policy decisions in education from the Secretary of the Department of Health, Education, and Welfare to a Board of Education having abundant opportunity to deliberate on the educational policies of the agency. It would raise the status of the Commissioner because basic policies of the agency and its administration would be made clear after deliberation by the Board on the basis of factually supported recommendations of the Commissioner. The Commissioner would become the top professional administrator for education without being subject to reversal by higher administrators with training and interests in other fields.

The proposed change would free the Commissioner for educational leadership. The Secretary of Health, Education, and Welfare and his staff would no longer make decisions in education on the basis of political reasons or pet ideas of their own. Examples of these have become more frequent recently.

A statement by retiring HEW Secretary A. A. Ribicoff is significant. "The man in my job," the Secretary said, "wears 20 different hats a day, runs 110 different programs, and is responsible for 75 separate budget items." The federal agency for education should not be counted among the programs the busy Secretary runs. The President of the United States is even more overworked. He should be able to learn more about education in less time through contacts with a Board and Commissioner than through a busy political middleman.

So we propose that Congress create by statute an independent agency consisting of a Board of Education and a Commissioner of Education. This Federal Education Agency should be limited by law to the following functions:

1. Those already exercised by the Office of Education and by the Commissioner of Education.

2. Those taken away from the U. S. Office of Education by the Department of Health, Education, and Welfare and its predecessor agencies, such as the education library, legal services for education, etc.

3. Additional duties as may be assigned by the Congress.

The agency should be prohibited by law from exercising any direction, supervision, or control over the administration, personnel, physical facilities, curriculum or instruction in any public or private educational institution, or over any governing board of such an institution. There are obvious exceptions, such as an educational institution established, financed, and administered solely by the federal government, or federal research and development contracts made with educational institutions to achieve specific federal purposes.

The Board should be authorized by law to appoint a qualified and experienced professional educator as its executive officer and as U. S. Commissioner of Education, and to fix his term of office and compensation within limits established by law. The law should authorize the Board to exercise general control and supervision of the operation of the Federal Education Agency, acting through the Commissioner of Education as its executive officer. It should have statutory authority to organize the staff of the agency, to appoint personnel upon nomination by the Commissioner in accord with Civil Service and other general personnel regulations of the government, to prepare and present the budget of the agency to the appropriate executive and legislative federal authorities, and to exercise other powers necessary to perform the functions of the agency.

Proposals for an independent agency for education have often been adversely affected by disagreements about how board members shall be selected. National election is usually regarded as impracticable. Election by state boards of education is a possibility, but they vary widely. A few states do not have such boards in any true sense. Policy of the Council of Chief State School Officers since 1948 has called for appointment made by the President on a nonpartisan basis for long overlapping terms.

Balancing theory and practicality poses two compromises that should be considered. One is Senate confirmation of board members. The other is to make the appointments "bipartisan" rather than "nonpartisan," as most people believe they would be anyway.

We need to define the federal role and to improve administration and underlying policies affecting federal programs in education. An independent Federal Education Agency is needed to accomplish these purposes. It would be great for educational progress if it could be established in any of the alternative ways we have mentioned, or in any other way that would permit it to operate appropriately.

NO!

BY STERLING M. MCMURRIN

Local and state boards of education control the public schools of America. They have the authority to determine what is taught and who teaches it. They would hardly seem to be appropriate models to be followed by the federal government in a nation that places a high value on decentralized local and state control of the schools and is fundamentally opposed to federal control. Nothing would be more damaging to our way of life than the development, whether intentional or not, of a monolithic national educational structure that would standardize the nation's public education and thereby destroy the pluralistic foundations of our society and culture.

Those who advocate a National Board of Education seem to ground their argument in at least three considerations:

1. That it would remove the Office of Education from political involvements and political pressure.

2. That it would overcome bureaucratic control of federal educational activities.

3. That it would bring order out of the confusion of federal educational activities.

These arguments are attractive but they are misleading and do not give the full picture. Here's why:

1. Any arrangement that would move the Office of Education outside the mainstream of the processes of government would be damaging to the status of education in the nation and would weaken the cause of education with the Congress. What is clearly needed is a movement in the direction of greater recognition of education and an even closer involvement of the Office with the White House and Congress than it has at present. Those who argue for a National Board of Education seem often to be quite uninformed about the nature of the political involvements of the Office of Education, apparently assuming that it is subject to undesirable political pressures. In the performance of its professional advisory function to the Congress and the Administration on matters of legislation and policy, the Office of Education is protected from unwarranted political interference by the Civil Service status of its staff and the enabling statute for the Department of Health, Education, and Welfare which gives it considerable professional autonomy. Insofar as support for American education depends on federal legislation, it is necessary that all sides be heard and that educational issues become matters of Congressional concern. Laws are not made in a political vacuum.

2. There is no reason for supposing that a National Board of Education would change the character of the Office of Education in the matter of bureaucratic versus lay control. The Office is staffed by people

of professional educational competence and through a network of "outside" advisory committees and panels it is kept responsive to the opinions and attitudes of the lay public as well as the educational profession. Moreover, whatever organizational structure exists, the Congress will continue to be responsible for enacting educational legislation and making appropriations. To remove the office from close involvement with the White House, making it subject to a policy-making board rather than to the President, would place education in a disadvantaged position in matters of legislation and appropriations.

It is apparently supposed by some that a National Board of Education would be more representative of the people than are the President and the Congress. This argument is so strained that it hardly deserves serious mention.

3. There is no reason for believing that the creation of a National Board of Education would provide an ideal instrument for coordinating federal activities relating to education. These activities will always be in great variety and associated with a diversity of agencies. Consolidation and coordination can best be achieved through an agency that is an integral part of the central Administration and is responsive immediately to the President. It should be recognized, also, that the proposal for a single board governing educational policies for all levels of education does not conform to our traditional structure of educational administration.

Finally, the role of the federal government in education is quite different from that of state and local governments, and the nation should not be looked upon as a great expanded school district. The Commissioner of Education is not a school superintendent for the nation, and the staff of the Office of Education is not analogous to the central professional staff of a school district. The proposal for a National Board of Education seems to suggest that this is the case. There is danger for American education in this proposal, the danger of encouraging a single standardized educational program for all our schools, and a single instrument for their control.

15

What Can We Do?

H. G. RICKOVER

Admiral Rickover is Assistant Chief for Nuclear Propulsion of the U. S. Naval Bureau of Ships.

The past months have been a period of rude awakening for us. Our eyes and ears have been assaulted by the most distressing sort of news about Russia's giant strides in technology, based on the extraordinary success she has had in transforming her educational system. All but in ruins twenty-five years ago, it is today an efficient machine for producing highly competent scientists and engineers—many more than we can hope to train through our own educational system which we have so long regarded with pride and affection.

We are slowly thinking our way through a thicket of bitter disappointment and humiliating truth to the realization that America's predominant educational philosophy is as hopelessly outdated today as the horse and buggy. Nothing short of a complete reorganization of American education, preceded by a revolutionary reversal of educational aims, can equip us for winning the educational race with the Russians.

Ours is a democracy. We cannot move forward faster than the majority of the people will permit us to go. But today the American people are aroused because they realize that something is fundamentally wrong with American education when a country—three-fourths illiterate a generation ago—can in twenty-five years catch up with us in so important a field of knowledge as science and engineering. In a

From the book *Education and Freedom* by H. G. Rickover (New York: E. P. Dutton, 1959). Copyright, ©, 1959, by H. G. Rickover. Reprinted by permission of E. P. Dutton & Co., Inc.

race it is of little importance how far ahead you are at the start when your opponent runs faster and the race goes on forever. A head start makes victory more certain only when the race is short.

Anxious parents who sense the ominous overtones of the news about Russian education have asked me: "What *can* we do?" I have also heard from people in all walks of life who do not have children in school but are still concerned enough to want to help and ask me *how* best to go about this. It has not been humanly possible for me to answer all these letters. My work in naval nuclear propulsion keeps me busy seven days a week and leaves me little leisure. For ten years I have hoarded my small amount of leisure and invested it in an effort to understand what went wrong with the American dream of universal education and how we might put it right again. There has been no time to answer letters, nor do I have a staff to help me in this leisure-time activity. I hope the many serious and conscientious people who never received an answer from me will take this chapter as a personal reply to their letters.

It is good to feel that one has friends when the enemies are so multi-tudinous and vociferous. In the great debate over American education, which started in earnest after the first Sputniks went aloft, there has been much evidence of a sense of outrage against the critics because they uncovered errors in judgment and in performance, and little awareness of the urgency of our educational crisis—little of the true patriotism which puts the larger issue of national survival above per-sonal sensibilities and job security. It is never pleasant to be told that one has not done his job satisfactorily. Most critics have been fair enough to place the blame not on the schools alone but on all of us. None of us is without guilt. But now that the people have awakened to the need for reform, I doubt whether reams of propaganda pamphlets, endless reiteration that all is well with our schools, or even pressure tactics will again fool the American people into believing that educa-tion can safely be left to the "professional" educators. If it be true that but yesterday our schools mirrored American mores and pleased most American parents, this is no longer so. The mood of America has changed. Our technological supremacy has been called in question and we know we have to deal with a formidable competitor. Parents are no longer satisfied with life-adjustment schools. Parental objectives no longer coincide with those professed by the progressive educationists. I doubt we can again be silenced. We are in a mood to make ourselves heard. It is tragic for our country that few of those to whom we entrust our children will face up to their past errors and join us in seeking ways to make ours the best educational system in the world.

Too long have we been discouraged from voicing discontent and offering suggestions for educational reform by being told that these are matters for the experts and which we are not competent to judge. This is a most undemocratic argument. In no other respect is democracy so clearly set apart from authoritarian forms of government than in the right and duty of each citizen to check and evaluate the performance of government, and to express his disapproval if public servants do not carry out the mandates of the people. This right and this duty are not limited to citizens having special competence equivalent to that of the public servant so criticized. We may criticize the police if they are derelict in their duties though we have no special criminological knowledge. We need not be tax experts to have strong views on taxation and to make them known in no uncertain terms. Like that of all public servants, my own work is under constant scrutiny by Congress, by my superiors, and by the press. It is work of a very technical character the details of which many of these critics may not fully comprehend, but what they can and do judge is the end product.

We render judgment every day when we buy one service rather than another; one product rather than that of a competitor. We are not interested in the philosophies animating the persons who provide the services or the manufacturers of the goods. We simply judge them by our powers as consumers. This we cannot do with public servants. Almost all of us must send our children to the schools we support with our taxes. We have no alternative; we are "captive consumers." If the end product of public education is unsatisfactory and if there is clear evidence that the reason for this sad state of affairs has something to do with the philosophies of the leaders of American education, then we are entitled to criticize and demand a change. Our educational leaders have never received a clear mandate from the American people to follow the theories of John Dewey and his disciples. We have never authorized them to change the objectives of formal education from teaching basic subjects to conditioning children for group life. Let us not be intimidated by claims of infallibility because of so-called professional status. Let us not be overly impressed by academic degrees. Not a few will turn out to have been won by such scholarly doctors' theses as, "The Technique of Estimating School Equipment Costs," "A Scale for Measuring Anterior-Posterior Posture of Ninth-Grade Boys," or "Public School Plumbing Equipment." Whatever their academic worth, such degrees open positions of influence in the school system which allow their possessors to decide whether a school will provide a solid course of study or one which slants the curriculum toward what one California school calls the "Essentials of Living." These particular "essentials" turn out to be such things as how to take care of a home, how to budget one's income, how to buy the right kind of food, and—not surprisingly, perhaps—how to make minor repairs to household plumbing.

I should like every American to get into the battle for better schools. In all fairness I must warn those who are willing to work actively in their local communities that they do so at their peril. The powerful leaders of American public education who have a vested interest in continuance of the *status quo*, whose jobs may even depend on it, have so far shown that they are more interested in retaining their positions and justifying their practices than in joining the American people in a thorough reorganization of our educational system. There are exceptions. Many classroom teachers in particular are on the side of progress. But power is in the hands of a relatively small group of men with strong convictions that they alone know how the child grows, how he learns, what he must be taught. They are adamant in rejecting all lay criticism. They deny the need of real reform. Their every public utterance repeats—as in an incantation—the "truth" as they see it, "our schools are the best in the world, the envy of the world." Since Sputnik there has been a slight modification in this article of orthodox faith: "Our best schools are still unequaled anywhere" is the revised version. They have convinced themselves and, in their righteous conviction, they are impervious to facts that call their faith in question. All they will permit you, the people, to do is to give them more money for more of the kind of education we now have.

If they can, they will punish those who publicly take issue with them. We have had an example of this attitude of the educationists. When *Life* and *Time* published excellent articles on American education this year, they naturally had to show that it was in need of reform. *Life* had published but the first of a series of articles when the influential National Association of Secondary School Principals issued a statement to its members containing the following passages: "We know from experience with another magazine a few years ago that *your most effective weapon will be to question the continuation of subscriptions* to the *Life* and *Time* publications *in your school* as long as they have an attitude and policy inimical to education. Also we suggest that you urge teachers, parents, and citizens to write similar letters to Mr. Larson [president of *Life* magazine]. *Of course, the force of your letter will be discounted if you indicate that you have been advised to write others such a letter.*" (My italics.)

The men who tried to enforce silence on two responsible and important national magazines by using the tax-supported school libraries as a weapon professed great surprise at criticism by the press. They declared virtuously that they had been completely misunderstood and claimed that "some have distorted the statement issued to our members, the principals of secondary schools [forgetting about the teachers, parents, and citizens who had been urged to join the censorship campaign!] as an effort to curb press freedom. Others have even characterized it as an attempt to organize a boycott against the publication!" Well, I believe it would be difficult to consider the action of the school principals' association as anything but attempted censorship and boycott.

This is not an isolated case. The National Education Association (NEA) is a powerful pressure group which wields great influence. Education is big business. One of my correspondents discovered this when he sent a short article on education—mildly critical—to the journal of a school board. The article had been accepted and set up when the editor went to one of the many conferences of educationists which periodically lay down policies for the schools. On his return, the editor sent the manuscript back because he had come to the conclusion, he wrote, that "it would do harm" to the writer since he was a supplier of equipment to the local schools. If published, the editor wrote, the article "would seriously affect any future business you might do" with the schools. He had discovered at the conference that "just now the public-school men are in a frame of mind that is entirely antagonistic to even the slightest breath of criticism of the schools. The technique is to call anyone who criticizes an enemy of education, and to treat him accordingly."

Finally, it must be understood by all reformers that if they do succeed in improving their schools these may well, in consequence, be "disaccredited." Thus, Holland Christian High School of Holland, Michigan, a small denominational school whose graduates have long done well at college, was told last year that its accreditation would be withdrawn unless it instituted courses in home economics and shop. The threat came from the North Central Association of Colleges and Secondary Schools which sets the standards for schools whose graduates are accepted without examination by colleges and universities in that region—nineteen states are included. The reason given was that the school was neglecting the needs of two-thirds of its students who do not go to college. In this particular community mothers in general are capable of teaching their daughers home economics, and shop training is available elsewhere. The community had the audacity to disagree with progressive notions of what subjects are useful to children and insisted that its school teach languages, mathematics, science, and history.

What gives the case special significance is that this association of educationists is charged with checking the schools in regard to the quality of their *college-preparatory course*, for it is on this course that accreditation itself is based. Instead, we find the association using its power of accreditation trying to blackmail a good school into wasting tax money on courses for which the community sees no need—money which it prefers to put into a good general education for those who do not go to college. The Holland High School authorities promptly voted against cluttering the curriculum with "know-how" subjects and the association just as promptly struck the school off its list of accredited schools. It is to be hoped that the colleges and universities in that region will disregard the action of the educationists and give special preference to students from so valiant a school. Unfortunately, in another case the association succeeded in browbeating a school. The Springfield High School at Springfield, Illinois, complied with educationist dictatorship and "strengthened" its home-economics and shop courses which had been criticized as inadequate by the association.

For champions of better education a hard year is ahead, so the *Wall Street Journal* warns. NEA is girding for a giant counteroffensive and has already upped membership dues from $5.00 to $10.00 to strengthen its legislative activity. The goal is to regain the people's confidence, so largely lost in what is called "a year of infamy." This is to be done not by a change in the progressive theories but by vigorous attacks against "unprofessional consideration of school programs"—in other words, expression of lay criticism of our schools. The counteroffensive is being organized from its elegant headquarters in Washington—as luxurious a home for the top leaders in education as is provided by the more affluent labor unions. I hope no American will let himself be intimidated. The welfare of our children and the future of our country are too important for us to give up the fight before it has made a good start. . . .

How are we to meet the challenge of Russian education when all our efforts to bring excellence back to our schools are shackled by the monumental selfishness of blind men?

Here is a field where you, the American voter, can take steps to eliminate an obvious evil in our educational system. Public pressure can induce state legislatures to coerce boards of education into relinquishing their iron grip on your teachers. For encouragement in pursuing the good fight I give you the case of Virginia. Something of great potential importance to American education happened there quite recently. Public opinion operating through the General Assembly forced the state board of education drastically to cut the number of "education" credit hours for teachers and to increase those required in "subjects" such as English, mathematics, sciences, and languages. A liberal-arts college graduate now needs but nine "education" credits to teach in high school. This in itself is a fine thing, but what really makes the Old Dominion a true pioneer for excellence in education is the new rule that even this nine-credit requirement may be waived by the state superintendent in cases where local communities wish to retain the services of retired professors and others qualified to teach who lack these "education" credits. If Virginia can do it, so can your state, if you will but labor patiently, rally public support, and move on the state legislature. . . .

It matters not whether you agree with my views on education. What matters is that all citizens get into the good fight to make our education the best in the world. Debates on facts or ideas are useful for they clarify the issues. Such debates must always be the preliminaries of far-reaching reform. We do not operate by executive, legislative, or "professional" fiat. We are a democracy. Now that we have been aroused to the dangerous effect which poor education has on our strength and influence as a world power, let not men of little vision with their soothing words hold back our righteous anger. We must sweep clean the temple of learning and bring back quality. For, as former President Sproul of the University of California warns us: "If we fail in our hold upon quality, the cherished American dream of universal education will degenerate into a nightmare."

Let us each make a beginning, however small. It takes but the moving of a single pebble to start an avalanche.

16

What Goes on Here?

JOHN KEATS

Mr. Keats, formerly a reporter for the Washington Daily News, *is now a free-lance writer.*

The fact that our professional educators cannot agree on the value of different courses of study to different individuals should not discourage you. If the pedagogues cannot agree among themselves, they need an umpire. Moreover, it is not their business to decide what shall be taught in your school—a matter which most of us do not seem to have understood. Very simply, public schools are *public* business; local school districts are directly responsible for local schools; if yours is a good school, you should be able to accept the congratulations; if there is something wrong with the school in your town, it is your fault and yours alone. The United States Constitution has not one word to say about the purpose of education in your home town. Educational matters are left up to the several states, and there, in varying degrees, affairs are bucked along to each of the nation's more than 60,000 school districts. Thus, it seems appropriate that any district really desirous of improving the quality of its education should establish a committee that is representative of the entire community to act as a perpetual, open grand jury on its public school.

This sort of action is often a bleak necessity, because most existing agencies in most communities are inadequate to serve the schools well. Too often the Parent-Teacher Association meetings are social affairs, or are used by school officials to bang the drum for more money. Too often school boards are too remote from the public to be responsive to the public will. (Indeed, some school boards refuse to hold public meetings on any school matters at all, and why this should be tolerated defies comprehension.) Too often school board members are entirely bemused with technical problems and leave the significant philosophical thinking up to the salaried school superintendent, who is usually a professional educator of one stripe or another. Since education of our young is too expensive and too serious a matter to be left only to the parents, or to the teachers, or to the school board, or to all three, we need to hear from everybody. One thing that often escapes attention is the fact that the public school is the entire community's baby. It is the concern of the child, the parent, the spinster, the bachelor, the elderly, the teacher and the appointed or elected officials. It is as much the concern of those who send their children to private or parochial schools as it is of those who do not, since they, too, are voters and taxpayers in the community and—much more important—since they are members of that society of which the school is merely one important function.

The citizens' grand jury should represent every point of view, social class and occupation in the school district. Most important, it should not come charging in to the schoolhouse ready to skewer the school board members or the superintendent to the blackboard, no matter what the apparent provocation. It should be formed with the idea of helping the school to become whatever it is the public thinks it should be. The idea for a citizens committee in charge of the school is certainly not new. The Quakers have been using it to govern their parochial schools here for the last two hundred years, and there is plenty of precedent for such committees on public schools. . . .

It would be delightful if our citizens committee could just whiffle through a bunch of bulgy books, taking an idea from here, a clue from there, and nail the result to the schoolhouse door and call it a curriculum. Unfortunately, matters are not this simple. Because the school is a function of the community, because the terms of education anywhere are dictated by the present reality of the locality, the first job of a citizens committee will be to study the community itself. We must know who we are and what we need and what we can do before we can decide how to jump.

Thus, we gather detailed legal knowledge of the local school situation, determining how much we can do at home, and how much we will have to pry out of the state. We compile facts relative to the school district's physical geography, trade patterns, tax base, sociology and cultural anthropology. In the process, we discover many facts relative to our financial abilities as well as many dealing with varying human needs, aspirations, cultural desires and interests. Working closely with the school superintendent and the school board members—all of whom should serve on the committee—we are further supplied with results of the school's findings about our children. We discover the intelligence ranges with which we must deal, and we find out how well the children are living up in achievement to their measured mental abilities. We also learn something of our children's desires, and while these might seem childish, they are none the less real, and deserve our serious attention.

After the facts are in, we begin to study the various educational philosophies in current coin and equate them with our situation. Next, we visit our schools to find out in the classrooms just where we might need a little jacking up. To check ourselves as well as to gain additional perspective, we should also spend hundreds of man-hours visiting other classrooms in other school districts. These classroom visits are crucial. Only thus can we see educational philosophy put into practice; the theories in the books take on three dimensions. We discover at first hand whether it is true that Johnny can't read, and if it is, we will see a practical demonstration of why he can't.

The citizens committee's last job, of course, is to make suggestions. Since the community maintains and operates the school in its midst, a committee truly representative of the community should legitimately expect to have all of its suggestions adopted, for surely it is no more radical to insist that our school literally follow our ideas of what our school should be than it is to say that the public should create its own laws and reserve the right of review.

None of this activity is easy. In the first place, it is difficult enough to establish any sort of public committee for any purpose. Then, you may well wonder how long we laymen must study before we can be expected to make intelligent suggestions in so apparently complicated a field as public education. I can only say that other communities have done the job, and that it took them a good, long time. Men and women unwilling to devote much of their leisure to a common task should not attempt this one. In New Canaan, Connecticut, some parents worked unselfishly, knowing all the while that *their* children would be graduated before hoped-for changes could be brought about in the school system. This is a job for genuinely interested, thoughtful people, and certainly not for crackpots and malcontents whose vision goes no farther than their own inferior darlings' reports that horrible old Miss Spence doesn't like them.

School board members, administrators, principals and teachers are usually more than happy to cooperate with any representative group of people whose interests in good education are as genuine as their own, and thus they can be of great help in speeding the layman's necessary education. Just as we depend on advice and cooperation from our elected and appointed corporation counsels, judges, policemen and social workers for the wise proposal and enforcement of our laws, so we depend on our schoolmen for much of the technical theory and classroom practice of education. In each case, it is the basic philosophy—the over-all policy—that is our particular province. That, and the right to review not only the practice, but the policy itself. The basic job is to decide why we want what taught to whom.

17

Who's Trying to Ruin Our Schools?

ARTHUR D. MORSE

Mr. Morse has been a journalist and free-lance writer. He is now Producer, CBS REPORTS.

Public education in America is under the heaviest attack in its history. This attack is not aimed at the improvement of free education. It is aimed at its destruction. So far it has struck at school systems from Port Washington, New York, to Pasadena, California.

"We place the greatest importance upon this attack," Dr. Willard E. Givens, executive secretary of the National Education Association, whose membership consists of 850,000 teachers, said recently. "In recent months campaigns against our schools have been intensified in number and effectiveness. Since they strike at the very roots of our system of free public education, they are a very real menace to democracy."

The most notorious success yet achieved by the forces that are undermining our schools was made at Pasadena.

Early in 1948 Pasadena's school board invited Willard Goslin, one of the country's most able and respected educators, to become superintendent of its public schools. Less than three years later the board that had hired Goslin asked for, and received, his resignation.

The shoddy developments that led to Goslin's ousting had nothing to do with his talents as an educator. His removal—as David Hulburd makes clear in his book *This Happened in Pasadena*—was the result of shadowy fears generated in the community with the aid of individuals and organizations as far away as New York City.

From *McCall's Magazine*, September 1951. Reprinted by special permission of the author.

The shame of Pasadena cannot be undone. Nobody knows what community will be next. . . .

Though the nature of the attack on the schools varies somewhat from place to place, the general pattern is identical. The attackers use the same techniques, the same literature and the same sweeping charges. They accuse teachers and textbooks of being subversive; they link modern educational practices with Communism; and they attempt to stampede parents into believing that our public schools are the breeding grounds of totalitarianism.

Chief among the groups that are exploiting the widespread misunderstanding of modern education and the consuming fear of Communism is Allen Zoll's National Council for American Education.

Many well-intentioned people, lured by the dual prospect of fighting Communism and reducing school taxes, have joined local groups which, like the Englewood Anti-Communist League, are linked to Zoll's organization. Anyone who is a member of, or has been invited to join, one of these groups should be interested in learning something about Zoll, whose career is not without interest.

Educators are usually cooperative in arranging interviews with reporters, but I found that in this respect, as well as in others, Zoll is not in the tradition. When I phoned his office, which is in New York, he was reluctant to grant an interview, until I pretended that I was in sympathy with his aims and wanted to gather material to further the cause. Then he agreed to see me.

"This will be the first interview I've granted since I've been in this thing," Zoll remarked and concluded by saying, "If you smear me I'll cut your throat." (This is not, of course, the kind of remark that one often hears in educational circles.)

Before seeing Zoll I looked into his background and found, among other things, that he was the founder and national commander of an organization called American Patriots, Inc., which appears on the Attorney General's list as a Fascist organization. The Patriots (now defunct) had their biggest fling during the years immediately preceding World War II, when Zoll, who cannot be accused of lacking a talent for opportunism, exploited the division of sentiment in this country toward the war. . . .

In 1948 the internationally known sales consultant, sensing a new market for a somewhat different brand of goods, organized his National Council for American Education. Ex-National Commander Allen Alderson Zoll now appeared as Allen A. Zoll, Ph.D.

The office of the National Council for American Education occupies a large room on the tenth floor of a shabby building at 1 Maiden Lane, in downtown New York. It has a staff of three: a receptionist, a typist and Zoll's secretary. The room is cheerless, sparsely furnished and undecorated except for numerous pictures depicting scenes in the life of George Washington. In the rear, partially blocked off by storage cabinets and stacks of old newspapers, is the small cubicle occupied by Zoll, from which he emerged to greet me.

At the age of 55 Zoll is a man of average height, weighs about 200 pounds and is growing bald. His eyes, which are his most distinctive feature, are narrow and glinting. His manner is restless.

At the outset I told Zoll that I was familiar with his main arguments against the schools: that "progressive education" is a menace, that most teachers and textbooks are subversive and that children are not learning the three Rs, which should be taught to the exclusion of virtually everything else.

"That's about it," Zoll said. "Most teaching and textbooks are Socialistic, and the teachers' colleges are implanted with Socialism. These Socialist plotters are deliberate saboteurs, and we're in serious danger from them—just as much as from the Communists. There are plenty of bad people who haven't joined the Communist party, and we're out for them too." Zoll leaned back in his chair. "You're either for individualism or collectivism. The middle is a barbed-wire fence. I tell kids that in my talks to them."

I asked just how he was attempting to improve this situation.

"Well," he began, "neither the FBI nor the Un-American Activities Committee knows what's being taught or what's in the heart of a teacher. The only person who knows that is the person right on the ground. I help these local outfits. . . . "

After Zoll had exhausted himself on the subject of disloyal teachers I asked what he was doing about subversive textbooks.

"We have an office in Wisconsin," he replied. "Their job is to review about sixty books a year. It's under the direction of our vice-president in charge of research, Verne Kaub."

I had run across Kaub before and knew that he, like Zoll, is a Johnny-come-lately to education. Until recently Kaub was working the religious side of the street, writing articles for the anti-Jewish publication *The Individualist*, as well as distributing a pamphlet titled "How Red Is the Federal Council of Churches?"

Zoll said that Kaub's job of ferreting out un-American propaganda in the children's books is sometimes pretty difficult. "Once," he said with a straight face, "we had to have a book reviewed eight times before we got a good analysis."

I asked Zoll what he believed the proper aims of education should be.

"That's a good question," he said. "I just sent a memo to our Board asking them to give me their ideas on that matter."

That didn't seem like a very good answer, but Zoll was indicating that he wished to wind up the interview.

"Any other questions?" he asked.

"Well," I said, "can you tell me what's right with the schools?"

He did not dignify that query with an answer.

I remarked that nearly all educational authorities agree that approximately 500,000 new classrooms need to be built within the next ten years, and asked Zoll if he also considered this a vital problem.

"That's a lot of fuddydud, about new buildings, when the old ones are just as good," he replied. "The factor of age has nothing to do with the efficacy of school buildings."

There seemed time for only one more question. Since Zoll now signs his writings "Allen A. Zoll, Ph.D.," and prefers to be addressed as "Doctor Zoll," I asked him about the degree.

"I got that from Temple Hall," he said quickly, and then seemed embarrassed by his hasty remark. He rose, and the interview was over.

After leaving "Doctor" Zoll I learned that Temple Hall College and Seminary (now defunct) was a one-man diploma mill operated by a man named D. Scott Swain. Swain's qualifications as an educator included the serving of a six-year prison term on six charges, including running a confidence game, obtaining property under false pretenses and passing bad checks. While running his "college" Swain conferred upon himself the title "Archbishop Primate." Probably the high point of his career was reached at a meeting in New York City, when the "Bishop" got roaring drunk and in a burst of expansiveness passed out Temple Hall Ph.D.s to his entire audience. The exact moment when Zoll was awarded his doctorate is unknown.

Zoll would be funny, if his aims were not so deadly. He cannot be dismissed as a harmless crackpot, for, though his statement to me that his organization has 10,000 members and is linked to some 400 local groups is an obvious exaggeration, it is nevertheless true that he has been a potent influence in every city whose schools have come under attack.

Zoll's influence is widely exerted through the pamphlets that he publishes and distributes. At the height of the school controversy in Pasadena, citizens picking up their morning newspapers found copies of Zoll's pamphlet "Progressive Education *Increases* Delinquency" on their doorsteps.

"So-called progressive education," the pamphlet said, "shot through as it is with the blight of Pragmatism, has had a very deleterious effect upon the original character of American education . . . The public school system in hundreds of cities and towns throughout the land . . . is fatally committed to these subversive principles of 'progressive' education." Zoll goes on to explain that modern education does not permit absolute truth, hence those who believe in it cannot be true Christians. And he makes the further observation that "currently it is popular to plug hard for the democratic equality of all men."

This pamphlet made such a vivid impression on the president of the School Development Council in Pasadena that he recited passages from it almost verbatim in his speeches attacking the school administration.

In Denver the forces attempting to oust superintendent Kenneth Oberholtzer (who is also president of the American Association of School Administrators—the highest honor his profession accords) presented copies of "Progressive Education *Increases* Delinquency" to each member of the Board of Education and to members of many other civic groups.

Other Zoll literature includes pamphlets bearing such titles as "They *Want* Your Child" (the Communists, that is), "Private Schools: The Solution to America's Educational Problem" and "How Red Are the Schools?"

The philosophy in these pamphlets is being advocated by the Parents' Council for Education in Eugene, Oregon; the Citizens' School Committee in Los Angeles; the Parents' Council in Minneapolis; the Three R Parents Committee in Columbus, Ohio; and by similar groups in many other communities.

Zoll's satisfaction in the wide distribution of his literature is not altogether spiritual. His most popular item, "Progressive Education *Increases* Delinquency," sells for 20 cents a single copy; 6 copies for $1; 1,000 copies for $60; and customers are offered a "special price on larger quantities." In all of his pamphlets Zoll makes a strong pitch for contributions. People who join his Council are rewarded with various titles, the rank conferred depending on the amount of cash they send in. They can become an Associate for $5, a Patron for $150, or a Benefactor for $1,000.

By the end of 1949, when Zoll was just swinging into action, his pamphlet sales and contributions had netted him an estimated $45,000. With the way his business is booming at present, there is no reason to believe that his efforts are not now being even more respectably rewarded.

Though Zoll's organization is the most important rallying point and serves as general headquarters for the enemies of education, other operators are busy turning out weapons for waging the attack.

One of the most destructive of these—a kind of secret weapon—is a quarterly publication called the *Educational Reviewer*. Edited by Lucille Cardin Crain, and financed by a lobbying organization with headquarters in Washington, D. C., the *Reviewer* has been used effectively in Englewood and in other widely scattered cities across the country. Its sole function is to try to discover subversive material in textbooks.

The methods used by the *Educational Reviewer* can be illustrated by its treatment of Dr. Frank Magruder's textbook, *American Government*. This text, which is on the recommended list of all 48 states, has been a classic in its field for a quarter of a century. It was appropriately selected for review in the first issue of the *Reviewer*, which appeared in July, 1949. The writer of the review was a woman named Edna Lonigan. How she made her point that the textbook is subversive can perhaps best be shown by comparing excerpts with which she purported to express Magruder's views with actual passages from his text:

MAGRUDER, ACCORDING TO LONIGAN:

Italy and Germany were dictatorships but not the Soviet Union.

The United States and the Soviet Union are equals fighting for "world leadership."

By democracy we mean that form of government in which the sovereign power is in the hands of the people collectively.

MAGRUDER'S ACTUAL TEXT:

Russia is leader of the dictatorial nations, most of which are Communistic.

The United States and the Soviet Union, the most powerful of the allies in the Second World War, now find themselves as the two only powerful contenders for world leadership.

By democracy we mean that form of government in which the sovereign power is in the hands of the people collectively, and is expressed by them either directly or indirectly through elected representatives.

In the last instance above, by deleting half of the sentence, Miss Lonigan was able to prove to her satisfaction that Magruder was an advocate of the collectivist state.

Unfortunately she proved it to a number of others, including radio commentator Fulton Lewis, Jr., who, a few months after the review appeared, read considerable portions of it on one of his broadcasts.

The response was big and prompt. The State Textbook Commission of Georgia immediately banned the book, as did the Houston, Texas, school board. Parents in Portland, Oregon, demanded that similar action be taken there. A newspaper in southern California quoted Lewis, attacked Magruder and concluded that the "public schools are bound to destroy this country." In places like Council Bluffs, Iowa, and Trumball County, Ohio, where the broadcast also caused a stir, some people took the trouble to read the textbook—and so avoided taking precipitate and foolish steps.

Referring to the *Educational Reviewer*, a report recently issued by a committee of the House of Representatives observed that "the review of textbooks by self-appointed experts smacks too much of the book-burning orgies of Nuremberg to be accepted by thoughtful Americans without foreboding and alarm."

That kind of talk infuriates the editor of the *Educational Reviewer*, Lucille Cardin Crain, who is convinced that any critic of her publication is a Communist.

Allen Zoll described Mrs. Crain to me as "a charming woman, very lovely"; and I found upon meeting her in her office, which is in a brownstone house on East 36th Street in New York City, that she does possess the most attractive figure in the antischool movement. She is 50, has cool blue eyes, a cameo face and a fondness for using rather fancy words. To indicate her personal interest in children Mrs. Crain sometimes says exuberantly: "I'm a grandmother seven times." This reference is to the children of her husband (who is 71) by his first wife. Mrs. Crain is childless.

Like Allen Zoll, Mrs. Crain joined the educational ranks recently. Her scholastic background consists of the equivalent of a high-school education, which she received at a convent in Minnesota. She is suspicious of most recognized educators who hold degrees, and she has expressed strong disapproval of what she calls our "compulsory state-operated educational system." What she is in favor of is a mystery.

When I asked Mrs. Crain what she thought the proper aims of education should be, she seemed to be pushed as far out to sea as Allen Zoll had been when I asked the question of him. After remaining silent for a spell Mrs. Crain, moved by a sudden inspiration, said brightly, "I like our little slogan on the *Educational Reviewer*." (This reads: "In the light of truth, objectivity and established Americans ideals, to examine the publications used in instructing American youth.") There seemed little point in pressing that subject further.

In other respects my interview with Mrs. Crain was not unusually rewarding, partly because she consumed most of it by delivering a diatribe against the National Education Association, which she thinks is subversive. Her reasons are not monuments of persuasion. Reading from an N.E.A. pamphlet, she remarked, "They say here they're 'committed to the democratic ideal,' " adding, as she tossed the pamphlet aside, "whatever that is."

The *Educational Reviewer* has been specific in explaining what it thinks democracy is. "Democracy," the *Reviewer* said in the October 15, 1949, issue, "is a government by demagogues leading to the tyranny of the majority over the minority."

A few steps behind Mrs. Crain is another foe of modern education—78-year-old Major General Amos A. Fries, Retired. The aged general is editor of a widely distributed monthly publication ironically titled *Friends of the Public Schools*. "Anyone who calls our government a democracy," this publication has pointed out, "is either completely un-American or a moron."

The general stands four-square against nurseries and kindergartens, health, welfare and recreational activities, services for handicapped pupils and vocational guidance, among other things. "Where one child is overworked," he says, "a thousand aren't worked enough."

The general's educational program, if such it can be called, stems from his apparent belief that things were better in the good old days when fewer children went to school.

These three—Allen Zoll, Lucille Crain, General Fries—by themselves would, of course, be ineffective. What enables them to carry on their programs is the support of well-meaning but misinformed people in communities across the country, who are frequently prompted to join a local, innocent-sounding school group because its main interest seems to be controlling school taxes or carrying out some other aim that appeals to the pocketbook or the emotions.

To provide facts enabling friends of education to improve our schools and defend them against unjustified attacks, there was founded in 1949 an outstanding organization called the National Citizens Commission for the Public Schools. President James B. Conant of Harvard was instrumental in its establishment. Roy E. Larsen, president of Time, Inc., is its chairman, and its membership includes many other leading American citizens. A nonprofit group, the Commission is financed by the Rockefeller Foundation and the Carnegie Corporation, and it works closely with all organizations devoted to better education, including the National Congress of Parents and Teachers and the United States Office of Education.

The National Citizens Commission stimulates and assists in the formation of local committees representing a cross-section of the community—business, labor, church, civic, women's and veterans' interests—devoted to improving the schools. The Commission furnishes its local committees, free of charge, a wealth of material that explains how to organize, what to look for in evaluating the schools, how to work with local educators and how to carry through a program of action. The Commission acts as a national clearing house of community experiences. One of its most valuable services is the distribution of case histories of school improvement in every part of the country. . . .

Our public schools are the firm underpinning of our democracy. Like democracy itself, they are in deadly danger.

"We are threatened from without," Willard Goslin said upon tendering his resignation as superintendent in Pasadena. "I think we are threatened even more from within. I know of no better way to wreck everything that we think is good in America than to begin to destroy ourselves one by one, institution by institution, community by community throughout the land."

18

Are We Educating Our Children to Be Socialists?

HOMER H. HYDE

Mr. Hyde is employed by the United States Civil Service as a Training Specialist in The Technical Writing Branch of Lackland Air Force Base, Texas.

Before a large, emotionally charged audience in the auditorium of Sidney Lanier High School in San Antonio, Texas, Representative John Alaniz of the Texas State Legislature, member of the Textbook Investigating Committee, remarked on April 3, "This Committee has spent hundreds of hours of testimony and has not come up with one real live communist yet."

This remark is typical of the newly styled "Non-Communist Left." Now, what Mr. Alaniz ignored was the fact that the Committee was not established to uncover communists, but rather to investigate the lack of patriotism in the history books being used in Texas schools, and the socialistic philosophies in other textbooks designed to make good socialists (or communists?) out of our youth. . . .

The attacks on our American way of life through textbooks include such socialistic philosophies as decrying the profit motive, condemning capitalism, spreading the wealth, destroying our feelings of nationalism and patriotism, destroying initiative and self-reliance, and making us all slave citizens of a One World Government. . . .

Several witnesses at the hearings exemplified the usual evasive tactics of the liberals, such as disregarding the evidence and resorting to

From *American Mercury*, April 1963. Copyright, 1963, Legion for the Survival of Freedom. Reprinted by permission.

name calling. This was true also of two of the five members of the Investigating Committee.

At the San Antonio hearings, April 2–3, Julius Gossenbacher, Jr., a former instructor in government at St. Mary's University, was quoted in a local newspaper as saying, "Since the committee is investigating textbooks, it would appear that more of the witnesses would be teachers, publishers, or other experts. . . . Surprisingly, I find this is not the case, and I am instead confronted by a *horde of vigilantes.*" (Emphasis supplied.)

Maury Maverick, Jr., son of the deceased Congressman, testified in support of a history text, *Our Widening World,* by Dr. Ethel Ewing, and after completing his testimony was questioned by members of the Committee. Maverick at one point had said he didn't think the Committee was necessary. Committee member Nelson Cowles asked Maverick if he didn't think the people who had requested the hearing in San Antonio were sincere in thinking the hearings necessary. Maverick replied he thought they were "completely sincere but don't understand the real meaning of the American dream." Now, after reading the testimony of the various witnesses, what do *you* think?

During the initial hearings at Austin, Committee member Ronald E. Roberts in a letter to the editor of the *Beaumont Enterprise,* said:

"As a member of the House Textbook Investigating Committee, I want to say a special 'thank you' for your recent editorial 'Texas Book Burners Still Seeing Red.' I sometimes feel that I am in a very definite minority as a member of the special textbook committee. It was most encouraging and refreshing to see a segment of the press give this situation some thoughtful attention.

"In my opinion these extremist groups that have been appearing before this special committee are far more dangerous than the Communists. These fanatical groups would actually destroy democracy because of the methods they seek to impose on our society."

Several professors from the University of Texas denounced the hearings, as might be expected. Among them was Dr. Benjamin Wright, Head of the History Department, who stated that the "ultraconservative Texans for America show a spirit which really isn't American." He was referring to the organization headed by J. Evetts

Haley which had initiated the state-wide interest in textbooks some two years earlier.

And just who were these people whose patriotism was impugned? The witnesses included executives of large business enterprises such as a railroad, oil company, light and power company, a foundry, a steel company, and a lawyer for the telephone company; also, teachers, doctors, housewives, and students.

In contrast, Committee member Robert W. Bass stated on 25 June, "We have heard enough to see what the trend is in our textbooks. It is obvious that the trend is toward socialism in many of the books used in the Texas public schools.

"We now have to take the poison out of the textbooks, and they're full of it. This country is heading toward socialism just as fast as we can go and they are trying to teach it through the books to our youth." (*Tyler Morning Telegraph*, June 26, 1962.)

As could be expected, speakers at the National Education Association meeting in Denver on July 5 told delegates to fight back against the "John Birchers," the "ultras," and the "extreme right wing." Refusing to face the evidence in actual textbooks, a panel of speakers told a special session on "Thunder on the Right and Education" that " . . . education has nothing to gain but much to lose by remaining silent in the face of attack." (*San Antonio Light*, July 5, 1962.) What the NEA speakers chose to ignore was that no one had attacked *education*, but rather the inclusion of socialistic indoctrination in educational *materials*.

RESULTS AND CONCLUSIONS

While the hearings were in progress, the Mel Gablers of Hawkins and and the J. C. Abbotts of San Antonio, prime citizen movers in the investigation, sent out thousands of mimeographed excerpts from the economics and history texts to business men and other interested citizens. As a result, hundreds of telegrams and letters were received by the State Textbook Committee, Governor Price Daniel, and legislators in Austin, urging remedial action. On May 7, the Textbook Committee met in Austin and rejected for readoption all five state approved economics texts . . . when the current contract expires in August 1963. Calls were issued for publishers to submit new proposed texts. Nothing could be done about the history text discussed, inasmuch as their contract extended from 1961–1968. However, it was anticipated that new home economics texts would be selected for the 1963 school year, since the contract for *The Consumer Investigates* expires in August 1963.

Early in March 1963, two bills were introduced designed to correct the problem discussed above, at least to some degree. One was a bill introduced by W. T. Dungan which would require the teaching of Americanism versus Communism in the state's high schools. Another one was jointly introduced by Nelson Cowles and Mr. Dungan which would allow more time for the consideration of proposed textbooks by the State Textbook Committee and simultaneously more time for individuals to protest the adoption of any book. Instead of the previous two or three weeks, the time would be increased to a minimum of three months. Mr. Dungan told me that he feels the latter bill has a very good chance of being passed, but was doubtful about the other unless more public support is aroused.

Are the rejected texts completely bad, you may ask? Of course not! Many citizens who examined them said, "Why, I see nothing wrong with this book." This is because they merely glanced at the glowing preface, introduction, and chapter headings, with perhaps a reading of some portions. The fact is, the content of these books is preponderantly American. You surely would not think the leftists to be so stupid as to write them completely pro-socialist, would you? Concerning this, Senator Nelson S. Dilworth, Chairman of the California Legislature's "Senate Investigating Committee on Education," stated: "A book with five per cent propaganda is heavily loaded, but the most dangerous are nearer two per cent."

What can you do? As an American citizen, you can do exactly the same thing that the Texan did. Examine the economics, history, home economics, and other texts being used by *your* children. Compare them with older texts of the 1920's. Prepare specific quotes with page references. Show these to your state representative, and ask him to introduce a resolution in the next session of the State Legislature calling for an investigation. Enlist the aid of fellow citizens. Contact patriotic organizations, such as the Daughters of the American Revolution, 1776 D Street, N. W., Washington, D.C., for information and guidance. Contact "America's Future," 524 Main Street, New Rochelle, New York, for sample evaluations on textbooks (they have made extensive studies). Write the Mel Gablers, P. O. Box 457, Hawkins, Texas. They will be glad to furnish procedural guidance.

It appears futile to bring up the matter in your local P-TA—but you may try. Mel Gabler, testifying in Dallas on May 31, stated:

"Article III, Section 2, of the By-Laws of the National PTA provides that 'local units . . . shall not seek to direct the administrative activities of the schools or to control their policies.' Members of local PTA units are not allowed to protest about textbooks or methods of instruction—such matters being 'out of order' under this By-Law. The group in charge of National and State Congresses of the PTA has practical power to manipulate the entire organization."

And what about talking to teachers? Speaking for himself and wife, Mr. Gabler said,

"It should be noted that in private conversations many teachers voice the same concern we have voiced in this testimony. However, teachers who are concerned are afraid to make their views public for fear of losing their jobs. In fact, each who has voiced concern to us has also begged that we do not disclose their names. This alone is a tragic situation."

You were right, Mr. Alaniz—the witnesses at these hearings failed to produce "one real live communist." But they did show how educators are educating our children to be socialists, perhaps ultimately good communists. And what kind of character will they possess? In a presentation which brought him a standing ovation from the audience, Dr. Forrest M. Smith, Jr., at the San Antonio hearings, pointedly described the probable character of our future citizens when he said:

"There is great pressure exerted these days from every side to make us equal in every respect—equality for the sake of equality. Yet in the traditional American point of view we are equal only before God and the law, as well as in the opportunities that our freedom guarantees us. But in all other aspects we are *unequal*, thanks be to God! For it is our very inequality in these other aspects that makes us *truly* free people.

"In fact, if we are forced by socialistic influences . . . to become equal economically, socially, intellectually, morally, and in every other way, why, we shall just simply lay down our sovereignty as free individuals and say: 'Give me a number, I no longer have a name.' 'Assign me a niche—I no longer desire to work.' 'Promise me security and all the fringe benefits and I will vote for you.' 'I can no longer continue to work out my own salvation—I'll get the government to do that for me!'"

Is that the kind of person you want *your* child to be?

19

The Teachers Take a Birching

DONALD W. ROBINSON

Mr. Robinson is Chairman of the Department of Social Studies, Carlmont High School, Belmont, California. He is also associate editor of *Phi Delta Kappan.*

The attorney, member of a leading Phoenix law firm, smiled with obvious relish as he said, "We've got them on the run, and we're going to keep them on the run." "Them" referred to Communists, Socialists, and liberals, all of whom he lumped together as dangerous. He considered liberals most dangerous, because "they are so firmly entrenched in government and education and because they pave the way for the Communists." . . .

When do we ignore and when do we respond to accusations from the lunatic fringe? Where is the dividing line between active citizen participation in school affairs, which we encourage, and vigilante pressures or meddling, which we resent? How far should we go in acceding to community pressures to decide what constitutes proper patriotic procedures in the schools? Who is a patriot?

The answers are not simple, and in many important particulars they will vary from district to district.

It seems almost futile to join the chorus of hortatory voices pontificating on the subject, but since the democratic process requires that all views be stated and re-stated and re-stated, it might be appropriate here to recall a number of the caveats with which we are already familiar.

Schoolmen should retain a sobering awareness that they have not yet succeeded too well in their goal of education for responsible active citizenship. Both the leaders and the followers of extremist groups are,

From *Phi Delta Kappan*, February 1962. Reprinted by permission.

by and large, products of the public schools, products who were preco-
cious in some of the less commendable qualities, exaggerating pride in
self-expression at the expense of intellectual effort. They are still
shirking the intellectual job and deriving a vicarious sense of participation from their presence in the jeering section.

Schoolmen should learn to accept criticism and dissent, perhaps
even personal attack, as evidence of a functioning democracy. Granted
that teaching efficiency is reduced when teachers are made to feel
defensive or pressured, teachers should be able to absorb some criticism—even some sharp and unfair criticism—without crying "foul."
When teachers too quickly admit to feeling pressured, they are con-
fessing a lack of faith in their administrators, school boards, professional associations, and in the ultimate good sense of the American
public. Any teacher who is fearful of having his teaching reviewed in
the court of public opinion just may be deficient in his faith in democracy—and that is the same charge he is leveling at the Birchers.

It is interesting to note that in nearly every community where the
film "Operation Abolition" became a source of controversy, neither
the defenders of the film nor its critics trusted adult American audi-
ences to analyze and interpret the film for themselves. Both sides felt
impelled to have speakers accompany the film to be sure that the audience was "given" the desired interpretation. Lack of full faith and
confidence in the ultimate good sense of the people is always a matter
for concern, the more especially when it emanates from staff members
of a democratic school system.

The muzzling of teachers must be prevented, but not by the muzzling of the patriotic groups. The name-calling campaigns must be
countered, but not by name-calling. The emotionalized hate-fear attacks must be met, but not in kind. . . .

Tensions always accompany change, and today the tempo of change
continues to accelerate.

The birth of the atomic age in 1945 complicated our loyalties by
making more imperative the relaxation of traditional concepts of national honor and survival in favor of a new commitment to human
honor and survival. The 1957 demonstration of superior Soviet techni-

cal skill provided impetus to the new trend to include a study of communism in the schools. A substantial reason for including in the curriculum well-planned instruction in the facts of communism is to reduce the necessity for reliance on other sources for this instruction. The report of the Fullerton investigation refers to the four-day "Anti-Communist School" sponsored by the Anti-Communist Crusade in Orange County in March of 1961 and includes the testimony of teachers who attended to the effect that the program was poorly planned and conducted and the speeches appealed to the emotions rather than to reason. "Many students and adults were left with the belief that there is a definite Communist threat, but without any guidance as to how to meet the threat. The fear this engendered has created a climate for acceptance of irresponsible criticism and unjustified attacks on the schools."

Such a comprehensive plan as that implied in the suggestions for attention to communism in the curriculum, clearly formulated policies for dealing with citizen complaints and for assuring teachers of support, plus a positive policy of honestly encouraging the dignified airing of differences of conviction can lead to satisfactory handling of tensions in any community where they arise. . . .

Index of Authors and Titles